The Realization of Life Aspirations Through Vocational Careers

THE REALIZATION OF LIFE ASPIRATIONS THROUGH VOCATIONAL CAREERS

Edgar Krau

Westport, Connecticut
London

Library of Congress Cataloging-in-Publication Data

Krau, Edgar.
   The realization of life aspirations through vocational careers /
Edgar Krau.
     p. cm.
   Includes bibliographical references and index.
   ISBN 0–275–95700–4 (alk. paper)
   1. Career development. 2. Vocational guidance. 3. Professions.
4. Occupations. 5. Self-realization. I. Title.
HF5381.K698   1997
650.14—dc20   96–20690

British Library Cataloguing in Publication Data is available.

Library of Congress Catalog Card Number: 96–20690
ISBN: 0–275–95700–4

First published in 1997

Praeger Publishers, 88 Post Road West, Westport, CT 06881
An imprint of Greenwood Publishing Group, Inc.

Printed in the United States of America

The paper used in this book complies with the
Permanent Paper Standard issued by the National
Information Standards Organization (Z39.48–1984).

10 9 8 7 6 5 4 3 2 1

Copyright Acknowledgments

The author and publisher gratefully acknowledge permission to use excerpts from the following:

Krau, Edgar and L. Ziv. "The Hidden Selection of the Occupational Appeal: The Paradigm of Nurses." *International Journal of Sociology and Social Policy*, 10, no. 7 (1990): 1–29. Courtesy of Barmarick Publications.

Various articles by Edgar Krau in *Journal of Vocational Behavior*, 1981, 1982, 1983, 1987, and 1989. Courtesy of Academic Press.

Krau, Edgar. "Motivational Feedback Loops in the Structure of Action." *Journal of Personality and Social Psychology*, 43 (1982): 1030–1040. Reprinted by permission of the American Psychological Association.

Krau, Edgar. "Turnover Analysis and Prediction from a Career Developmental Point of View." *Personnel Psychology*, 34 (1981): 771–790. Courtesy of the publisher.

Krau, Edgar. Article in *Bulletin of the International Test Commission*, no. 18, 1983. Courtesy of the International Test Commission.

Contents

Preface

This book deals with the formation and the implementation of life aspirations. It is a process in which people realize the project of their lives, attaining the goals they set for themselves in external achievements and inner development, as they become the kind of person they want to be. Wishes and aspirations change over time and according to culture and fashion. However, the studies that led to this book, extending over a period of 40 years, of people living in various parts of the globe and under different socioeconomic régimes showed that the striving after life meaning is one of the enduring things in the world: In hyperdemocracies, as in the affluent society or under a communist totalitarian régime, people want to give meaning to their lives.

In our conception the *meaning* a person seeks in life is his or her self-realization. It is not a task that suddenly appears after all other needs have been gratified, but a life project that crystallizes in adolescence and thus precedes the full gratification of needs in the various life domains. People do not choose their life meaning arbitrarily. We realize ourselves in a society with a cultural environment dominated by certain values. Society and its values determine the direction of our self-realization and of the meaning we are seeking in life. Construing life meaning amounts to an equation uniting objective reality and its subjective valence. This fact may be concealed from the external observer, with the result that only one aspect is emphasized—usually the subjective side. This is not astonishing, because we all are pleased to hear encouraging opinions on the power of our mind and will in shaping our fate. Says Howard (1993): "We are the novelist creating the novel of our lives, and we are risking our life on that particular story." These are beautiful words, but they express only one side of the equation. The novelist indeed creates a reality, but the "playwright" of the life scenario is only participating in the "writing of the plot." While certainly influencing it, the playwright has also to cope with forces and situations impossible to control.

Individual life meaning rests on social acceptance and approval, which is granted for what benefits society. In the social mainstream groups, *work* benefits society, as it produces the material and spiritual goods necessary for raising the general living standard. Therefore social approval, retribution, and social success recompense work performances in the various domains. People's lifelong working conditions and work experiences constitute their *vocational career*, in which the social and the individual utilities converge. Work careers create socially needed utilities and in this very activity permit the gratification of individual life aspirations, bestowing meaning upon people's lives. The vocational career is a main instrument for achieving self-realization, the embodiment of life meaning.

The concept of career belongs to a developing capitalist society in which work has been stripped of its former religious meaning and power. Therefore, it is senseless to ask whether Michelangelo had a career or whether Jeanne d'Arc was a career woman. Although, objectively, their activity had the characteristics of what we would today label *careers*, subjectively those people experienced more the calling to perform a religious imperative. While the ethical content of work has not disappeared, as also attested to by the etymology of the words "vocation" in English, "Beruf" in German, "profession" in French, and the like, which all are close to the sense of *calling* or a declaration of faith (cf. "vocare," "profiteri" in Latin, "Berufung" in German), it were nonetheless an oversimplification to clothe medieval realities in the concepts of our culture. Bertolt Brecht did it, writing about the "Business of Mr. Julius Caesar," but the result was a mediocre parody very far from a truthful scientific description or even from good literature. It follows that the concept of career should be used to refer to the occurrences of modern times. Herein it refers to the phenomenon of work performed by an individual throughout the life span.

The much-trumpeted disappearance of careers or their dissolution into leisure activities are fashionable slogans, hastily drawn conclusions better fitted to the needs of scoop-hungry journalism. Since for all material times work is necessary to keep society going, careers cannot disappear. They are the sum total of people's work tasks and work experiences throughout their life span. Patterns of careers change in response to economic conditions, but as long as people work, they have careers. For a majority the meaning of their lives is tightly linked to careers, either to performing the vocational activity as such or to the various collateral gratifications achieved through careers, such as money, status, and affiliation. Only for a minority are life aspirations not linked to work, but they too have to compromise over some form of work careers in order to gain the material freedom necessary for pursuing aspirations and meanings in other life domains.

Our starting point is the analysis of the phenomenon of *self-realization*. We see the vocational career as a main instrument for its fulfillment. In this perspective the shaping of life aspirations expressed in an *end-state image of self-realization* is the person's primordial choice, not the vocational career. The latter's role is secondary and subordinated to that of life-meaning fulfillment. Career decisions (as well as undecidedness) are in the first place determined by the characteristics of the self-realization image. Concealed aspects in this image and also in the occupational requirements cause difficulties in understanding the choices made by the individual in construing a career.

We are putting forward the following theses: (1) Life choices are wholesome, with domains not clearly separated; the criteria of choice are also mixed, reflecting the wholesomeness of the desired self-realization end state. However, for a majority, work is an important element of life choice. (2) Life choices for the future concern images. People have an image of themselves performing the roles of life, which include the vocational one. While the image of the vocational role may undergo changes, the end-state image of self-realization, once formed, will remain stable in its main features. (3) The real motives of life choices are generally hidden to the external observer. For the person, concealment of motives used to follow from lack of clarity in the end-state image of self-realization and from fear of privacy invasion.

As in a "Looking-Glass War" by John Le Carré the aspirational image is compared and matched not with the vocations and their requirements as such, but with another image the individual creates of them after yet another image that public opinion holds of those vocations. None of these images is an exact replica of reality. Wishfulness, defensiveness, and social desirability are sovereign in changing characteristics and in shifting emphases. This explains why there are so many mismatches and career choices ending up in frustration.

A central idea of the book is that career success depends on *career planning* and that essentially the image people form in adolescence of the situation they want finally to achieve constitutes a life project. Generally the image of future self-realization is blurred and only some components stick out. However, in people successful later on, this aspirational image becomes a conscious plan, which extends to the intermediate steps leading to the finally desired situation. Counseling for self-realization may help this process, and it must be anchored in the prediction of the probable course of people's careers. The book provides a *prediction model* and methods for its computation.

The model rests on the assessment of the career ingredients referred to career ladders with intermediary steps and to their requirements. The following *career ingredients* will be discussed:

Motivational ingredients. We look first at the image of an aspirational end-state of self-realization. Achievement motivation and promotional dynamism spur the person to an ascent career type. Their absence or weakness furthers a career of a horizontal type. Values and especially work values are the culturally accepted expression of the person's aspirations and provide the conscious motivational steering of behavior towards desired ends. Also included are attitudes toward work and authority figures at the place of work. Positive attitudes essentially express the absence of characteropathic drawbacks. We then consider people's affiliation to a socioeconomically active (or passive) social milieu of origin and any motivational brakes such as neuroticism and negativistic attitudes.

Instrumental ingredients. These include, first, the instrumental career ingredients belonging to the person, such as vocational aptitudes and learning aptitudes, general employability skills and habits, vocational knowledge and skills, and a becoming physical appearance and manners accepted by groups significant for the person's career. Second, the instrumental career ingredients offered by society include existing occupations and their structure, the situation of the labor market, career paths in society and in organizations, and the socially conditioned career start. Third are instrumental brakes such as inaptitudes, habits contradicting society's values, or vocational requirements. The book discusses the possibility of reciprocal enhancement and compensations among these various career ingredients.

Though a career may not be predicted in detail, it is possible to predict a dichotomous career type of social and vocational ascent or horizontality. The difference between them is not between success and failure, but essentially between different kinds of self-realization aspirations. In both career types there are people who realize themselves and others who do not. The final results may be predicted out of the assessment of career ingredients, the career type, and the probabilities of coping with the requirements of a certain career ladder.

What are the possibilities for the planful realization of careers? It will be shown that successful *planning* and implementation of life careers rest on several premises: (1) The clarity of aspirations. In adolescence aspirations are usually expressed in an image of the future. This image must become a plan, as it not only refers to the desired end state of self-realization but also contains the intermediary steps by which the desired end state can be reached. Lack of awareness that intermediary steps are necessary or contradictions within the aspirational image predict failure. (2) The match between people's career types based on their ascent score (in the assessment of career ingredients) and aspiration image. Mismatches predict failure. (3) The availability of counseling. The literature has repeatedly stressed that in view of the very complicated problems involved in correct career decisions, people have to receive help from vocational counselors.

Failure in the attempt to realize life aspirations expresses failure in meeting environmental requirements and in adjusting to developmental tasks attuned to those aspirations. This constitutes a serious problem causing feelings of maladjustment and frustration, with possible repercussions on the individual's personality and mental health.

It follows from the key role work plays in people's life that the bulk of maladjustment problems will originate, be related to, or find their expression in the person's vocational career. Therefore, we should be entitled to consider a *psychopathology of the process of career development* as it deviates from acknowledged career problem solutions and results in vocational failure, maladjustment, or frustration. We put forward three theses characterizing the psychopathology of the process of career development:

Normal and pathologic behavior are meant to cope with problem situations. The difference lies in the social adaptive value of the behaviors.

Maladjustment is a devolutionary process starting with superficial, mild forms of suffering, a feeling of dissatisfaction and frustration, and it progresses toward more severe forms wherein satisfactory functioning is hampered. Usually behavior on the job is the first to be affected. Because the leading human activity is vocational, it puts strain on energy reserves and often has an imposed character, with regard to both the nature of the work and the social relationships involved.

Personality disturbances are mobile and have a certain fluidity between one another as dysthymia and characteropathy (psychopathy) mingle. In the different phases of the devolutionary process one of these disturbances appears as the dominant one. It should be added that, when speaking of disturbances, reference is made only to psychogenetic disorders, that is, those not caused by primary substratum damage (psychoses, certain severe psychopathies).

As adjustment on the job is the result of a concerted action of a multitude of factors, maladjustment is also a "composite" disturbance, in which one symptom usually sticks out. A second analogy concerns the evolutionary process, the way adaptive behavior gradually develops in a chainlike process wherein each stage is dominated by a key phenomenon (e.g., no adjusted behavior on the job without prior skill acquisition, no skill acquisition without previously developed abilities and interests, and so on). So does maladjustment evolve and grow in a spiraling process, with dominant key phenomena in every stage.

The main instrument for assisting people in achieving the realization of their life aspirations and life meaning is *counseling*. In order to intervene in a process of such complexity, counseling must give multilateral consideration to inner and outer processes and occurrences. Using only the clients' cognitive map for the reconstruction of their life theme, counselors may be stonewalled by the existing occupational realities and reminded that counseling is neither psychotherapy nor essay writing. Life does not follow counseling theories; it is the latter that have to adjust to life.

If the task of counseling is to assist people in their quest for self-realization, it cannot be limited to choosing a vocation or a college major in younger years. It must include the crisis-and failure-counseling of later years, in which the clinical aspects are evident. Nevertheless, clients usually see their problems as vocational, they present them to a vocational counselor, and only an approach labelled vocational has face validity in their eyes. This means that vocational counseling is of a more complex nature than accepted hitherto, both conceptually and methodologically. Analysis and understanding of the developmental process will have to precede any methodological consideration of counseling. In this book the reader is first invited to join in the venture of discovering how people shape and try to implement their life aspirations. We shall then proceed to the analysis of career planning and prediction, subsequently discuss the causes of life failures, and then review the required counseling interventions.

Above all, this book is about planning for the personal future and learning how to construe it.

> Let us, then, be up and doing,
>   With a heart for any fate;
> Still achieving, still pursuing,
>   Learn to labor and to wait.
>   (Henry Wadsworth Longfellow, "A Psalm of Life")

1

Self-Realization: The Attainment of Life Goals

From time immemorial human beings have been preoccupied with finding the sense and purpose of their being. Kant systematized these thoughts in three well-known questions: "What am I capable to know?" "What shall I do?" "What can I hope?" Answers have varied between the quiet acceptance of a fate that can be neither explored nor changed and an active involvement with life. Today, in our agitated, dynamic age, impetuous in its transformations, we move away from the stoic ideal of a serene peace of mind and come closer to the Aristotelian concept that considers happiness a never-ending activity in accordance with the laws of nature. There will always be unsatisfied desires, but, even so, happiness is people's supreme purpose in life.

Throughout the generations, many valuable ideas have been expressed on happiness. For Epikuros it is related to the avoidance of pain; for Descartes and Spinoza happiness is directed inward and appears in the restraint of our passions, which leads to spiritual perfection. However, Spinoza admits that for common people it is linked to wealth, honors, and enjoyments and that only a few chosen are capable of arriving at *amor dei intellectualis*, the intellectual love of God, the state of supreme felicity.

Despite the various definitions, humanity has always returned to the basic idea that happiness has to be sought in the real life, where people have to cope with the problems of their existence. It is in this sense that Hegel in his "Philosophy of Mind" ridicules Rousseau, who claims a natural, indolent, happy state in which wants are gratified without striving. Hegel points out that happiness is a natural desire for all humans and that it has to mean a permanent pleasure and joy, not the satisfaction of every whim, but satisfaction on the whole or at least for the realistic maximum in a prolonged life period.

In modern psychology, this philosophical idea of happiness is upheld by Erich Fromm (1947), who states that it is achieved through inner productiveness. Criticizing Freud, Fromm points out that happiness is not the satisfaction of needs springing from a physiological or psychological want, but rather the accompaniment of all productive activity in thought, feeling, and action.

Despite this lack of agreement regarding the substance of happiness, there is a general consensus that happiness is people's supreme goal, which has to be achieved in the framework of general human moral standards. The meaning of this condition may be to make one's community or society as a whole a better place to live but also to achieve self-perfection through what has been termed *Pareto's utility*. The Italian sociologist demanded the building of a social structure in which every individual would achieve the greatest utility for himself without jeopardizing the utilities of others (Pareto, 1919). More often than not, such cautioning is forgotten nowadays, as is the other conclusion regarding the problem of happiness in the history of philosophy: namely, that there are various paths leading to happiness, which essentially remains an individual experience.

It follows that all people must have the right to choose, by themselves and for themselves, the goals that they wish to attain in life, without being told under what conditions they will be regarded as being successful and self-actualized. The problem is one of both cultural and individual differentiation. Today it is an acknowledged fact that the qualitative differences between cultures do not entail a ranking on a superior-inferior dimension (Kluckhohn, 1962; Hofstede, 1980). There are no axiological differences between cultures, and life goals cherished in one culture are neither superior nor more important than the life goals widely pursued in another culture.

In Hofstede's research some cultures appeared to be individualistic, some collectivist. They are distinct, but neither is superior to the other. The recent economic boom in Japan fully proves this statement. Collectivist societies call for a greater emotional dependence of members upon organizations and for the responsibility of the latter vis-à-vis their members (Hofstede, 1980). It is clear that in such a setting life goals will not be identical with those widely pursued in a Western achievement society. Ronen (1979) points out that in the United Kingdom, Germany, and Canada, self-actualization includes autonomy as a central value, while self-actualization is linked mainly to self-esteem and recognition in Japan and France.

It is generally accepted that "personality and life style are sensitive to the historical moment" (Rychlak, 1982) and that there is no absolute freedom in the establishment and pursuit of life goals. At the same time society has no moral right to impose the life goals of the majority upon a differently thinking minority, nor has it the right to depreciate such people, despising them as "losers." In the United States the so-called Santa Fe Experience (cf. Sarason, 1977) has become widely known. After reading a newspaper article titled "Prominent New York Banker Turns Waiter," D. L. Krantz went to Santa Fe and found there many educated people with highly successful records as stockbrokers, TV producers, art directors, and so on now working as farmers, small-business owners, or construction workers. These people all felt that there are more important values and goals than an affluent life: It was the freedom from external constraint allowing them to be themselves. They sought a life not defined by property, work, or family; the major significance of the jobs they now held was only to sustain the life they led.

What has been said does not mean that the individuals described in the Santa Fe Experience were free of cultural bonds. In organizing their lives in ways that were not appreciated by the culture of the majority, they yielded to other cultural influences. People have to be free to choose the culture they want to adhere to, without exposing themselves to scorn and degradation. However, no one is free from cultural influences and from social bonds in an absolute manner. Life-goal achievement and self-realization take place within social bonds and in accordance with socially acknowledged ways. One recalls Hegel's definition of happiness as a fusion between desire and duty, feeling and reason, freedom and necessity, subjective inclination and objective institutional life, especially of the State, as it evolves to higher forms ("The Phenomenology of the Mind").

Happiness as a life goal has been an object of inquiry less for the scientists of our time than for philosophers. Although the work of Campbell, Converse, and Rodgers (1976) has focused attention on the phenomenon of happiness itself, the problem has been dealt with mainly by theories of self-actualization, which serve as examples of concepts of happiness. The most popular of these theories is Maslow's (1954), which equals self-realization with the attainment of happiness and full psychological health but limits this achievement to a few chosen people capable of first satisfying all their previous needs on Maslow's pryamid of needs.

The discovery of the pyramidal character of the human needs structure has been one of the major breakthroughs in the psychology of motivation, and yet this strength of the Maslowian conception is its undoing. It has been conceived and presented as a model of human motivational processes, but it is only a paradigm. The most striking reality is the differential, the individual character of the need pyramid. Jeanne d'Arc willingly sacrificed her life for her country, Giordano Bruno for the truth. Romeo and Juliet for love—and for the sake of truth Galileo Galilei was willing to waive his status and security, but not his life. This does not mean that happiness ceases to be related to self-realization. It does mean, however, that the content and the place of self-realization in the hierarchy of human needs differ from one individual to another, while the person is still abiding by the sociocultural and moral norms of society.

Three major theses in Maslow's theory of self-realization prevent it from adequately reflecting real-life events and constituting an efficient instrument for fostering action that aims at self-realization in wider social strata:

1. The pyramidal construction of human needs as having a fixed model of stepwise realization allows for self-realization to occur only after the gratification of all previous need steps of the pyramid.

2. Self-realization is the attribute of a "successful person," the winner in social

competition, who is motivated by achievement motivation. Only such a person is able to enjoy success and to be fully satisfied and happy.

3. The main avenue leading to self-realization is the vocational field, which is also the main area of competition, where people must prove themselves and realize all their potential in order to achieve self-actualization.

In its best-known version, Maslow's (1954) need pyramid consists of five steps: physiological needs, security needs (physical and economic), the need for love and affiliation, the need for recognition (for competence and/or social power), and the need for self-actualization, demanding that people be active in the field appropriate to their abilities and do what they can do best: A musician shall make music, a painter shall paint, a poet shall write poems. "Man has to be what he can be" and reaches self-actualization only if and when all the other steps of the need pyramid have been gratified. Therefore, only the very few are capable of reaching this stage.

As a matter of fact, this basic principle of a stepwise progression through the pyramid of needs is not Maslow's alone. It does not even matter that Maslow himself, seeing the incongruency of his theory with real-life events, introduced changes into the structure of his needs-pyramid model and later spoke of deficiency and growth motivation (Maslow, 1962). Alderfer (1969) also described not a five- but a three-step pyramid consisting of (a) existence needs that include all the various forms of material and physiological desires, (b) relatedness needs involving relationships with significant other people, and (c) growth needs to which belong all the needs that involve people causing creative or productive effects on themselves or the environment.

From our point of view, there is a definite progress in the definition of growth needs by Alderfer, admitting the possibility that they may be gratified not only by competition winners and not only in the occupational area. Moreover, even failure is acknowledged as an experience that may lead to the enrichment of the personality. Nevertheless, the pyramidal progression in need gratification is maintained. Growth needs come into focus only after the gratification of relatedness needs, which in turn begin to function after existence needs are plainly satisfied. Seeking relatedness needs when there is little gratification of growth needs amounts to regression. Therefore, de facto, growth needs belong neither to the domain of relatedness nor to the area of existence. The principal content of Maslow's conception thus remained untouched.

Interestingly, such theories have been proposed in spite of contradictory research findings. The very thoroughly planned empirical verification of Maslow's theory by Hall and Nougaim (1968) found almost no support for Maslow's thesis. In a longitudinal study lasting over five years with management trainees of the American Telephone and Telegraph Company, the authors tested the hypothesis of preponderancy in higher needs, as lower-order needs are being satisfied and decrease in strength. In particular, it was assumed that in the last year of the research successful managers would be lower on need strength in

Safety and higher on need strength in Achievement Esteem and Self-Realization. Nothing of the kind happened. The research did not support the hypothesis of the need pyramid, not even in a two-step hierarchy. Changes in needs were unrelated to any objective measure of gratification in the Safety, Achievement, Esteem, and Self-Realization areas. It appears, therefore, that needs continue to motivate even after their gratification. In other research with samples of women, Betz (1984) found that self-actualization ranks first both in women managers and in homemakers, although the former category of women may have lower scores in their needs for safety-security and the latter category may have more wants in their esteem needs. None of these empirical verifications supported Maslow's conception of self-realization.

We certainly do not need scientifically controlled research to tell us that the attainment of self-realization does not have to await the gratification of all other needs. Who would doubt the self-realization of Heine, Schiller, Pushkin, Modigliani, Mozart, Beethoven, Virginia Woolf, and other giants of humanity? However, it is general knowledge that most of the basic needs of these outstanding people were never satisfied. The appalling want in means of subsistence that caused Modigliani, Mozart, and Schiller to end their lives in dreadful circumstances, the frightful loneliness of Heine or of Beethoven, in addition to an uncomfortable material situation, the abasing scorn and political oppression in which Pushkin lived, or perhaps Virginia Woolf's feeling of being in exile everywhere—do these testify to an all-encompassing need gratification? Self-actualized people are "happy, healthy animals, full of lust and who enjoy life," Maslow points out (Maslow, 1954). Were Beethoven, Heine, Schopenhauer, or Spinoza happy, healthy animals full of lust? Not even Toulouse-Lautrec fits into this category, although the satisfaction of lust was not absent from his life goals, as it was in the case of the stern, dark, pessimist Schopenhauer or the slender philosopher Spinoza, destroyed by consumption. To the contrary, history and literature show many cases of people suffering from distress and anomie, the lack of values, precisely because all their needs have been permanently and too easily satisfied. In the French aristocracy of the "ancien régime," such ease led to degeneration and not to self-actualization. It paved the way for the characteristic "spleen" of the beginning of the nineteenth century, depicted in the tragic torments of Byron's Childe Harold and Pushkin's Eugene Onegin.

For the sake of fairness it must be said that Maslow himself saw the shortcomings of his theory. He intended to publish a paper in 1964 on the nature of happiness and in 1966 a critique of the self-actualization theory. In these intended and posthumously published papers, Maslow stressed the pluralism of individual differences and his conviction that real happiness necessarily implies difficulties. He wrote, "It is a privilege to undergo the misery of creativity, even the related insomnia and tension" (Maslow, 1991a). Let us pass over the fact that difficulties and tensions are related to the process of creation and are not abasing and mean problems of everyday life. The point is that Maslow *did not publish* these papers; they appeared in 1991, edited by E. Hoffman two years after the publication of my own book on self-realization (Krau, 1989a).

As a superior mind, Maslow saw the flaws of his theory, but his previous beliefs drew him back, and he could not overcome his own psychological resistance. In the same outline on the nature of happiness, he redefines happiness, "to include the good fortune we take for granted and which may therefore lapse from everyday awareness." Is it not again the "healthy, lusty animal," with all his needs satisfied, who happily blinks through these posthumous redefinitions?

The pyramidal self-actualization theory of Maslow introduces a socioeconomic criterion for evaluating the content of self-actualization. A general gratification of all previous needs is feasible only at the higher echelons of the social hierarchy. To all others this right is denied. Realizations in the realm of the arts or spiritual activities are recognized by this theory as self-actualization only if they ensure a comfortable life to the artist or the thinker, with some allowance for insomnia and creative tension. The falsity of the first thesis of the pyramidal self-realization theory is related also to the falsity of the second thesis, according to which self-actualization is the winner's reward. We have to ask: winning in what? So Mozart lost in his competition with Salieri—does this mean he did not actualize himself, while the mediocre Salieri did? Did not St. Peter and St. Paul lose their legal battles and their lives? Was not Nelson Mandela in prison for 27 years? And does this mean that they are losers who did not achieve self-actualization? The obvious conclusion is that only in the cultural pattern of the achievement society is self-actualization related to success in competition. Today there is a growing awareness of the limitations of this culture.

Pervasive changes have taken place in the value system of the Western society, the postindustrial society. Its substance lies in the services offered to the public, and knowledge provides the axis for social stratification (Bell, 1973). Today the spread of education has attained unprecedented levels, including higher expectations, and there is a definite trend of increase in the number of occupations termed professions. All this produces shifts in the values of society.

In Inglehart's (1977) formulation the modern trend is expressed in more liberal values, in greater openness to innovation, and in a greater emphasis on knowledge and on professional standards in comparison with organizational ones—in short, a delegitimization of traditional values is occurring at present. This phenomenon leads to a change in the sense of success. The new ideas of success revolve around different forms of self-fulfillment, self-expression, the actualization of potential (Yankelovich, 1974). The point is that these ideas are new only for us, not for people living in other cultures—in India, in China—and we have seen that important thinkers in the Western culture of the past held identical views.

In his book *Culture's Consequences*, Hofstede (1980) documents that achievement motivation is not a universal category and that to stress the ubiquity and/or the superiority of achievement motivation amounts to ethnocentrism, an exaggerated tendency to see characteristics of one's own group or race as superior to those of other groups. Maslow categorized human needs according to the U.S. middle-class culture pattern, Hofstede argues; he adds that there is no reason that economic and technological development should suppress cultural variety.

An objection to this argument could be made by referring to McClelland's (1961) research proving that in cultures relying substantially on achievement motivation there is a greater rate of material progress, expressed in the consumption of electric power and the number of registered patents. However, in our discussion, material advancement is not the only form of success and not the single condition for satisfaction and life happiness. In collectivist cultures, the latter goals are possible at low levels of achievement motivation (Krau, 1985).

It follows that we ought to reject also the second thesis of Maslow's theory on self-actualization. Neither competition nor the achievement motivation related to it appears as a universal condition of success and of the satisfaction and life happiness that should follow from it.

The change in the meaning of success entails a shift in its locus, too. By 1956, Dubin had documented that work is not the central life interest for a majority of the working class (Dubin, 1956). About 20 years later this conclusion was upheld in the prestigious work of Campbell, Converse, and Rodgers (1976), especially in the case of people with lower education and lower income. However, lack of satisfaction also seems to grow among professionals (Sarason, 1977), and it appears that work has lost much of its attraction and that its instrumentality in obtaining satisfaction has decreased. This is true especially of the young, who are hit worst by unemployment. The result is either self-devaluation or the loss of importance of work for the individual. In parallel, the role of nonwork grows in shaping the personality (Lévy-Leboyer, 1986). This means that work is not the only avenue for achieving self-actualization and happiness although, as will be seen, neither can be obtained unless people are adjusted to their work.

Our contention is (Krau, 1989a) that in order to avoid the flaws of the present theories on self-realization, one has to conceive a theoretical structure in accordance with research data and daily life experience. The importance of self-realization lies in the fact that it is synonymous with the attainment of the person's life goal, and it leads to happiness. We put forward the thesis that self-realization is a matter of individual choice achieved within the framework of adjustment. This basic sentence comprises several meanings expressing the complexity of the phenomena of self-actualization and adjustment. Five of these meanings are discussed below:

1. Self-actualization is achieved in social interaction, and therefore people who enter this path should have full control over their mental faculties and use them without infringing on the principle of Pareto's utility. This means that self-actualized people have to be normal from a psychological and moral point of view. The need of self-actualization must not be used as an excuse for inflicting harm and sufferance on other people. Self-actualization is not only a psycho-

logical but also a social phenomenon. There has to be adjustment to the moral standards of humanity, not just to those of a contemporary society. Otherwise, one could think of Himmler as adjusted to the standards of Nazi Germany and achieving self-actualization as he rises from the status of a poultry rancher to the position of an all-powerful police chief of the German empire. Adjustment to the condition of mental and moral sanity is the first meaning of the adjustment required by the process of self-actualization. This criterion is liberal enough not to bind the individual by the rules of his membership group in society, but nonetheless it is restrictive enough not to allow interpretations of the human condition or of moral standards that are unacceptable to the mainstream of human conduct throughout ages.

2. In mentally sane people, self-actualization means the attainment of a much-valued goal, an objective success, even if its meaning is the achieving of mental peace or the overcoming of psychological problems. Nevertheless, the ultimate and intimate meaning of self-realization is subjective: It is the condition that bestows overall satisfaction and happiness upon the individual. Nobody save the mentally and morally sane person has the right to judge whether he or she is self-actualized and happy.

Success and glory have proved fallacious many times in history. Charles V, the Ruler of Two Worlds, gloomy and disappointed, renounced his empire and in 1556 retired into a monastery, where he ended his days as a simple monk. Newer research in history tends to ascribe this demeanor also to the emperor Tiberius (cf. Prause, 1969). Axel Munthe in his *Story of San Michele* describes Tiberius as leading a lonely life, "an exhausted ruler of an ungrateful world, a gloomy old man with a broken heart." Modern times have also produced the mystery of prominent, successful men taking their lives; we need mention only the tragic suicides of Ernest Hemingway or of the Russian novelist Fadeev. To the contrary, Diogenes felt happy in his barrel; in the twentieth century, England's Edward VIII abdicated his throne and willingly went into exile "for the sake of the lady he loved," as Nostradamus had prophesied 400 years earlier in his famous "Centuries."

The subjectivity of the self-realization judgment does not free the individual from the necessity of having objective success. It means, however, that each person alone will choose the area of activity in which realization (or failures) are central to his or her self-image. In these salient domains of life, objective achievements must be obtained for self-actualization to take place. In other, nonsalient areas, a compromise is possible, as the person adjusts to existing constraints. This is the second meaning of the basic statement that self-realization functions in the framework of adjustment. Perhaps that is its most spectacular meaning, borne out in every episode of human history. Socrates, the giant of human thought, had to put up not only with the intrigues of his detractors, who eventually took his life, but also with the sour Xantippa, his wife. Nevertheless, he was happy until his last breath and was considered the bright ideal of a thinker throughout the following 2500 years, up to this very time. Until his Russian defeat, Napoleon Bonaparte had every reason to be content with his success as a statesman and as an army commander, but his love life was one great deception that even today constitutes the subject of scornful comedies.

There is no all-encompassing success, nor an all-encompassing and everlasting happiness. Happiness lies both in fulfillment, with achievements in salient life domains, and in compromise, adjusting in parallel to the conditions existing in the nonsalient areas of life. Schiller, the poet, said that he saw no man merrily ending his life as the gods strewed their gifts upon him with full hands all the time.

> Noch keinen sah ich fröhlich enden,
> Auf den mit immer vollen Händen
> Die Götter ihre Gaben streun
>
> ("Der Ring des Polykrates")

The same idea had been expressed by Henry Wotten, sixteenth-century English poet:

> Count no man happy
> until you know the
> end of his days.

Three necessary conditions must be fulfilled for self-realization to become possible: (a) Objective achievements that are subjectively recognized as such, in life areas salient to the person's self-image, (b) No frustration or serious complaints in the other areas of life. Self-actualized people have to be adjusted to the conditions of their existence; it contradicts common sense and the postulated requirements of mental sanity if frustrated people who feel miserable pretend that they are self-realized. At any rate, it is highly improbable that they will pretend to be. (c) The state of self-realization is related to a lasting feeling of overall satisfaction and happiness, despite the compromises in areas not salient to the person's self-image. Horace expressed this thought as he wrote in a poem that a happy man is not the one who possesses much, but one who uses wisdom, who fears dishonor, and who is not afraid to die for cherished friends and fatherland:

> Non possidentem multa vocaveris
> recte beatum; rectius occupat
> nomen beati, qui deorum
> muneribus sapienter uti
> duramque callet pauperiem pati
> peiusque leto flagitium timet

non ille pro caris amicis
aut patria timidus perire.

(Odes and Epodes IV.9.45)

3. It has been stated so far that the gist of self-actualization lies in subjectively acknowledged objective achievements in the area chosen by the person. This thesis needs further clarification as to the nature of those achievements. If the emphasis is on the subjective acknowledgments of the person's achievements, how can they be measured and objectively assessed as such?

Although individually achieved, success is a social category; it is a social reward for achievements of a certain kind. Success does not exist without a public whose values are fostered by certain actions and which rewards them with different forms of social recognition. Each community or society has norms not only for punishment or failure but also for acknowledging and rewarding behaviors that advance its values, its ideology, and its patterns of life. In this light, the acknowledged success of an individual contributes to collective solidarity and enhances the generally accepted common values. However, not every outstanding deed is appreciated as such or, at least, not always at the time it is performed. The success of Jeanne d'Arc, France's national heroine, is relatively recent: Her canonization was pronounced in 1920. In 1431, however, after receiving the learned opinion of the Sorbonne, a French ecclesiastical tribunal sentenced her to death for heresy. Ernst Thälmann was executed as a traitor in Nazi Germany, but he was a national hero for Germans who identified themselves with the struggle against the Nazis and especially with the parties of the left.

This means that not only the area of self-realizing achievements is a matter for individual choice, but also the social reference group from whom the individual seeks recognition. It is not the standards of the membership groups by which achievements can and should be measured in issues involving judgment on self-realization, but the standards of the reference group freely chosen by the individual. Such a reference group may have actual physical existence in the individual's own culture or in another one or a presumed existence in posterity. Again, this criterion is both liberal enough not to chain people to the beliefs and the way of life of their membership group and rigorous enough to have to have them abide by certain social norms and to measure their actualization against these norms. Here appears the third meaning of the basic sentence that self-realization functions in the framework of adjustment.

4. Hitherto we have stressed the element of choice regarding the life domain in which the person's self-realization takes place, and we have criticized the existing theories of self-realization also on the grounds that they limit the phenomenon only to achievements in the area of work. This is not to say that work has lost its importance for self-actualization. On the contrary, regardless of whether work is or is not the individual's central life interest, it remains the dominant activity in his or her life (American Assembly, 1974; Hall, 1976). There are two reasons for this perennial primacy of work in people's lives. First,

human society relies on work for the maintaining and raising of its living standard. Work was already proclaimed as source of the "wealth of nations" in the eighteenth century by Adam Smith and François Quesnay; it has preserved this role in Keynes's (1936) *General Theory*, probably the most influential book on economics in the first half of the twentieth century; and it maintains this role today in the era of computers and robots. There is a consensus nowadays that the modern information and communication technologies have to be brought into line with human work activity (Docherty, Fuchs-Kittowski, Kolm, and Mathiassen, 1987) and that, if the living standard is to continue to rise, productivity growth must contribute more in the future (Baily and Chakrabarti, 1988).

As work is central to the welfare of human society, there are severe standards for adjustment to its requirements; people who do not comply with them are "selected out" (Krech, Crutchfield, and Ballachey, 1962) or brought into a marginal position, in order to allow better-suited individuals to fulfill the social expectations linked to the job. This marginalization entails social condemnation and contempt. For the individual, the most likely aftermaths are frustration and maladjustment, which certainly prevent self-actualization.

Second, as Sarason (1977) points out, work is a kind of developmental drama performed on a stage onto which every major aspect of human behavior, aspiration and feeling may be cast. It is a main opportunity and a general instrument for the development of human talents, capabilities, and motivations. This aspect has been stressed by Russian psychologists (Rubinstein, 1962; cf. Bauer, 1982). It follows that even if people do not choose work for their self-actualization, it cannot be neglected. People have to be adjusted to the requirements of their jobs. Only if this is done may they pursue self-actualization through their vocational careers or use their careers as a basis enabling them to devote their thoughts and feelings to the areas of leisure, family, or community life, as they are free from possible threats or frustrations originating in their jobs. The adjustment to the requirements of one's work activity is a *condition sine qua* for the possibility of self-realization. Such is the fourth meaning of the basic sentence that self-realization functions in the framework of adjustment.

5. If work constitutes an adjustment basis for self-realization, either within or outside the vocational career, people will have to be adjusted also to the general developmental requirements of the latter. These requirements have been linked to life-cycle characteristics (Erikson, 1963; Sheehy, 1976; Super, 1980) or more specifically, to the developmental stages of the vocational behavior as such (Bühler, 1933; Levinson, Darrow, Klein, Levinson, and McKee, 1978; Hall, 1976). The point is that regardless of the content of their experiences or their jobs, people in every stage of their lives have to cope with certain tasks. Havighurst (1964) coined the term *developmental task*—one that appears in a certain period of the individual's life; its successful negotiation leads to happiness and to success in later years, while failure leads to contempt from society and to difficulties with events in later life. Examples of such tasks may be the stages described by the Levinson group: Getting into the Adult World,

Settling Down, Becoming One's Own Man (Levinson et al., 1978). In the latter's view, the mutual interaction between individual development and society leads to a universal sequence of phases, each with a typical time of ascendancy and each culminating in a critical turning point called crisis, which is followed either by greater health and maturity or by increasing weakness. There are eight such phases, among them autonomy versus shame and doubt, initiative versus guilt, industry versus inferiority, identity versus identity confusion, generativity versus stagnation, and so on. The best known of these stages is ego identity, which refers to people's feeling, of knowing who they are and what their aims are.

Munley (1977) applied Erikson's theory to the problems of career development. He pointed out that failure to develop a favorable ratio of autonomy, initiative, and industry may result in particular kinds of vocational choice problems in the identity stage: inappropriate vocational choices, vocational uncertainty. It is clear that such problems will make adjustment difficult and will therefore prevent the person's self-actualization. Adjustment to the developmental task of the life cycle is a precondition for self-realization. It is the fifth and last meaning of the basic sentence that self-realization functions in a framework of adjustment.

Although, according to the theory put forward here, work is not the one single avenue of self-realization, the vocational career maintains a particularly important role in this process. The theory of self-realization to be achieved within the framework of adjustment requires the person to make three important choices, and in two of them the vocational career is a main focus of attention. The first choice concerns the area of self-realization and has to be based on a thorough knowledge of a person's abilities and the requirements of that person's career. It is the decision in favor of the career rather than any other area as a focus for self-realization; and it is a weighty decision, because there is need for a painstaking evaluation of one's psychological potential and abilities vis-à-vis a convincingly founded preference order of interests. The target of these evaluations is more often than not the vocational activity, while the process itself regularly takes place under the guidance of a vocational counselor.

The second choice refers to the selection of the group of reference. This decision is not overtly linked to vocational behavior, although Münsterberg (1913) has demonstrated that the vocational activity has a determining influence on people's belonging to a certain social milieu and on their social relationships.

In addition, there are important repercussions of the decision regarding the choice of a reference group upon people's vocational careers. Krau (1985) has shown that the norms of the social reference groups influence behavior in competitive occupational situations and in career aspirations and satisfactions. Persons behaving in accordance with the norms of collectivist cultures evince less achievement motivation, and their life aspirations center less on career advancement. If, as a result of a change in their ideals and affiliations (e.g., in immigrants), they adopt the values of the Western achievement society, a deep modification occurs in their interest focuses and aspirations and in their actual behavior, while in the transitional period there is a drastic reduction in satisfaction. Career success then becomes a central life aspiration, even if its meaning is only instrumental to achieving need satisfactions and actualization in another life area. In immigrants a strong work commitment accompanies the entire process of absorption into the host society, as work is the only means they have to rebuild their lives and gain status and recognition (Krau, 1984). At the same time, in research on Israeli immigrants in the first period of their new lives in the country, the main variance of satisfaction stemmed from abiding by national religious values, which they thought were the main values of the Israeli society (1983b). This behavior expressed the adjustment to an imaginary reference group. As they became acquainted with the real situation, a sharp change in their values took place and consequently also in their behavior and aspirations, which went through a process of adaptation to the real norms of the host society. However, during this whole complicated evolution, work remained a central focus of concern.

Whether work is the avenue for self-realization or a base instrumental to achieving it in another life area, the choice of a vocation that matches the person's abilities and preferences is a necessary condition for attempting to achieve self-actualization. It is the person's third choice, and it obviously concerns most directly the vocational activity.

It has been pointed out that the absence of frustration is essential for achieving self-realization and life happiness. Work can be an important source of satisfaction but also of frustration, and this depends upon how well people are adjusted to their jobs. Maladjustment at the job spills over to other life domains. It has been characterized as a behavior disorder that deviates from the accepted sociocultural standards, and as such it is harmful for the individual, for society, or for both. Behavior disorders may shorten individual's lives, reduce their efficiency and happiness, or make all these things happen together (Zubin, 1967).

This discussion leads to a further important point. If self-realization is situation-bound, as it is achieved in the framework of adjustment to the constraints of life situations and social standards, then it is plausible that for a number of people the meaning of self-realization and happiness would be in defeating the threats and adversities in their lives, in so to speak "making the best of it." In research published by Tausky and Dubin (1965), half of the investigated middle managers held a "limited success view," as they evaluated their career achievements by the distance covered from their career starting point up to their present position. This gave them a sense of achievement and satisfaction contrasting with the "unlimited success view" of another and actually small group of predominantly younger managers and experts who emphasized the goals they still had not achieved.

In this sense self-realization may also lie in adjustment itself, if it entails the overcoming of serious difficulties, especially in the development of a vocational career. Once more self-realization and the vocational career appear tightly linked together. Lastly, work *is* people's dominant activity.

2

Work and Career as Tools for Self-Realization

From the beginnings of human society, few things have appeared so persistently controversial as work. Praised by Hesiodos in his book *The Works and Days*, it was despised by Aristotle, who said that a man who performs physical work is incapable of moral and intellectual life and even less of participating in public affairs (*Treatise on Government*). In accordance with the Bible, the Middle Ages considered work as imposed upon humanity as punishment for the original sin. However, being imposed by God makes work sacred. It is interesting that in some people this duality of attitudes is preserved even today, when it may express only contradictory feelings without any religious motives.

There is no doubt that every progress of civilization is conditioned by an increase in society's work output. Work improvement is the only way to tackle the problem of economic underdevelopment.

Work comprises all activities undertaken in order to produce or to facilitate the production of material goods and to render services to human society, on the condition that this activity be recompensed with a certain fee and that certain rules regarding quantity and quality standards as well as an obligatory time and duration of the performed activity be observed. These conditions are important in order to differentiate between work and hobbies or play, in which the activities are performed without any imposed standards and with no expectation of fees. While work entitles people to a material remuneration, their reward may in addition consist in their advancement to a higher position, in an increase of competence or social power, or in the mere interest arising out of the content of work. It ensues that work links together economic and technological, social and psychological aspects.

Because work is related to the progress of human society, it can be presumed that as a result of the advancement of science and technology, the necessary work activity could be performed more and more by robots guided by computers. Consequently, there would be less and less need for human work, which would hold less and less potential reward for the human person. Already today, in the main industrial countries, entire sections of plants in the steel and the automobile industries are wholly computerized, and the programmed work activity is performed by robots. We have airplanes flying without pilots and ships sailing without a crew on board. However, all these systems use remote control, and one must not confuse remote control perfomed by a human operator with complete automation. Humankind is not relinquishing work, but changing its role and its place in the system. It is the heavy physical work and the repetitious drudgery that are now being performed more and more by machines, while the remaining human work becomes more complicated and interesting. Even the functioning of computers is conditioned by human work input. Computer programming, supervision, and maintenance are essentially human activities. No computer or robot can take the human being's place in creative work in making decisions in human problems, or in organizing or leading social processes. This is so because computers have no human feelings and little flexibility. They merely execute the commands they are programmed to do and are not capable of adapting to sudden unprogrammed changes or of acting in situations of uncertainty (McCormick, 1964; Ward, 1966; Bedni, 1975). Norbert Wiener, the founder of cybernetics, foresaw that we might possibly build something like the external expression of emotions (Wiener, 1961), but such constructs are not the emotions themselves guiding our behavior.

Above all, the human brain is superior to the computer by its potential, by its construction, by its combination of analog and digital mechanisms, and by the language it uses. This thesis put forward by von Neumann (1958) has been found to hold true ever since. It ensues that computers and robots are auxiliaries designed, created, and made by human beings and supervised and repaired if they break down.

The human use of advanced technology is by all means beneficial to society as it increases the potential for production and services. However, in the short run, automation and computerization are causing social problems questioning the necessity and even the possibility of the population's general participation in the workforce. There are data attesting to the fact that the transition to the new computerized technology has caused an increase in the number of unemployed (Schaefer, 1983; Herr, 1984).

The existence of unemployment does not mean that work becomes less necessary. In every society there are unemployed who would like to work but cannot, and idlers who do not want to work even if they could. This is by no means a normal situation, and the voluntary or compulsory absence of work in people's lives has a damaging effect on their self-image and/or on their psychological integrity. Research attests to the loss of a job being followed by a decline of psychological and physical health proportionate to the length of unemployment (Warr and Jackson, 1984). The damage appears gradually (Friedmann, 1961; Tiggemann and Winefield, 1984), moving from the initial shock and optimism to indifference, a sense of personal powerlessness, the loss of time structure, depression, and an inferiority complex. It is true that work and employment are not necessarily the same thing, even though for many people the two coincide (Jackson, 1986). Man's dominant activity is not employment, but work. This is the best framework of *agency*, conceived as the endeavor to assert oneself, to initiate and influence events on the basis of planning ahead in accordance with one's view of the future as well as one's memories of the past (Fryer, 1986). Free play is too whimsical to allow for the consequent realization of plans. When a socially useful activity is performed according to plan, despite difficulties that arise, we are dealing with work, even is some would call it otherwise out of vanity, rebellion, or shame.

For long there has been argument about the possibility of escaping or at least reducing the influence of the job on a person's lifestyle through the choice of and involvement with avocational activities. Reference is usually made to Wilensky's (1960) theory of leisure's compensating function in relation to work activity, especially in a job with limited horizons. Nonetheless, it seems that the compensatory possibilities offered by leisure are limited. It has been pointed out that the functions of leisure are relaxation, entertainment, relief from boredom, and personal development, as leisure time permits a broader social participation and the cultivation of the physical and mental (Dumazedier, 1967). However, these latter functions are attained only if the job activity does not impoverish the person's capabilities for self-expression (Meissner, 1971). Parker (1971) also arrived at the same conclusion, when he pointed out that, far from being a compensation, leisure is more often than not an extension of occupational life, and what people seek in leisure depends upon what they found or did not find in their work activity.

It, therefore, seems that the best chances for self-realization are offered by work, although other life activities certainly must not be excluded. The most modest work activity may allow for self-realization to be achieved and felt, if this activity is the subject's free choice. Weber (1930) grasped this phenomenon when he spoke of the Protestant Ethic comprising diligence, effort, restraint, and thrift unrelated to whether or not these are followed by blessing and material achievements. In the Protestant faith, the individual cannot know whether he is chosen to receive God's blessing, but he is bound to behave as if he were.

In more prosaic terms this means that people may choose to realize themselves in work, even in the most modest work, but even if they choose another life domain for self-actualization, they must still adapt to their work and emotionally accept it. Then and only then family and leisure may fulfill a compensatory role. For people frustrated with their work activity, leisure is not the answer (Friedmann, 1961; Parker, 1971).

We have already pointed out that the importance of work for the individual stems from its economic importance for society, acknowledged by rewards of various kinds. To individuals, work appears not only as a collection of activities they are bound to perform, but as social roles conferring a certain status. With every change in the role goes a change in status. Thus, a person's vocational life is made up of a sequence of job roles expressed in a sequence of statuses and in the subjective experiences that go with them. They constitute the person's vocational career. The social and economic rewards for work are attached to these role and status sequences, which, beyond the present gratifications, permit the anticipation of future satisfaction. When speaking of self-realization, such an anticipation is essential because it gives a sense and perspective to the events of the present. We may conclude that the vocational career and not work as such is the canvas of adjustment and self-realization.

Careers have been viewed as the series of positions occupied by people during their lifetimes. However, opinions are divided as to the content and the time range of the concept. Hall (1976) stresses its multiple senses, but actually his career stages encompass the ages between 22 and 65, when the person is engaged in real work activity. Charlotte Bühler (1933) and later Super, Crites, Hammel, Moser, Overstreet, and Warnath (1957), who introduced the concept, also stress the primacy of vocational activity in defining the content of people's lives. Though the career is the sequence of vocations, jobs, and positions occupied by a person for a lifetime, the analysis of careers has to extend beyond the active vocational life to include antecedents in the prevocational stages that influence the choice of career. It may be appropriate to consider the vocational career as embedded in life activity, and therefore it can be understood only in this broader context. A person's career is the result of influences, processes, and decisions made before entering work, and it is intimately connected with all aspects of the individual's total life sphere. The understanding of this fact explains Super's evolution toward a life-span, life-space approach to career development (Super, 1980). He describes nine roles (child, student, worker—including unemployed as ways of playing this role—leisurite, citizen, spouse, homemaker, parent, pensioner) performed in four theaters of life: the home, the community, the school, and the workplace. Each role is typically played in one theater, but may also be played less often, sometimes less congruently in one or more other theaters. However, the excessive enlargement of the career concept referring to the lifetime evolution of the individual in his or her total life space may lead to the loss of the phenomenon's specific features and to the difficulty of delimiting it. Using the total life-space approach, the study of careers easily becomes a philosophical theory dealing with the human person's general evolution, like Driesch's (1921) reinstatement of the Aristotelian entelechy (the condition of realization in a potentiality) in a vitalist perspective or Erikson's (1963) evolution stages through crises from basic trust versus mistrust to ego integrity versus despair. However, approaching specific career problems from the point of view of life should be beneficial, as recently proposed by Cochran (1994), because the vocational career is part of people's wholesome life, and only this perspective can help them in coping with their problems and fulfilling their life aspirations. This integrated perspective does not alter the fact that work activity is dominant in human life and therefore occupies a special place among the roles performed in the person's life space during his or her lifetime. Hall (1976) emphasizes that the notion of career has not been designed and used exclusively by psychologists. The concept is broadly used in day-to-day language, having several senses:

1. Advancement. Of successful people it is said: "They made a career."
2. Certain professions are called careers (medical career, law).
3. A lifelong sequence of jobs. No value judgment is made about the type of occupation or the direction of movement.
4. A lifelong sequence of role-related experiences (the changing aspirations, satisfactions, self-conceptions). In this sense Hughes (1958) coined the term *subjective career*, which refers to the particular experiences that people have on their jobs, as contrasting with the objective career expressing the lifelong sequence of the jobs themselves.

Hall's approach stresses the unity between the objective and the subjective aspects of the career phenomenon, between "what people do and what they feel." This is an important step in understanding human behavior. However, the enumeration of senses in which the concept of career is used suggests the necessity to clarify another aspect sensed by the common language: the connection between career and success. It is expressed in two of the four sense connotations. We are told that "career" simply means success or that only certain professions are characterized as careers. Why physicians and lawyers, why not peasants, locksmiths, or dustmen? Obviously, because the professions called careers are related to people's image of success. Correctly, Hall rejects the success approach to the definition of careers, and so it should be. From an objective, scientific point of view, the dustman also has a career. However, the problem reappears when dealing with the relationship between careers and self-realization. The conception underlying the common language connotations is elitist. Physicians, lawyers, and military personnel have careers because they are supposed to be able to gratify all their needs. Industrial workers or clerks are not considered to be able to do so: They have no careers.

To arrive at this absurd conclusion, the content artifact already described had to be matched by a methodological one. It consists of judging careers from without, from the observer's point of view, and not from within—the subject's own evaluation. If we agree, however, that the judgment concerning the person's self-realization must be made by him or her alone, then obviously so must the evaluation of that career. The truth of this latter statement depends upon the possibility of demonstrating that (a) there is a variance in the subjective conceptualization of career success, (b) objective career success is not based solely on hierarchical advancement or the gain of power, and (c) vocational lives also constitute careers without an objectively acknowledged success, without continuity in a certain occupation, or even in the status of unemployment.

Research has brought into evidence at least two different views of career success. Some actors are oriented to career-long occupational advancement with the purpose of arriving at or near the peak in an occupational structure, while self-esteem is lost if this aim is not achieved. Such is the unlimited-success view, which contrasts with the limited-success perspective, by which actors consider themselves satisfied either to maintain their positions or to make modest progress within an occupational structure (Parsons, 1954; Hughes, 1949). A majority of people conceive of their careers as a continuous series of events related to the sense of their life achievements and embodying a subjective sense of success.

The question is whether one can predict the series of events composing people's careers together with the feelings of satisfaction or of failure and frustration attached to them. To do so, one will first have to take a look at the different career ingredients. They may be divided roughly into two groups: (a) dynamic factors that provide the motivational impulse to enter a certain vocation, to undergo there a process of socialization, to strive for vocational mastery and advancement, and to hold out despite the difficulties that inevitably appear, and (b) instrumental factors that provide the psychological tools of capability to perform the required occupational activity and the social tools of existing vocational avenues, organizational career paths, and job requirements.

The dynamic factors comprise the person's value system, vocational interests and aspirations relating the person's self-image to a certain occupational status. These psychological phenomena appear in the process of socialization and social interaction. Thus, to get a thorough picture of the dynamic factors of an individual's career, one will have to include also the agents of socialization: the family and adult acquaintances, school, peers, and the mass media.

The factors instrumental to the attainment of status in a specific occupational area may be divided into instruments belonging to the individual and to society. The former are vocational aptitudes and the knowledge and skills built on them, in addition to a positive attitude toward work and authority figures at the place of work. These factors compose the "personal dowry" people use to build their careers. If taking into account that a vocation means not only a field of activity but also its level and the institution where it is performed (Anastasi, 1964) and that in addition its main characteristic lies in its shape or mobility pattern, then the skill factor will be of utmost importance in leading to self-realization or for easy adjustment permitting self-realization in another area.

It should follow that career attainments are largely a function of the person's education. Such a contention would be rebutted by the growing practice of personnel reduction today. However, if speaking precisely of self-realization, one may say together with Fitzgerald (1986) that education has never been defined only in terms of its relationship to work. Thus, it is possible for somebody to be overqualified, but not to be overeducated, especially if the alternative to overqualification is to be unemployed.

With this last problem we are again reminded that the realization of a career relies not only on motivational and instrumental factors characterizing the person but also on the instruments existing at a given time and at a given place in society. These conditions determine the direction of aptitude development and mainly the existing possibilities and directions in which to use them. With all its innate basis, even the expression of a vocational calling is shaped by society. It is most doubtful, Freyre de Andrade (1965) points out, that there might be natives with a vocational calling for electronic engineering in the Amazon region or Germans with a calling for snake tamers. The societal instrument of career realization appears in a double aspect of challenge and constraint as the structure of existing vocations, which enable the performance of specific activities, in opportunities in the labor market to find employment in certain occupations rather than in others, and in the existing paths for career advancement. Today the meaning of career realization is mainly an organizational career path, while advancement by free change of positions appears to be rather an exception taking place after wars or social upheavals. In the past it was a most-favored aspiration and was seen as the expression of the "American Dream." At the present time this dream itself is changing and adjusting to the organizational career characterized by Milkovich et al. (1976) as a patterned sequence of positions through which organizational members move in a set order. In their view, careers are a structured property of the organization. This is only partially true. The career is also an individual phenomenon, because even from an organizational point of view "the organization is the people who are working there" (Perrow, 1970). Organizations themselves may be understood only when we have the conception of people located in various positions within them. This means that, apart from being a challenge for the individual, the career is a socialization constraint (van Maanen, 1978). In order to realize themselves through an organizational career, people must learn what is expected of them and behave accordingly. Society offers the individual an instrument for self-realization. The outcome depends on the degree of mastery of this instrument. The career is the meeting point of social and individual investments, and the purpose of the latter is to serve society as well as the individual. If one does have a genuine superiority, George Meade (1967) writes, one is a good surgeon, a good lawyer—but it is a superiority of which one makes use in the community.

This means also the taking of a position against all kinds of escapist manifestations. A "civilization of leisure time" in which work is despised and neglected is detrimental to society as well as to the individual. Amusement begins to function not only as a substitute for work but for activity itself (Janne, 1967), as more passive forms of leisure occupations start prevailing.

Society should give all people the opportunity to utilize their abilities, but they should know their abilities and aspire to a career activity in accordance with them. If Cooley (1967) is right that adolescent development includes the fit between aptitudes and interests, whereas the stronger component decides the direction of aspiration development, it has to be said that the two components have a different flexibility. Interests are easier to modify, while the aptitude inventory rests on native premises. What is lacking may be compensated but only to certain limits. Even a strong interest has to adjust not only to strong abilities but also to weaknesses, which means renouncing optimistic aspirations and changing them. In practice, the individual may refuse to do so and then make desperate efforts to avoid failure and keep up appearances, while the price to be paid is premature burnout. In his well-known book on stress, Selye (1956) pointed out that the energy reserves of the human body are limited, and thus also the resistance to stress. An important characteristic of aptitudes is that they permit the performance of activities with a reduced effort. A correct career plan will take into account the possibility of resisting stress for a long period of time. This and only this creates the premises for self-realization. In Napoleon's time it was said, ''Better a live drummer than a dead emperor.'' It ensues that one must not hold on to a job that definitely surpasses one's aptitudes, no matter how interesting it may be. People should be sincere with themselves; as to the others, a plausible motive will always be at hand to justify the renouncement.

The centrality of career in people's life depends upon the expected gratification of needs the career is able to provide in each anticipated sequence. What is unconditional is that society itself relates the work career to need gratification and self-realization.

3

The Holistic and the Hidden Aspects of Career Choice Linked to the Quest for Self-Realization

The new concept of self-realization functioning in the framework of adjustment is based on a holistic view of the human person and deals with the self-actualization of Everyman and not just of a social elite. It deals with real life as it leads to success but also causes stress and distress. Only such a broad view can explain the phenomenon in its complexity and possibly control it. If the vocational career constitutes a main vehicle of self-realization, the same holistic conception will have to be applied to its analysis.

The traditional concept of careers relies on the separation between work and nonwork and on the clear differentiation between life domains. This approach has definite advantages, as work is different from leisure and one should certainly not mingle the two and also keep separate work and family preoccupations. Yet, psychologically, such separations are difficult to make, because it is the same unitary and unique person who works, enjoys leisure preoccupations, and at the same time also tries to fulfill aspirations in family life. In order to live a satisfied and fulfilled life, some kind of congruence among these roles and activities has to be worked out.

In the last decades the link between work and the nonwork domains of life has been stressed again and again, as the leading role was ascribed to work spilling over upon leisure activities (Meissner, 1971; Cherns, 1973; Super, 1980). Even authors supporting the view that leisure has a compensatory role (Wilensky, 1960) claim that the meaning of leisure is secondary to work, as people want to get from leisure what they are not able to get from work. It is in this sense that Parker (1971) asks for the integration of work and leisure. Such a request was voiced earlier by Balchin (1970), who asked for the elimination of the factors that separated work from pleasure. He complained that nobody has introduced the drama and excitement, the colors and the showmanship of a football match into industrial work.

More recently there is a change in conceiving of the linkage between work and leisure as a consequence of the devaluation, the desacralisation of work (Yankelovich, 1974; Lévy-Leboyer, 1986). Work is no more considered a moral obligation. Unemployment hits people whether or not they are motivated and industrious. Past decisions seem to have no instrumentality because economic recessions could not be foreseen or forestalled. Therefore a shift appears in the place work occupies in the person's life sphere. Because of the advancement of technology, more time is available for nonwork activities. Stoetzel (1983) and Warr (1982) have found between 60 percent and 70 percent of men and women in Europe and in the United States who said they would be happy to stop working if they were able to receive a sum of money equivalent to their present salary. Lévy-Leboyer (1988) concludes that work motivation should be examined from a wider angle, including other activities. She points out that the motivation responsible for the quality and the quantity of work performance is due to factors both inside and outside the organization.

If one looks at the human person as a whole, there certainly is no ground to sever work from nonwork as far as meaningfulness of life is concerned. It is also an acknowledged fact that the roles of worker, family and community member, or leisurite change emphases in the process of development, as indicated by Super (1980). But then, this holistic "wider angle" (with the term used by Lévy-Leboyer) should be applied to the whole of career development, especially if the focus of interest is self-realization. It would shed new light on the process of career choice and on the development of career patterns linked to career images, to the orientation toward basic life and career satisfiers.

As already stated, self-realization is not a final objective appearing after the gratification of other needs: It is an omnipresent and continuous striving that affirms its successful climax when the conditions of objective success and adjustment are fulfilled. Self-realization as an end state is the result of a process.

If so, then the three choices on which self-realization relies also have a developmental history. To review, these are the choice of a salient life domain—more specifically, the choice between the career vs. another life domain as the area of self-realization—the choice of a reference group, and the choice of a vocation. Traditional career psychology kept these choices apart, although reciprocal influences were recognized. Murphy and Burk (1976) introduced a special career stage of renewal as a result of changes in self-image in midlife. Lyon (1965) spoke of serial careers to accommodate the changes caused in lifestyle by family or cultural events. Nevertheless, in the existing literature, even if reciprocal influences are acknowledged, the original choices are dealt with in separate developmental processes.

We are saying that the developmental process is holistic and choices are interwoven. What the person chooses is a track for self-realization, for attainment of her objectives, including the performing of activities she desires. Charlotte Bühler (1933) grasped this phenomenon when she entitled her book on careers as dealing with the "Lebenslauf" (one could translate it into English as "life development"), although she remained a prisoner of the general conception that life development is determined by one's vocational career.

The initial-life track choice with self-realization in view is an additional argument against Maslow's stepwise appearance of needs. One does not first aim at satisfying the need for security, then of affiliation links and love, and then of status: People make their early life choices having in mind a wholesome picture of all that they want in order to be self-realized and happy.

In this light, from the individual's standpoint, the choice of a vocation is not the capital and main choice of life. It is secondary and derived from the holistic picture of oneself in a self-realized end state. This is close to Cochran's view on the narrative paradigm. He writes, "We live in a story, we represent life in a story, we explain paradigms through a story" (Cochran, 1990). From an objective vantage point, the choice of a career is one of the most important life decisions as a main instrument to attain the desired end state. Yet, the isolation of the vocational career from wholesome life leads to the misunderstanding of the developmental process within its meaningfulness for the person.

The literature of our century has given attention to the development of the personality through the stages and passages of life (Erikson, 1963; Sheehy, 1976; Levinson, Darrow, Klein, Levinson, and McKee, 1978). Super (1980) has offered a synoptic view on life roles and outlined their interaction in different age groups. However, the problem at this point is not the objectively assessed interaction between roles, nor the progress through universal psychological stages of identity development but the individual's developmental process as it is forecast and realized by the individual himself and oriented toward the image of the end state hovering in his mind.

In this sense, and not without certain qualifications, the choice of a career could be considered indeed as being the translation of the person's self-concept into vocational terms, as it has been seen by Super (1963) and advocated recently by Vondracek (1992).

However, precisely as Vondracek senses it, career choices is not the whole translation of a self-concept into social practice but a contributing part, since self-identity also comprises ideological, family, and sexual orientation. It has to be defined in structural terms as a systematic link between all parts of the personality growing together in a proper development. It should be added that in adolescence, when the choice of a career is finalized, more often than not self-identity is not a clear concept but an image with agglutinated characteristics, and the choice of a career is intended to contribute to the transition toward another end-state image of oneself as a self-realized person.

We put forward the following theses: (1) Life choices are holistic. The domains are not clearly separated and the choice criteria are mixed, reflecting the wholesomeness of the end state. (2) Future life choices concern images. One has an image of oneself performing the roles of life, which include the vocational role. Although the image of the vocational role may undergo changes, the *end-state image of self-realization*, once formed, will remain stable in its main features. (3) The real motives of life choices are generally hidden from the external observer. We shall later deal with the problem of to what extent they are hidden from the person. At any rate, it is not an unconscious and repressed drive in the Freudian sense but more of a secret kept for fear of privacy invasion. Nonetheless, concealment of motives also used to follow from lack of clarity in the end-state image. (4) The individual's choices are based on the match of images. In choosing a career he matches his end-state image with an occupational image existing in public opinion. Career crises, psychological problems, turnover, and organizational problems with employees appear when the match reveals itself as having been illusive from the beginning or disintegrates.

We studied the evolution of careers over many years. It is a very difficult task because scientific accuracy would require longitudinal studies encompassing the whole of a career with statistically significant samples. The difficulties of such a task are nearly insurmountable. On one hand are geographical mobility within a society in transformation and socioeconomic difficulties halting the research; on the other, the natural limits of the searcher's life span may be shorter than the careers of his subjects. For all these reasons not all intended research projects could be completed, and what has been done extends over a very large span of time.

We shall start with the presentation of the following investigations: (a) a longitudinal follow-up over 40–some years (between 1948 and 1990) of 14 people well known to the author; and (b) a 12–year-long longitudinal follow-up of 25 female high school students during the years 1958–1970. Both these studies were conducted in Romania, but several members of the first sample emigrated to Western countries and were followed up there. A series of interviews were taken over time, and objective events linked to the subjects' life careers were registered and subjects were asked to evaluate them.

One could argue that they are very serious differences in values and culture between those samples and contemporary society. It is my conviction that neither political doctrines nor time changes the fundamental mechanism of human choices; they may add or modify the external constraints or content of values, but not the process of choice itself. The events, ideas, and ideals are only a canvas onto which choices and plans are applied. Humanness is universal over meridians and over time.

The sample well known to the researcher (see Table 3.1) comprised nine males and five females. Save for two, all of them obtained university master's degrees in a variety of fields. Table 3.1 epitomizes their life careers, starting with the dream-image of self-realization and continuing with life events until retirement. The life histories reveal the existence of three groups: (a) the group marked with * for whom self-realization lay in the chosen vocational activity comprised four subjects (29%); (b) the group marked with ** for whom self-realization was not linked to a specific vocational content but whose vocational career was essential for realizing their material and status aspirations comprised seven subjects (50%); and (c) the group of three subjects (21%) marked with

* * * for whom self-realization was not linked to a vocational career as such. While for the first two groups, totaling 79% of the sample, the vocational career was the salient life domain, for the third group it was not. Their life objectives comprised material comfort, marriage with a person of prestige, traditional life in community, or family life in general. The vocational career was of secondary importance. Nonetheless, they all had a satisfactory vocational record, as they were adjusted to their jobs, although the central domain in their lives was not the job, which they readily renounced or changed if family interests so demanded. Such an attitude fostered good family relations, and they all considered themselves finally as realized.

While the life objectives of the first group centered on a specific vocational activity, the end-state image in the second group focused on work perquisites and concomitants such as status, power or social salience, money, and material comfort. These objectives are not linked to an occupational activity of a specific content, yet the vocational career as such is instrumental to their attainment and a necessary condition. This group had the largest percentage of failures (43% as compared to 25% in the first group). Because of the small sample size, these differences are only indicative.

In the third group the choice of a vocation, imposed by society and economic needs, was nevertheless purely accidental and aimed at not interfering with the main direction of the subject's self-realization. In persons whose self-realization depended on a career but not on a specific vocational activity, the choice was determined by collateral characteristics of the chosen vocation that linked it to the wholesome images of self-realization, not to the vocational activity itself. To cast the problem in terms of differences in involvement as theorized by Kanungo (1982) and Jans (1982), the first sample group manifests career and also specialty involvement, the second group only work career involvement, while the third group manifests neither the one nor the other.

In our sample, psychology was chosen as a career by four subjects, but for only two of them was it a life objective. The other two chose psychology because, according to regulations existing at that time, it enabled them to become teachers, and this occupation was desired because of the comfortable working hours and conditions (e.g., long vacations) related to teaching and not for the sake of educating the younger generation. Being a teacher also meant a respectable position in the community, one suiting a "doctor's wife" or commanding respect from fellow citizens. One member of the sample (**M.E.**) chose teaching history because it permitted a career in which she could use higher education, the latter being a main component of her self-realization image. She chose history because she had entered a job after leaving school, and the university entrance examination in history was the easiest to prepare. When 25 years later she emigrated, she became an accountant and was very unhappy until her former higher studies were recognized. Since then she has been satisfied with her life.

Because of emigration **S.B.** also became an accountant. Earlier she had thought to become a teacher of chemistry, again because of the comfortable

Table 3.1
Life Careers of 14 Well-Known People

No.	Subject	Image of self-realization	Studies	Career entered in late 1940s and 1950s	Follow-up in the 1960s and 1970s	Follow-up in the late 1980s and early 1990s	Realization of initial dream
1.	B.*	To immigrate to Israel. To be a respected well-off medical man, to have a religious lifestyle.	Medicine	Country physician in Romania. Refuses to marry to facilitate emigration.	Country physician in Romania. In Israel, physician in social security. Married at age of 40.	Physician in social security. Not satisfied. Some problems with family.	No
2.	E.*	A respected and successful professor of psychology at a university.	Psychology	University assistant. Political dismissal. High-school teacher. Married at 29.	University teacher and well-known scientist. Head of research institute. Trouble with the regime. Emigrates.	University professor in Israel with known scientific activity. Satisfied.	Yes
3.	G.*	To be a Catholic bishop serving the Church. To live in comfort and to be sympathized with by women.	Vatican College "Propa-ganda Fide"	Unable to bear celibacy. Returned to Romania as a Greek-Catholic priest and married. The regime forced him to relinquish priesthood. Became a geography teacher.	Teacher emeritus. Has his own house (very important to him) and a romantic affair. Satisfied.	After retirement and the 1989 upheaval, activist for the restoration of the Greek-Catholic church in Romania. Satisfied.	Generally yes
4.	I.***	A doctor's wife living in comfort.	Psychology	High-school teacher. Waits for a doctor to marry.	High-school teacher of defective children. Marries a doctor at the age of 38.	High-school teacher. Satisfied. Lives in comfort.	Yes

28

No.	Subject	Image of self-realization	Studies	Career entered in late 1940s and 1950s	Follow-up in the 1960s and 1970s	Follow-up in the late 1980s and early 1990s	Realization of initial dream
5.	J.**	A communist activist having communist friends. To do intellectual work.	Chemistry	University nomination. Marries a former communist activist who became research fellow. Active in the Party.	University teacher in chemistry. Husband dies. Active in the Communist Party.	After the 1989 up-heaval forced into retirement because of past communist activity.	Yes
6.	M.E.***	To have a comfortable life. To have an academic title.	History	Junior high-school teacher. Marries at 26.	Junior high-school teacher. Comfortable housing. Emigrates and is very unhappy.	Office worker with academic title recognized. Advancement. Comfortable housing. Satisfied.	Yes
7.	M.V.**	A wealthy spender. To be a respectable citizen.	Chemistry	Administrative position. Marries at 20. Money troubles.	Administrative position. Lives beyond his means on borrowed money. Emigrates.	Employed in temporary research projects. Continues to show off.	No
8.	N.**	To become an applauded politician. To live a life of comfort without making efforts.	Philosophy	Activist of the Communist Party; dismissal because his parents had been well-off people. Became a teacher. Marries. Wife of "unhealthy" origin. Party frowns.	High-school head-master, again dismissed by the Party. Out of protest asks for transfer into a junior high-school.	Junior high-school teacher. Frustrated. Retirement and early death.	No
9.	O.**	An elegant wealthy man. To work with machines. To be a "ladies man."	Machine Engineer-ing	Research fellow in metallurgy. Marries at 23 the first girl who really loves him.	Research fellow in metallurgy. Frustrated but tells everybody how appreciated he is. Gives up thinking of love adventures as he fears his wife.	Idem. Asks for retirement at the age of 60. Shows off but inwardly feels hurt.	Very partially.

Table 3.1 (Continued)

No.	Subject	Image of self-realization	Studies	Career entered in late 1940s and 1950s	Follow-up in 1960s and 1970s	Follow-up in the late 1980s and early 1990s	Realization of initial dream
10.	R.M.*	To do research in psychology. To have success with men. To work for the Party.	Psychology-Education	College teacher. Very little success with men. Favored then abandoned by Party.	Research fellow. Marries in her late 30s. Bad marriage, divorce. Neglected by Party. Asks for retirement then emigrates aged 55.	Counseling psychologist in an important hospital in Israel. Satisfied.	Generally yes.
11.	R.**	Be a wealthy fashionable man. To work in the field of economics.	Economy	Works for the Party. Research fellow in Economic Institute. Attracted by high living standard in the U.S. and emigrates.	Recruited by the CIA to make propaganda against communist regimes. Receives death threats from communist secret services.	Nervous break-down. Receives new identity in the U.S. Retirement.	No
12.	S.P.**	Be a respectable citizen, living in a healthy condition (was ill in his youth).	Mathe-matics	High-school teacher. Marries a girl who attends to him during an illness.	High-school teacher. Enthusiastic about his wife, who is given honor by the Party.	Idem. Tells everybody how well-off and respected he is. After retirement sees he has realized nothing.	No
13.	S.B.**	Comfortable life with family; thinks of becoming a teacher of chemistry.	High-school only.	Emigrates. Marries. Housewife, then office worker. Again emigrates with husband.	Accountant. Gets promotions, happy with family.	The same until retirement. Satisfied.	Yes

30

No.	Subject	Image of self-realization	Studies	Career entered in late 1940s and 1950s	Follow-up in the 1960s and 1970s	Follow-up in the late 1980s and early 1990s	Realization of initial dream
14.	Z.N.**	To be a leader. To have social and economic success.	High-school	Becomes Party activist. Party frowns upon his Jewish origin and he emigrates to Israel. Marries.	Enters politics. Is promoted to managerial position in one of the trade-union-owned enterprises.	Top promotion refused. Plant in economic difficulties. He is offered early retirement under very favorable conditions. Becomes business man. Satisfied.	Yes

*   Self-realization lies in chosen vocational activity.

**   Self-realization not linked to specific vocational content, but vocational career essential for self-realization.

***   Self-realization not linked to vocational career.

31

working conditions this occupation offered. Unlike **M.E.**, she was immediately satisfied with accountancy, as she had also been with simple office work. All these jobs gave her the means to contribute to the comfortable life of her family. In all these cases the choice of history, chemistry, or accountancy was purely accidental and was easily reversed or changed. What counts for these people are the concomitants of the occupational choice, and the subject's only striving is to hold them constant across changes.

On the contrary, persons whose self-realization is linked to a definite occupational activity would not change it voluntarily. If such changes are forced upon them, they would revert to their beloved activity as soon as circumstances would permit. Of this group **B.**, **E.**, and **G.** had periods in which their desired career activity had to be changed. **B.** failed at his entrance examination for medical school, **E.** had to teach Russian instead of psychology and prepared his Ph.D. in psychology while teaching Russian in high school, and **G.** returned to his ecclesiastical preoccupations after a forced interruption of 40 years.

At the time all these people were in high school and spoke of their future, it was an image that they conveyed in all discussions: an image of oneself as a physician, a university professor of psychology, and the like in those who chose a vocational activity as a tool for self-realization, and an image of oneself as an elegant wealthy person working with machines or people (here the nonwork situation dominated but work remained an important component of the picture), or as a woman living a traditional life, marrying a physician, if work played nearly no role. However, asked directly about their vocational choice, all would come up with the name of a vocation. Out of shyness people are reluctant to reveal their dreams about the future, and they talk of vocational careers because of social desirability. Real intentions are at least partially, if not entirely, covered, and direct questions usually prove misleading.

With the exception of a few cases of a pronounced vocational calling based on early manifestations of outstanding aptitude, in most people the end-state guiding image of oneself lacks integration. That is to say, all desired elements are there, those belonging to work and those not belonging to it, but the person does not try to link them together in a unified plan and may pursue them separately or fail to see that they are contradictory to some degree. We may refer to **M.V.**'s image as a wealthy tippler and also a respectable citizen, **G.**'s image of being a high-ranking Catholic priest but also sympathized with by women and living in comfort. The more integrated the elements of the guiding image are, the greater the person's chances to realize it, and vice versa: the more contradictory they are, the greater is the probability of failure.

It appears, therefore, that the end-state image is not the kind of constructive representation of craftsmen and skilled workers (Krau, 1970b) in which the image of an object appears as the integrated result of work operations by which this object has been produced. Constructive images are precise guides for planning and subsequent skilled execution, because they are based on the knowledge expressed in the partial images conveying the sequence of work operations.

Thus, lathe operators who want to carve a given metal piece must have the representations of the metal after each partial transitory lathe operation until the desired form and dimension are reached.

People thinking of their future lives generally lack the knowledge of partial stages toward self-realization and have only the image of the end-state. This image seldom is the integration of clearly articulated phases, but people have "the feeling" of what they ought to do in order to realize it. The girl **I.**, whose life purpose it was to marry a physician, felt she must go out with doctors, and this is what she did; but **O.**, who wanted to be an elegant wealthy man and work with machines, entered a career in metallurgy that left him neither wealthy nor elegant, although he was definitely talented. His image was too unspecific to constitute an effective tool for planning and planful execution. First, machine work and elegance are incompatible; second, he entered research, where wages are lower than in industry, and became an entrepreneur only as he passed the age of 60.

It would be possible to reach a better articulation of the guiding image, were the subject willing to discuss it openly, but this does not happen. People are reserved when talking about their future life projects, and curiously enough real life-career choices are revealed mainly when they speak of their leisure preoccupations. Asked about her future vocation, **I.** would say she wanted to be a psychologist, but she spent all her time meeting and arranging dates with physicians or talking about such dates. Yet **R.M.**, another girl who saw herself as a future psychology researcher and indeed became one, used to talk about her studies and intended research projects even in her leisure time.

In discussing future occupational plans, **M.V.** praised his affinity for chemistry, however, in his leisure preoccupations the only matters of interest were nightclubs and card games. All the time there was much talk of borrowing money for these salient preoccupations. His self-realization image presented him as an elegant spender and a respected citizen. Subsequently he finished university studies in chemistry and married early in order to be a respectable citizen. Thereafter, all his life he chased rewarding administrative positions, while constantly trying to enlarge his financial resources by borrowing money, which he never paid back. All his acquaintances knew his flawed character, and nobody wanted to have anything to do with him, let alone lend him money. Finally, he gave up a good position in the hope of getting an even better-paying one through emigration, but his dream was not borne out. Such was the realization of a career choice in chemistry.

Leisure preoccupations in adolescence tell far more of life objects than discussions of the specific topic of occupational choice. Manifestly, occupational choices are made with the intention to realize the image that leisure preoccupations project, obviously because of their strong emotional load. Only if the vocational career is capable of commanding such an emotional load will it be the subject's salient and planfully realized life activity embodying self-realization.

At any rate, the guiding end-state image is always a complex one containing vocational and nonvocational elements, whereby the choice decision is determined by the emotionally loaded components of this image. In persons desiring to realize themselves in a specific vocational career, the emotional load extends to the vocational activity as such. The word "extends" is not accidentally used in the previous sentence. It means that also in the case of a strong career involvement the main emotional load is on the concomitants of the vocational activity. This phenomenon clearly appeared in our first (career and specialty involved) sample group. They saw themselves as *successful* research fellows, *renowned* university professors, or *respected* physicians; and the emotional emphasis lay on these concomitants. Nevertheless, for this group the special vocational activity as such offered the means to achieve the desired end state, while this was not the case with the others.

Relating the choice of a career to the person's self-image, Super (1963) considers that after the self-image is formed, the person translates it into the choice of a vocation whereby work entry marks its implementation. In the light of what has been said, this theory is congruent with reality only for people for whom the vocational career is instrumental for obtaining a self-realization status in which the vocation as such is a secondary attribute. Only for this group is it necessary to translate the self-realization image into vocational terms. This is not so for the groups whose self-realization is constituted of a specific vocational activity nor for those who see it in an entirely different life domain. For the former, no translation is necessary, as their self-image is essentially cast in vocational terms (even if concomitants play an important emotional role); for the latter group, the two are not linked, and the vocational choice is purely accidental, as Roberts (1968) would hold. The occupational career may be changed or interrupted with no influence on the individual's self-image, since such interruption has no detrimental impact on the roles and factors essential to self-realization.

This linkage between self-concept and the end-state image of self-realization is in line with recent research in which self-identity was related to paid employment perceived as challenging, varied, and goal achieving and to feelings of satisfaction with the nonwork aspects of life, but not to job satisfaction nor to work involvement (Brook, 1991). In the light of our theory, these specific findings were produced by a sample in which for a majority self-realization was not linked to a particular vocational activity and via a statistical generalization by which the life philosophy of the majority was forcefully applied to the minority.

In order to prove our contention that time and space have no influence on the basic condition and laws of human life goal-setting, the reader is invited to compare the groups of self-realization goal-setting analyzed so far on a sample from the 1940s in communist Eastern Europe with samples investigated at the end of the 1980s in capitalist Israel. The investigations were conducted in 1987–1988. The first sample comprised 60 subjects with various occupations:

12 engineers, systems analysts, technicians

12 physicians, psychologists, psychiatrists

6 educational workers

5 public servants, students

7 clerical workers

3 army officers

3 scientists, librarians

3 salesmen, insurance agents

7 production workers

2 entrepreneurs, artists

The mean age was 42.5 years, with a standard deviation of S.D. = 9.5. The subjects were asked to define what self-realization meant to them and to rate their achieved self-realization on a 7–point scale. They were then asked to motivate their ratings and to tell what they thought should happen for them to be able to fulfill their aspirations.

The salient feature in the definitions of life goals in the sample was their abstractness, and not only in persons belonging to a higher socioeconomic level. Compare, for instance, the definitions given by a former waiter and now owner of a pub and by an active army officer. The pub owner's definition of self-realization was "to realize myself in all life areas and mainly in work." The army officer's definition was "the capacity to receive in order to give—the capacity to help others—to accede to a task in which I shall have to use all the knowledge and experience I accumulated." Both definitions are quite abstract and reflect moreover what the subjects had read or heard about self-realization. The cherished end state of self-realization is carefully hidden, and only by hints is it possible to deduce the existence of an image depicting a superior army officer who helps his men and uses all his knowledge in the battlefield. The pub keeper's definition also stresses his work activity, but has even less the characteristics of an image and remains an abstract statement. At any rate, such definitions may be categorized as belonging to the group of self-realization in a definite vocational activity, matching the first group of our 40–year follow-up sample.

The abstractness of life-goal definitions is not so much an indicator of high striving as it was interpreted by Emmons (1992), but of concealing one's real motives. However, it is true that the phenomenon occurs much more frequently in the group that sees their self-realization in a particular vocational activity, which may create the impression of high striving.

The following vocational definition of self-realization was given by a motor mechanic and although it stresses work concomitants and is therefore somewhat more concrete, the level of striving is by no means low: "To be satisfied in my work, to develop myself, to care for my family, to see my grandchildren, to become self-employed." If we relate this definition to the previous follow-up study, it may be categorized as belonging to the second group, who strive to achieve concomitants of work career situations.

To the third group of aspirations, not related to work, belongs the definition given by a building entrepreneur: "To increase my leisure time in order to occupy myself with things not linked to work, to have a high-level income." This man was not satisfied with his progress toward self-realization, but this is not astonishing if somebody gives leisure first preference while still aspiring for a high income.

A satisfied systems analyst defines her self-realization thus: "To live well and enjoy life." Work is not even mentioned in the all-encompassing aspiration to enjoy life. Is it a low or a high aspiration? The answer is not easy and involves considerations of a philosophical nature. In a more concrete form the idea was expressed by a hotel cook: "To care for my family, economic security, happiness, hobby preoccupations, joy of life, grandchildren, to see my daughters married." Although she intended to be adjusted to her job in order to achieve "economic security," essentially her life aspirations were not linked to the domain of work.

The distribution of self-realization categories in this sample is very similar to that of the 40–year follow-up sample:

Group I. Self-realization in a definite vocational activity: 17 subjects = 28.3%

Group II. Self-realization in material and status concomitants of career positions: 32 subjects = 53.3%

Group III. Self-realization in areas not linked to work: 10 subjects = 16.6%

Where is the place of self-development in the self-realization typology? If it is linked to what has been termed by Stefflre (1966) the *occupational persona*, the individual aspiring to self-perfection will belong to our first group of self-realization, in a given vocational activity. If the meaning is a general *experiential living* (Toffler, 1970), then such persons will belong to our third group, whose self-realization is not linked to work.

At this point the reader may ask for some statistical proof of the differences among the aspirations of individuals belonging to the three groups of self-realization. To this purpose the subjects were administered the Value Scale of the Work Importance Study (WIS) elaborated by an international team in which the author of these lines collaborated. The instrument measures 18 values with 5 items for each, and the subjects are asked to evaluate each item on a 5–point scale (Krau, 1989b). Table 3.2 presents the results of this examination and the comparison between the three groups.

Though the three groups are different with respect to their value preferences, the differences are better articulated between groups I and II. A one-way analysis of variance between groups I and II yielded an F coefficient of 4.69 significant

Table 3.2
The Rating of Self-Realization in Aspirational Groups

Aspirational Group	N	Mean Self-Realization Score	SD
I	17	5.58	0.93
II	32	4.87	1.14
III	10	4.77	1.09
t I - II	2.33	p = 0.03	
t I - III	1.89	p = 0.06	
t II - III	0.25	nonsignificant	

at $p = 0.05$. The difference was $F = 3.12$ between the groups I and III, and $F = 3.05$ between groups II and III, both significant at $p = 0.07$.

The aspirational orientation in Group I, which seeks self-realization in a definite vocational activity, mainly comprises ability utilization, authority, autonomy, intellectual stimulation, prestige, risk taking, and variety, that is, the intrinsic characteristics of the vocational activity. Compared with the other groups, Group I members are less interested in aesthetics, social interaction, economic rewards, participation in decision making, and physical activity.

Group II, seeking self-realization in work concomitants, emphasizes social interaction, economic rewards, intellectual stimulation, participation in decision making, supervisory relations, and physical activity. These are conditions of comfort that a work life may offer to people not particularly interested in excelling in the vocational field.

Surprisingly, Group III presented a generally high involvement with values. These are people who "want it all," but without making the effort required by a work career. They want achievement, intellectual stimulation, creativity, and economic rewards, but without ability utilization, prestige, or physical activity. They are higher in social interaction and altruism and also in aesthetics than the others. These latter characteristics clearly point to the nonwork domains of life.

What is the link between aspirational groups and their actual self-realization? The data presented in Table 3.2 show that the clear goal direction of Group I gives its members a substantial advantage over the other groups. Though there is no significant difference between the satisfaction scores of achieved self-realization in Groups II and III, both rate their achievements lower than Group I.

It is true that these results are based on self-ratings and not on an objective assessment of achievements. However, self-realization has to be subjectively assessed, and recent research by Seidlitz and Diener (1993) has demonstrated that differences between happy and unhappy people in the recall of positive versus negative life events primarily result from differences in the interpretation of life events.

Other recent research in the United States has confirmed the deleterious effect on the actualizing tendencies of the self of an exaggerated focus on financial success (Kasser and Ryan, 1993). This idea was expressed earlier by Deci and Ryan (1985) with regard to what they called the *control oriented* personality style, looking for external sources of regulation for behavior and attitudes. In Kasser and Ryan's research conducted with students, the relative strength of aspirations for self-acceptance and community integration were generally associated with greater self-actualization, whereas an emphasis on financial success aspirations was related to lower psychological adjustment. However, these findings are in contradiction with Bandura's (1989) approach intimating that when people feel self-efficacious about obtaining highly valued external rewards, better adjustment should result.

Our conception of the three groups of self-realization aspirations offers a unifying framework to these contradictory conceptions, as they reflect the link among aspirations, their implementation, and the psychological well-being of different people. All kinds of aspirations are legitimate and *may* lead to self-realization *if* recognized and implemented according to their internal logic and if the person does not feel violated by an existing cultural pattern.

One might object that the link between self-realization aspirations and work, as expressed in the three-group typology, is largely status bound and that so are the achievements reported and rated by the three groups. This is so only to a certain extent, and we may refer to the case of the waiter/pub-keeper who, despite his lower socioeconomic status, belongs to the first group of self-realization in a definite vocational activity. Nonetheless, the problem remained whether the already-known division into aspirational categories would also be found in persons belonging to the upper echelons of work organizations or whether this status would produce only aspirations of self-realization in their work career. We therefore investigated a sample of 216 mid-level managers, people who had already made their entry into the upper social hierarchy but had not yet fulfilled all their aspirations. The sample was drawn from organizations of various sizes, working with various kinds of technology and belonging to different ownership categories. As a matter of fact, the main aim of the research was to find the characteristics of tomorrow's manager, and this wider aspect is discussed in Globerson and Krau (1993), but since the roots of people's future achievements should be found in their life aspirations, the managers were also administered the already familiar questionnaire on self-realization.

In Table 3.3 we find the familar groupings of self-realization goals: self-realization in the manager's vocational activity, in concomitants of power status and prosperity achieved through work, and in goals not linked to work. It will be remembered that in our first sample of youngsters, this last group comprised some 20 percent of the subjects, but it is not astonishing that in managers it will be smaller, comprising only 5.5 percent of them. The difference seems to have

Table 3.3
Middle Managers' Definitions of What Self-Realization Means to Them
(N = 216)

	Definition Examples	N	%
A.	Self-realization in a definite vocational activity	69	32
	Interesting, enjoyable work		
	To become a specialist in my work		
	Realization of my entire potential		
	Freedom in decision making on the job		
	To achieve the goals I set in my work career, in family life, in studies		
B.	Concomitants achieved through work	134	62
	Wealth, property, the achievement of a high living standard		
	Achievement of an important position		
	To succeed in all my undertakings		
	To make plans and to realize them		
	Satisfaction of all my needs and desires		
C.	Realization of goals not linked to work activity	12	5.5
	To be able to attend to my favorite hobbies		
	To work only 8 hours a day and feel good		
	To feel good every day		
	To enjoy good health		

enlarged the second group, that choosing concomitants achieved through work. Again, this group was by far the largest also in the longitudinal follow-up sample.

Self-selection into the managerial career produced a certain influence on the distribution of the self-realization aspiration categories but, very significantly, the same groups and the same proportions between them were found in this research too.

At any rate, 40 years after the first investigation in quite another geographical area and in a radically different socioeconomic system, the same behavior pattern became evident in life-goal setting. One might ask why we went into such a detailed analysis of the first sample with events that occurred a long time ago, when there was quite recent material at our disposal. First, in the investigation performed at the beginning of the 1990s, there are definitions of the personal meaning of self-realization but not a 40-year follow-up of their implementation. For the study of self-realization through vocational careers such a follow-up is very important, but at this stage it cannot be repeated because, presumably, the recently interviewed subjects will live much longer than the experimenter. Second, the definitions of grown-up people are much more abstract and sophisticated, as they deliberately try to hide their real intentions out of social desirability or as a resistance to the perceived invasion of privacy. This does not happen in conversations of one peer youngster with another. For all these reasons, we prefer to go back to our first sample of well-known people for whom date are available on their entire process of career development, and not just cautiously formulated definitions. We may pursue the analysis more confidently now: Time and space do not change the basic human condition and the psychological laws of behavior.

The analysis of future projects and "dreams" of life careers in retrospective reveals that the process starts early in childhood under the influence of significant adults and peers. At a certain moment one of the games reflecting adult roles becomes a favorite, and the child says, "When I shall grow up I shall be a—." Such vocational attractions are very unstable and more of a dream. The child does not think of them as a means of earning a living. When he becomes aware of this latter characteristic of vocational roles the dream becomes a vocational preference, but the motives that produced the dream remain and will be transferred to the newly expressed preference.

Between the years 1967 and 1974 we performed a comparative analysis of two groups of high school students: Group A with initially 130 high school students was followed up from the fifth to the twelfth grade, and in group B with 118 high school students anamnestic data were collected. In the fifth grade 75 percent of the subjects were able to indicate a vocational activity they would like to exercise. In the seventh grade this proportion grew to 90 percent. Recollections of senior high school students indicated the fourth grade for 42.3 percent of them as the moment when they began to think of a future vocation.

However, expressed vocational preferences have little stability at that stage, and even should they have, it is more of a verbal response learned under the influence of parents and teachers. From the point of view of an independent judgment, seventh grade is an important turning point and, indeed, more than half of the expressed options remained stable until the last grade of high school, when many students had second thoughts. As the moment of implementation approached, this tendency got stronger (see Table 3.4). Finally one-third of the options expressed in seventh grade remained stable and were implemented. This percentage is congruent with the one that appeared in the first sample group of the 40-year follow-up, the group for which self-realization lay in a specified vocational activity.

It follows that changes in the development of vocational preferences occur mainly in individuals for whom the vocational career is only instrumental to achieving certain concomitants of a vocational status or is not at all linked to the desired end-state.

Vocational preferences are stable only to the extent that they are the gist of the end-state image. However, it is understood that preferences must not be

Table 3.4
Stability of Vocational Preferences during High School
(in percentages)

From grade 5 to grade 7 N=130	From grade 7 to beginning of grade 12 N = 96	From beginning of grade 12 to the end of grade 12 N = 94	From beginning of grade 12 and implementation of decision N = 93
53	54.2	38.4	33.3

conceived narrowly. If somebody dreams of being a physician, and there is no way he could afford lengthy studies, he enters the paramedical profession; here one certainly can speak of stability in the development of vocational choice. Whether this is self-realization or not is quite another problem, and we shall discuss it later.

The test for the meaning of the vocational career for the individual's self-realization is the approaching of implementation, of leaving school and entering the world of work. Table 3.4 shows that the largest loss of stability in vocational preferences occurs during the last year of school. In this period nearly 25 percent of a years-long stability in preferences is lost. The moment of implementation is the moment of truth, marked by what German literature used to call *Torschlusspanik* (the panic of being trapped, as the gates of the town are closed in the evening). Contributing to this phenomenon is the enlargement of occupational information, which the individual now actively seeks. The point is that job realities will not deter persons who see in a vocation the fulfillment of a dream. They will scare off those for whom the career is an instrument to attain concomitants, because they will ask if such concomitants could not be attained with less toil.

The following excerpt of an interview illustrates how an instrumental career is forsaken when in new conditions the instrument ceases to be useful; as the logic of the Middle Ages held: Sublata causa tollitur effectus (if the cause is taken away, the effect vanishes).

G.V., 10TH GRADE, OCTOBER 1960

In the previous winter, **G.V.** traveled home on the stairs of the train and got sinusitis. She was operated on, but the disease would not disappear. She had strong headaches, she was not able to read or to understand what was being taught at school, and her school record was poor.

When I was little I wanted to learn at the music conservatory because I can sing. My older brother promised me he will help me with money. Today I do not want anymore to learn music because of my illness. I feel I must care for my health. In the hospital I asked how could I learn medicine, although formerly I did not like it. I decided to be a paramedic. My mother wants it too; she too lost her health at the age of 14. Since then she suffers from lung ailments, and even today she has not regained her health. Medicine is the only vocation which attracts me, because for all what you do in life, be it a physical or an intellectual activity, you need good health!

In later years the student's health improved, and so the basis for the passionate desire to learn medicine dissipated. In October 1962 she declared that she felt repulsion toward the medical profession because ill people in hospitals cry and complain all the time. The next summer **G.V.** entered a training school for chemical laboratories.

The lack of stability in vocational preferences may finally reflect temperamental characteristics based on what Pavlov (1951) has called the traits of Higher Nervous Activity. Here is the story of a student whose excessive nervous liability had been assessed also by psychological testing.

M.A., 10TH GRADE, NOVEMBER 1960

I want to be a teacher because I like being with children. I so resolved in the fourth grade when our teacher asked us what we want to be. Previously I had other preferences too. I wanted to be a medical assistant, and this because what I heard in one of our educational hours last year on the health profession. However, I changed my mind, because we learned anatomy and it is difficult, and I won't make it. Last summer I thought of becoming a journalist. I talked it over with my classmates in the dormitory [of the boarding school] and I renounced because they told me that it is tiring work in the newspaper office at night.

What teacher do you want to be?

Geography and Romanian.

These two specialties do not go together.

Then geography.

The vocational evolution of the student was as follows: In June 1961 she opted for medicine, in September 1962 (the beginning of the eleventh grade) it was the faculty of medicine, in 1962 geography and appeared again. After finishing school she entered a chemical training school for enterprises and later on got a corresponding job.

One could certainly ask whether in such cases there really is a guiding image at all. The answer is positive. An attentive analysis of the excerpt reveals in all expressed preferences the desire to work with people and to have comfortable conditions, and there is heavy emphasis on avoiding effort. These are her guiding elements for self-realization, and they may be applied to hundreds of jobs as her temperament of excessive lability dictates. What job she takes up is not important to her as long as the guiding elements of her self-realization image remain constant.

Stable or not, the vocational preferences expressed in the fourth or fifth grade do not appear out of the blue; they are prepared by the child's previous experience. It is of interest to follow how these things happen, through retrospective interviews, with questions tailored to the specific case, what in French psychology used to be called "the clinical method." Such interviews were conducted with 25 female tenth-grade students, who were subsequently followed up for a period of at least twelve years (1958–1970). The following interview excerpts shed light on how vocational dreams crystallize and grow into preferences.

B.M., 10TH GRADE, MAY 1958

B.M. wanted to be a teacher of history-geography (the two qualifications were paired in the Romanian curricula at that time), and indeed her school record was good in these subject matters. She liked books about places of historic significance and foreign peoples. She often listened to the radio programs of "Music of Peoples of the Globe" (a popular radio program at that time on which Western music could be heard) and "Merry Excursionists," even if they lasted until late in the night. She then wrote letters to girls who gave good answers in the "Merry Excursionists." In these letters she wrote on books and movie pictures and on life in her school. In school vacations she used to accompany a relative of hers on a truck carrying building stones from a nearby quarry.

Do you like to travel much?

I like excursions. When I was in a youth camp I liked it. I wish I could travel to Italy, India, Africa.

Is there somebody in your family who used to travel much?

She said that her father was a truck driver and had seen many places. When he returned he used to talk about the places he saw. In her childhood her father was seldom home. When he came back from his trips, he would bring her something and tell her where he had traveled. When the experimenter asked her to tell of an event of her life that had impressed her particularly, she recalled that once she lost her way in the Youth Camp: she and a girlfriend got lost in the woods.

In the coming years **B.M.** realized her vocational preference. She finished university studies and got an appointment as a high school teacher. Using our previous classification this would be a vocational choice based on a salient career where experiences linked to the specific vocational activity compose the image of self-realization. However, the emotional load that produced the career choice rests on the nonvocational components of her self-realization image, travelling and knowing strange places as her father did.

Not all people of this category succeed in realizing their dreams, and they have to compromise, as in the following example.

S.V., 10TH GRADE, MAY 1958

> I should like to be a pharmacist, but this is not my final decision. I chose this vocation only to name a choice. As a matter of fact, I am still undecided. When I was little, I had other thoughts. I wanted to be a ballet dancer, but I did not succeed. I went to the city of C. to register in the choreographic school, but I was not accepted because they receive children only up to the fourth grade and I already was in the fifth.

In the following discussion she said she liked an artist's life. She had an aunt who showed her much love, and this aunt had been a ballet dancer and used to tell her many stories about that life. The student added, "I did not change my thoughts even now. I cannot enter this vocation but I still hope. One hopes until one dies."

After finishing school, **S.V.** became a teacher of language and literature in a rural school. This was the closest she could get to the arts.   Let us now consider a case in which the love for literature reflected other preoccupations, which determined the final career choice and its implementation.

V.A., 10TH GRADE, MAY 1958

V.A. declared that she would like to be a teacher of literature, as she liked reading much. (She was indeed a good student.)

What do you read?

War stories. (She said she liked reading about how people kill each other. In those days of puritanic communism, crime stories were nonexistent because in the eyes of the régime they set bad examples.)

Are you really so tough and bloodthirsty?

Oh, no! (It appears, however, that at home she used to kill the chickens for meals when her mother had no time.)

She was especially devoted to her father. In his young days he had worked in a leather factory: They cleaned and tanned the hides. Afterwards he entered the gendarmerie (a very repressive police force in Romania before World War II). He often told stories of those days to other people, who would listen respectfully. "When he told them, I always sneaked in and listened," the student remembered, and added that to her he told tales about dragons. Her mother also told tales about dragons, but her father did it better, because he embellished them. When asked to tell an event of her life, she recalled a case when she nearly caused a girlfriend to drown.

In the years after finishing school, **V.A.** became an enterprise accountant working in internal controls. In a communist régime this was an organ of repression: They brought people to courts for the slightest financial negligence or misdemeanor, and sentences were disproportionately harsh. In a certain sense it really meant killing people. Additionally, her job was office work with people, where **V.A.** had "to read much," so all her desires came true, but in an entirely different arrangement. Her vocational career was a means for realizing concomitant preoccupations and desires. She might have found her happiness in a dozen other occupations where she could play "the dragon."

These cases illustrate how vocational preferences appear. The main mechanism is emotional reinforcement. This link of the chain usually disappears from the memory of grown-ups when they say: "When I still was a child I liked literature, arts," and it is in this sense that the real motives of choice stay hidden even from the person speaking. In a given culture, tales for children are very similar. One could assume that **B.M.** was also told tales with dragons, but she was particularly impressed by the stories her father told her from his travels, as he always *brought her presents* when coming home. A conditioned reflex links together gifts and travels and results in an attitude of positive evaluation and selection of certain experiences. The same process took place in **V.A.**, whose emotional gratification was linked to contents of repression and bloodshed, or in **S.V.**, where love for art originated in the loving care of her aunt who had been a ballet dancer.

It would indeed cause an awkward feeling, if the person would have to admit that the basis for a life career in geography is the presents brought by her father from his travels. In other cases, the linkages of life motivations for self-realization may be even more embarrassing.

B.V., 10TH GRADE, OCTOBER 1960

> I should like to enter a training school in the health profession because I like this work and I see how appreciated health personnel are.
>
> When I was in the fifth grade I thought of becoming a seamstress. My teachers convinced me to continue in senior high school but my parents were opposed. They said they were unable to support my studies.

However, as **B.V.** was a good student, she had no difficulty in getting a stipendium. She said she had an aunt who was a dressmaker. She often used to be at her aunt's and used to watch how she sewed. The aunt made dresses also for her. When she put them on, all would admire how nice they were.

How did you think of choosing a health vocation?

I participated in health courses and won first prize in the district contest and third prize in the regional contest. I was responsible for the Red Cross in our school.

Why do you think a health worker is more appreciated than workers in other occupations?

Every doctor or paramedic, when they arrive in a village, all love them. My aunt's husband got ill, and a paramedic treated him. After he cured him, my aunt started to like him.

After finishing school **B.V.** married a handsome, well-off man and remained a housewife. It is not astonishing that the student was more influenced by her aunt than by her parents, who rejected her. It is also not astonishing that the only and heavily sexual emphasis of her quest for self-realization (the identification with the aunt who cheats on her husband with a handsome paramedic) is hidden there. The point is that the entire "official" vocational story she tells is perfectly plausible; only the "unravelling of the plot" is surprising and confusing, but natural in light of her hidden motivation.

The meaning of "hidden" is not that the person forgets, rejects, or represses the events. As the interviews show, the latter are neither forgotten nor repressed, but the person deemphasizes the linkage. The chain of motives remains hidden to the environment and not under a clear focus of consciousness for the person herself. In other words, it remains imagery that is not spelled out, clarified by language, by what Pavlov (1951) called the *second system of signalization*. Paradoxically, in staying imagery and not being the object of conscious judgments, the influence of these motives grows. All events related to them may become irrelevant later, as Allport's (1937) theory on the functional autonomy of motives would hold, yet in every life decision of importance the original emotional load linked to former *significant others* will play a role of utmost importance.

Research has consistently held up the capital importance of the father for the development of his children. Psychoanalysis saw in children's relationships with their fathers a fundamental element in forming their personality. Even if today some smile at the idea that fathers' strong influence upon children rests upon a castration complex, that influence itself has been proved over and over. Much evidence has suggested that the father is the parent most concerned with the adoption of cultural values and traditionally defined sex roles (Lamb, 1976). It is not astonishing therefore that in the first two recorded cases the crystallization of vocational interests was linked to behavioral patterns elicited by an identification with the father.

While psychoanalytically nuanced theories prefer the term *identification*, learning theorists would speak of a process of *modeling*. They predict that a child will be more likely to imitate a model about whom it feels positively than one of whom it is afraid (Lamb, 1976). However, many studies have failed to prove behavioral similarity between the father's masculinity and the son's.

Therefore the term *identification* seems more appropriate if its meaning is a motivation to become like another person (Bronfenbrenner, 1960).

However, important as the figure of the father may be, the reinforcing gratification that shapes the child's interests may be linked also with other persons who play the role of significant adults. This was the case with the aunt of **S.V.**, but peers may also be regarded as significant others if they impress the subject with their greater experience and offer emotional satisfaction. Be the significant others who they may, their influence as norm setters on the person's behavior is considerable (Vallerand, Pelletier, Deshaies, Cuerrier, and Mongeau, 1992).

G.S., 5TH GRADE (MALE STUDENT), MAY 1969

I should like to become a teacher of physics because I like the radio amateurism I practice together with my cousin. He is the president of a circle of radio amateurs. He is also an excellent student and all admire him.

(One may conjecture who really are those ''all'' who admire him.)

D.V., 10TH GRADE (FEMALE STUDENT), OCTOBER 1960

I should like to be a doctor. I decided so because I am much attracted by this profession. I have a (male) cousin who studies medicine. In summer vacations he used to tell me about doctors' work for the sake of people and about methods to cure illnesses. Because of their devoted activity, doctors are loved and respected everywhere. When I was younger my dream was to become a teacher. I was very impressed by the teaching methods of my female literature teacher. I changed my mind 2–3 years ago, when I read books dealing with the life of physicians and how they treat ill people.

In the following discussion it appeared that these books were supplied by the already-mentioned cousin and that she did not remember any of the titles. At the interviewer's insistence, she remembered that one of the books was on cancer. She had a grandfather she loved much because he had raised her, and he died of cancer. There was another book on students' lives.

Apart from your cousin, do you know other students?

No (pause). In our village there is only one from the Polytechnical Institute (with disdain in her voice).

After finishing high school, **D.V.** entered the faculty of medicine and the last follow-up showed her as a well-appreciated physician, ''respected and loved'' as she had dreamed of.

Two matters of interest appear in this excerpt. **D.V.** was not raised by her parents (divorced) and had to seek for a significant adult elsewhere, first her female literature teacher, and then her male cousin, a medical student. The shaping of interests by the latter, having very probable romantic overtones, was deemphasized by the subject, who attributed it to reading books (which she did not remember). One may wonder whether to some extent the process may not even be hidden from the subject herself, again as a defensive measure aimed at asserting independence in making decisions of life importance.

Be this as it may, the high school student chose the medical career out of an entire complex of motives in which the vocational activity is only one component, and probably not the main one. This girl was attracted previously to teaching literature when the "cousin" came along, enveloping all kinds of tales about the importance of medical men with his personal charm, with the special attention he gave her in speaking with *her* (of all the girls of the village) and giving *her* books (perhaps there was even more between them, but for our purpose this is enough). At that time the girl had no other significant adult, as she had been raised by a grandfather who had passed away. For an excellent student, the switch from literature to medicine was possible. We have there the choice of a career for the sake of its activity, but in making this choice the activity was only one component in a holistic image dominated by nonvocational components.

The functions and qualities of the significant adults were investigated by Rodriguez-Tomé (1965), who concluded that they supply the developing personality with indications of self-knowledge with emotional implications. In adolescence self-search is a search among other people, although it develops within the individual. Significant adults reflect a positive image of the adolescents, they offer understanding and support. They are appreciated for their understanding character, for their intelligence, and for the success the subject thinks they achieved.

It follows that identification with the significant other is part of a process of information seeking and social comparison, but in contrast to the behavior of adults, where upward comparisons are ego-threatening and lead to negative affective reactions (Wheeler and Miyake, 1992), the upward comparisons in childhood and adolescence with closely related persons are ego-shaping and induce positive emotional reactions.

By the essence of the educational process, nature and society reserve the role of significant adults to parents and teachers, who should offer understanding affection and positive evaluation to the young they raise. Only when parents and school fail to fulfill these legitimate expectations is the role taken up by other people: uncles, aunts, grandparents, or elder peers on whom the adolescent bestows the role of educators. This may not be a positive phenomenon, but it is congruent with the laws of the personality's psychological development through positive reinforcement by affection and other gratifications.

Identification with a significant other may lead to choosing the same occupation, but it does not necessarily do so. **B.M.**, who because of her father's influence developed a strong interest in unknown places and landscapes, wanted to be a teacher of geography and not a truck driver like him.

Identification with the significant other concerns *only the behaviors reinforced emotionally.* Apart from this, the crystallization of the guiding image for self-realization is influenced by several ingredients. Cultural factors in the social environment play an important role, as does the self-evaluation of the subject's abilities, again relying on a process of social perception. However, the significant other is the integrator of the self-realization image and thereby of the basic characteristic of the life career to be chosen and implemented.

Holland saw this holistic characteristic of the career-choice process when he spoke of the whole personality in search of an occupational environment capable of gratifying its wholesome adaptive orientations. However, Holland takes up the analysis only at the point when these adaptive orientations are already formed. He writes that at the moment of vocational choice the person is a product of interaction between one's heredity, with a multiplicity of cultural and social factors and agents including parents, friends, significant adults, and one's own social status, and the physical environment (Holland, 1966). One may agree with this thesis but still ask how the "product of interaction" came into being, since precisely the characteristics of the crystallization process essentially determine the choice of the career and its implementation towards the self-realization end-state.

To complicate the matter further, the analysis of the crystallization process of the self-realization image meets with tremendous difficulties because the person's guiding image has components hidden from an external observer and even from friends. To reveal them would mean an intolerable invasion of most intimate thoughts; the individual fears ridicule and/or social sanctions. This may explain why Holland works with a sort of "finished product" and gives the subject the task of performing a self-directed search of career avenues. Such an endeavor is no threat to the subject's privacy and cannot reveal hidden motives; consequently, in the counseling process one gets the counselee's full cooperation.

One should not look at the crystallization of the end-state image of self-realization as a stepwise agglutination of elements taken by imitation from significant others. The process is one of interiorization, the way character traits, or what Freud called the *superego,* are formed. The process may not always be devoid of consciousness, as Freud thought. In some instances we consciously want to be like our significant others, but this aspect is less important. What counts is that, once interiorized, traits and aspirations become a basic framework of the personality's behavior. Just as self-concept has been found to resist change and maintain stability (Swann, 1983, 1987), it is difficult to change the crystallized end-state image of self-realization. Personal striving has been found to be very stable over time (Emmons, 1992). This is not because our behavior is determined from the unconscious; we may be quite conscious that we are shy or aggressive and even know why we are so, but by the same token we know perfectly well that we cannot change it, because "this is how we are."

Tice (1992) has recently found that cognitive dissonance and public interactional behavior were among the factors contributing to changes in self-concept. History offers the examples of St. Paul, St. Augustine, or Tolstoy. Yet, many times the change concerns self-presentation and not the self-concept, the area of activity and not the basic behavior pattern. Above all, aspirations for self-realization are the most resistant to change and the most cherished and guarded aspects of the personality. After repeated failures one may say, "I am a nobody," and behave accordingly, but in one's most secret thoughts still hope that one's aspiration dreams will come true. Frequently what changes is only the direction of self-presentation, not the basic behavioral style. Even in religious matters there is an anecdote relating that although Saulus became Paulus, the fanatic remained.

The political upheavals in Eastern Europe just after World War II and at the end of the 1980s saw many people who changed their political allegiance in order to stay in a position of social power but who stuck to old behavior patterns of intolerance. We shall present a story of such an apparent change of self-realization aspirations in the prosaic setting of everyday life. It is one of 54 cases of maladjustment investigated by us between 1982 and 1984 in Israel and is discussed in Chapter 8.

J., AGED 32

J.'s parents had separated, and neither of them had been much concerned with her upbringing. She had spent all her youth in boarding schools in the countryside. The family was well-off; at the time of the research her father was a successful businessman in the United States. In school J. was a mediocre student. She could have done better but invested all her energy in social relationships, while giving no thought to her future vocational career. All that she wanted was "a normal family" and a life in the countryside. She indeed married early in Tel-Aviv and worked in all kinds of temporary jobs until she and her husband resolved to move to one of the new agricultural settlements. There she got a job as secretary of the settlement's council, a job with considerable social prestige and power. She was very satisfied with her career, but then she separated from her unfaithful husband and felt she could no longer remain in the place where he lived. She returned to Tel-Aviv where she sought a position as a senior company secretary in order to have the same power and influence. But the job she got was dull, and she complained that she actually had nothing to do but answer occasional telephone calls. Her neuroticism scores indicated maladjustment, and she was deeply dissatisfied. She said that her experience as a council secretary had whet her appetite for interesting work.

Apparently we have here a case where an initial self-realization aspiration belonging to Group III, referring to a domain not linked to work, changed to one belonging to Group I, self-realization in a defined vocational activity. Only the concealment of the true aspirations contributed to this impression. As a matter of fact, her father remained her significant other, and her true aspiration was for power and social influence, while the domain of these aspirations proved nonessential and was taken from her frustrated youth experience, to prove herself in a "normal family" and in the agricultural setting where her humiliating boarding-school experiences had taken place. Until her clash with life situations, her true and lasting aspirations remained unclear, if not hidden, even to herself. In reality she did not change her aspirations but tried to move them from one area to another. Initially the family setting (with the husband) prevailed over all others. Her response to difficulties was flight, and in the end she became maladjusted.

The end-state image of self-realization is the blueprint of a life plan, which despite all its intricacy and lack of clarity has to be systematically carried out in order to ensure life success. A modification of the image components in later life stages threatens to annul all the preparations the person has made during lengthy periods of time. This makes achievement in completely new avenues very difficult, and a majority of people will be too frightened to try.

In order to complete the analysis of the psychological mechanism of career choice we have to enlarge its perspective. The crystallization of a future path for self-realization, of which the vocational career is a part, appears as a process embedded in sociocultural relationships. It is not only an act between individuals, the person and her significant others. The latter are agents of socialization, and the values they transmit are decisively influenced by their social environment, in content as well as in their order of preference (cf. Krau, 1987, 1989b).

The choice of a significant other means more than just the acknowledgment of a personal reinforcer. The significant other is an authority of reference whose opinions and values are interiorized by the subject and become standards for evaluating oneself and the world. Moreover, the membership group of the significant other becomes the reference group of the subject. Their values offer the standards against which success and failure are evaluated.

In our study of the theory of self-realization (Krau, 1989a), we mention objective success as one of its basic conditions, adding that for the subject success is an achievement acknowledged as such in the eyes of the person's reference group. Now we may add that the reference group is chosen through the person's choice of a significant other, which represents and personifies all genuine and social reference authority. This is a new link between the process of career development and self-realization; the latter choice is primary and dominant, the former secondary and derived. The person's life and career success concerns achievements congruent with the values of a significant other, i.e., of the significant other's membership group.

4

Occupational Images in Public Opinion: The Hidden Selection of the Occupational Appeal

Traditionally, the process of choosing a vocation has been presented as the match of a person's interests and aptitudes with occupational requirements. However, it has already been shown that the individual's body of reference and acceptance for his career choice is an image, his end-state image of self-realization, of which his intended career is a part. This is to say that the end-state image of self-realization is confronted and matched with the image the individual has of a particular career. The present chapter will investigate how this latter image is formed and what role it plays in the "self-selection into an occupation" (Krech, Crutchfield, and Ballachey, 1962). Maintaining the individual's role as an agent, we shall now give attention not so much to the push factors but to the pull factors, that is, to the occupation's motivational "valence," to use a term coined for a social context by Lewin, Dembo, Festinger, and Sears (1944).

Generally it has been considered that occupational appeal is a function of the area, the level, and the institutional characteristics of a certain occupation (Anastasi, 1964). However, occupational characteristics do not directly influence people who choose their occupation without on-the-job experience. In this case their impact is mediated through the occupation's image in the public. It is a well-known fact that people used to choose a vocation in accordance with its public prestige while neglecting specific information on the requirements of the job (Paterson, 1957; Lofquist and England, 1961; Poole and Cooney, 1985; Taylor and Pryor, 1985). This means that the individual choosing an occupation is exposed rather to what constitutes the reflection of the occupation's objective characteristics in public opinion.

The investigation of occupational images in the public must reveal the common features existing beyond the occupation-specific content, the characteristics actually motivating vocational behavior, and not only those declared out of social desirability. The best method to start with seemed to be eliciting free associations in which censorship and the "editing" of responses are reduced to a minimum, people being asked to tell everything that comes to their minds in connection with the name of an occupation.

We performed such research with 52 subjects (34 sophomore students in psychology and 18 students in education). They were asked to respond to the word-starters "psychology" and "teaching," so that we could obtain the key associations evoked in each by their own occupation and by the other one. The subjects approximated the condition of public opinion because in their own vocation they were not so advanced as to have the understanding of a specialist, and of the other occupation they had only a scanty notion.

All subjects were interviewed individually. In a first data processing, idiosyncratic associations were eliminated and similar statements were grouped together. As a result 200 statements on psychology and 120 statements on teaching were obtained. More statements were made on the subjects' own occupation than on the "other occupation"; those on the latter also included a high percentage of its shortcomings (see Table 4.1).

The public image of psychology appears to be strongly influenced by the emphasis placed on clinical psychology by literature and the mass media. Only 3% of the subjects mentioned the less-popular social, industrial, or child psychology. In a majority of associations, psychology was related to the assistance given in mental illnesses and the solving of intimate problems by a "bearded man" "leading an interesting life." It is fair to assume that these are traits of prestige and power, appealing to people who choose psychology as a vocation. Teachers are less outspoken, but the prestige traits are there, modestly concealed within the description of their activity: They have pupils whom they examine and to whom they give homework, which plainly means power; and they have long vacations, for which they are envied by people working in other occupations. It follows that the gist of public occupational images is constituted of traits of power and prestige, emphasized by people actually aspiring to those rewards. In this sense there is a linkage between prestige and personal characteristics as dimensions of the occupation's cognitive map (Gottfredson, 1981).

Gottfredson (1981) pointed out that people generally share a common perspective on the occupational world based on the social meaning of occupations. (This perspective constitutes a *cognitive map* with a three-dimensional anchorage: the perception of the occupation as more fitting for men or for women, its prestige level, and its correspondence to particular psychological and social characteristics. Jacobs and Powell (1985) and later Kanekar, Kolsawalla, and Nazareth (1989) found a relationship between the occupational sex type and prestige, as male occupations seemed to have greater prestige in the public eye; but Taylor and Pryor (1985) brought evidence that the problem should be considered in a more differentiated form. Thus "realistic" occupations in Holland's classification are of low prestige, although characterized as male jobs, while supportive and artistic occupations are of medium prestige, although sex-typed as female.

Table 4.1
Associations Obtained on "Psychology" and "Teaching" from Sophomore Students

PSYCHOLOGY			
Seen by psychology students	N 184	%	Examples
Characteristics fitting clinical psychology and counseling	98	53.2	Mental illnesses, empathy, stress, solving problems
Understanding the world	28	15.2	Knowing yourself, studies, the science of the soul
The psychologist's image	26	14.1	Beard, pipe, interesting life, interesting person
Shortcomings	26	14.1	Too much studying, disappointing, irresponsible, speculations
Psychology of the child, social, industrial	6	3.2	Improving society, understanding the development of children
Seen by nonpsychologists	14		Examples
Neutral statements	6	42.8	Treating problems, good language skills
Shortcomings	8	57.1	Not a science, preaches things – does not give solutions, haughty
TEACHING			
Seen by students in education	N 68	%	Examples
Satisfying work	8	11.7	It is hard work but satisfying
Describing teacher's activity	26	38.2	Pupils, exams, homework
Material rewards	8	11.7	Long vacations
Love of children	10	14.7	Love of children, education with love
Shortcomings	16	23.5	Noise, different schools – different students, lack of appraisal
Seen by nonteachers	52		Examples
Material rewards	12	23.0	Long vacations
Teachers are mischief makers	8	15.3	They are on strike all the time
Teachers are boring	16	30.7	They repeat themselves over and over, boring
Today it is difficult to teach	10	19.2	Lack of appraisal, insolent students
Teachers are losers	6	11.5	Only who does not achieve something more becomes a teacher

The subject is additionally complicated by the fact that the concept of prestige itself needs to be analyzed and explained. Duncan (1961) saw its gist in level of education and income, as the two are independent from one another and their impact is balanced. Curry and Walling (1984) objected to this opinion on the ground that the influence of education on prestige is strongest at the lower and upper ends of the social occupational spectrum, whereas income is related to prestige in the social middle ranks. Generally, however, education without income is not related to prestige. In more recent research with high school students Dickinson (1990) found that in adolescence occupational prestige is linked to the importance of the occupation's contribution to society, the effort it requires, and the necessary educational level. It has to be added that as a sociological concept prestige is culture bound. Its meaning and evaluation criteria differ with traditions and socioeconomic systems (Kapr, 1969; Adler and Kraus, 1985), and its impact on individual behavior also seems to be subject to dominant cultural influences (Krau, 1987). All these difficulties in the definition of the concept prompted redefining it for the culture in which the investigations herein presented took place.

In a research experiment conducted at an assessment center with 60 candidates for the positions of production engineer, chief bank economist, sales promoter, and bank teller (15 candidates for each occupation), a questionnaire with the following questions targeted the perceived prestige of the occupations that the subjects sought to enter: (a) What is the measure of prestige inherent in your occupation? Justify the rating by telling how people working in this field would describe this occupation. (b) How would people working in other fields describe the measure of prestige inherent in your occupation? Justify the rating by relating how they would describe your occupation. (c) How much influence do you think you will have on your advancement in your occupation?

The answers were scored on a 5-point scale. The results are presented in Table 4.2. They show significant differences between the occupational groups regarding the prestige of their occupation, as perceived by themselves and allegedly by other people. While engineers and bank economists were constantly high in both evaluations, bank tellers occupied the lowest rank, although they tended to ascribe a higher evaluation of their jobs to public opinion than the one they were willing to make themselves. Sales promoters occupied an intermediary position. Their self-evaluated prestige tended to be higher than the one allegedly made by public opinion. Said one salesman, "I know that this job is viewed as exhausting, heavy work which does not require special education, but in my opinion not everybody is capable of working in this field. I get from it great satisfaction, and I am proud of it." Bank economists also ascribed a lower opinion of their job to public opinion than the one held by themselves. In the overt questions they emphasized the job tasks that made them belong to management, while the public would perceive more the office work, the service to customers, working hours both in the morning and the afternoon, and the like.

There was no significant difference between the sample groups in the per-

Table 4.2
Evaluated Prestige in Four Occupations

Measures of prestige	Engineers		Bank Tellers		Bank Economists		Sales Promoters		ANOVA comparison
	X	SD	X	SD	X	SD	X	SD	F
Perceived prestige	4.13	.19	2.46	1.30	4.13	.99	3.26	.79	9.26*
How others perceive the prestige of this occupation	3.93	.59	2.86	1.24	3.66	.97	2.80	.77	5.62*
Measure of influence on advancement	3.66	.81	3.53	1.06	3.80	.56	3.53	.63	nonsign.

* p = .01

ceived measure of influence on advancement. A differentiating tendency appeared when the sample was divided into a group with work experience and another without it (F = 3.63 significant at $p = 0.06$). People with no work experience felt they would have a greater influence on their advancement than did those who already knew what was going on.

In regard to the perceived criteria for advancement, engineers and economists mainly referred to intellectual abilities, which constituted a significant difference vis-à-vis the other groups ($\chi^2 = 11.39$ significant at $p = 0.01$). Tellers significantly emphasized seniority ($\chi^2 = 10.40$ significant at $p = 0.01$) and regular attendance compared with sales promoters. Interestingly, sales promoters gave a prominent place to the criterion of loyalty to the organization (F = 7.25 significant at $p = 0.01$). These findings underscore the opinion expressed by Beehr, Taber, and Walsh (1980) that employees who were promoted used to perceive the characteristics in which they were strong as the criteria used by their employers for intraorganizational mobility. We may add that the same applies to candidates who do not yet know the organization but who aspire to promotion.

At any rate, the inquiry has proved that there is a "public evaluation" of the measure of prestige comprised in the various occupations. It is based on the occupational image existing in public opinion. The various occupational groups may have had a different evaluation of the importance and the prestige of their job. They emphasized job characteristics that do not appear in the public image or appear there in an ancillary role. The important fact is that the difference is not only between people who are working in an occupation and know it thoroughly and those who know it from hearsay only: All the sample subjects were candidates who had not worked previously in those jobs, and some of them had not worked at all. When they applied for a job, they already had a definite image of it and particular expectations of what they should do and the way the organization should respond.

At this point the analysis had to give a more precise description of the content of the occupational image; it had to explain how the differences appeared among the occupational images in public opinion, in individuals, and in occupational groups and what the significance was of such differences. The first question to answer was whether these differences were a function of people's occupational information. We decided to revisit the already investigated profession of psychologist (occupational psychologist) but to control the degree of information held by the subjects about the vocation. Accordingly, the research sample comprised occupational psychologists with a seniority of several years in the field, psychology students at the beginning of their specialization in occupational psychology, and professionals as well as semiprofessionals from fields of activity not related to psychology: engineers, teachers, and managers. There were 10 subjects in each sample group.

In accordance with the material obtained in the previous two investigations via free associations and open questions, it was hypothesized that the content of the occupational image would comprise the following items: (a) task content, (b) evaluational characteristics such as prestige or income, (c) the necessary abilities and skills, and (d) difficulties encountered in the occupational activity. The research started with an inquiry into the image of an ideal occupation using projective sentences such as:

People say an occupation is good if . . . .

People are successful in their occupation when . . . .

An occupation is frustrating if . . . .

Then the subjects were asked about the motives for choosing their actual (i.e., real) vocation, what the tasks of the occupational psychologist were, what abilities and skills were required, which traits favored and which ones hindered the exercise of the profession, what measure of prestige was attributable to it, and what the difficulties were with which a psychologist had to cope. The results of the inquiry were submitted to a z-test for comparing proportions.

Table 4.3 compares the evaluative characteristics of an ideal occupation in all sample groups with those of industrial psychology as perceived by the subjects who chose this career. The table shows that many more features are desired in an ideal occupation than are found in the real job of occupational psychologist. Nonetheless, the number of characteristics mentioned for an ideal occupation by nonpsychologists is smaller than the number given by psychologists and psychology students. The vocational attractions of students focus on interesting

Table 4.3
The Evaluative Characteristics of an Ideal Occupation as Opposed to the One Actually Chosen

| | 1. Students | | | 2. Psychologists | | | 3. Other professionals | Z-value comparisons | | | |
| | | | | | | | | Real occupation | Comparisons Ideal occupation | | |
	Ideal	Real	Z	Ideal	Real	Z	Ideal	1-2	1-2	1-3	2-3
Interesting work	10	7		5	2		10	3.89*	3.93*		3.93*
Income	9	2	4.42*	5	0	2.76*	8		2.17*		
Prestige	6	2	2.23*	6	1	4.42*	10			2.23*	2.23*
Ability utilization	6	2	2.23*	2	2		10		2.17*	2.17*	4.63*
Variety	2	0		7	0	4.44*	6		2.76*	2.17*	
Contribution to others	5	8		7	9		2				2.76*
Chances for advancement	5	4		2	1		6				2.17*
Labor market	0	0		2	1		0				
Satisfaction	6	0	3.93*	8	0	4.64*	6				
Normal healthy people	0	0		0	5	2.76*	0	2.76*			
Acceptance in occupation	0	2		0	1		0				
Visible results	0	0		0	0		3			2**	2**
Influence	0	0		0	3	2**	0	2**			
Other	1	0		0	3		1				
Total	50	27	3.47*	44	28	2.43*	62			1.70**	2.54*

* p = 0.01
** p = 0.05

work, income, prestige, and ability utilization; and they basically maintain these characteristics in the image of their actually chosen vocation (occupational psychology). We may therefore conclude that the above-mentioned characteristics are part of the occupational image of this profession and constitute its occupational appeal for newcomers. Psychologists with seniority have a more selective image in which they underline the pride they feel comparing themselves to clinical psychologists: They are dealing with a normal, healthy population, and they have real influence (what they intend to say is that they influence hiring and firing in organizations).

The task content of the profession of occupational psychologist as seen by the three sample groups is presented in Table 4.4. It is natural that the job tasks mentioned by psychologists with seniority are significantly more numerous than those mentioned by people who do not work in this profession, or not yet. Neither the students nor the group of other professionals include guidance, research, or human resource management among the tasks of the occupational psychologist. However, these very tasks are stressed by psychologists, and they convey connotations of social power. Presumably herein lies the real occupational appeal, but for connoisseurs only. Public opinion tends to see the tasks of the occupational psychologist in counseling and organizational intervention. True, nonpsychologists mention selection less ($z = 4.27$, significant at $p = 0.01$), probably because it is a more specialized term.

The opinions on vocational abilities and skills needed by occupational psychologists are presented in Table 4.5. The very instructive finding of this table is that the bulk of significant differences appears between the psychologists and both the other samples, including the students in psychology. This means that the image of an occupation held by those who work in it is not the one appearing in public opinion, and that during vocational training people still hold the public-opinion image of their vocation.

The differences between the public image of occupational psychology and that of the experts concern the need for openness and flexibility, diagnostic ability, decision-making skills, and expression skills. These are the traits stressed by psychologists, but they do not think they are in need of much knowledge. The public image of occupational psychology, as it appears in professionals and students, comprises features of helping and understanding, readiness, analytical and diagnostic skills, and knowledge. It is "leaner" and less nuanced than the psychologists' own occupational image.

It will be remembered that the psychologists and the students were also asked which traits and skills were especially helpful in occupational practice. Again, the psychologists gave richer answers ($z = 4.72$, significant at $p = 0.01$). The most important traits they mentioned were the ability for interpersonal communication, sensitivity and listening ability, analytical and decision-making skills, and the ability to influence people. Students agreed with the first two traits only, but added responsibility (no psychologist mentioned it). Once more, we see the features with power connotation appearing at the core of the occu-

Table 4.4
The Tasks of the Occupational Psychologist

Occupational tasks	Total	1. Students	2. Psychologists	3. Professionals	Z-value comparisons		
					1-2	1-3	2-3
Counseling	9	9	10	10			
Selection	17	6	9	2		2**	4.42*
Organizational interventions	13	4	3	6			1.70**
Diagnosis	11	5	3	3			
Listening	7	0	0	7		4.86*	4.86*
Guidance	5	0	8	0	4.93*		4.93*
Writing reports	3	1	1	1			
Research	2	0	2	0			
Human resource management	3	0	3	0	1.70**		1.70**
Total	93	25	39	29	2.35*		1.68*

* p = 0.01
** p = 0.05

Table 4.5
Personality Characteristics, Abilities, and Skills of Occupational Psychologists

Abilities, skills	1. Students	2. Psychologists	3. Professionals	Total	Z-comparisons		
					1-2	1-3	2-3
Readiness to help	8	8	7	23			
Understanding, listening	5	4	5	14			
Sensitivity	3	3	7	13		2.00**	2.00**
Psychological strength	3	2	4	9			
Openness, flexibility	1	6	0	7	2.76*		3.89*
Inventiveness	1	4	2	7			
Patience	2	3	1	6			
Analytical ability	6	6	4	16			
Diagnostic ability	3	8	4	15	2.59*		2.00**
Knowledge	6	2	4	12	2.00**		
Decision making skills	2	6	2	10	2.00**		2.00**
Inter-personal relationship	1	4	3	8			
Leadership	1	2	4	7			
Expression skills	1	6	0	7	2.76*		3.89*
Total	43	64	48		3.17*	3.00*	

* p = 0.01
** p = 0.05

pational image in persons who chose the vocation of occupational psychologist and achieved seniority in it. Obviously these traits constituted the real occupational appeal for them, but surely they are not the ones emphasized by public opinion.

Another question put to the subjects concerned the traits that would hinder the exercise of the profession of occupational psychologist. This time too the psychologists gave the richer answers compared with students ($z = 4.07$, significant at $p = 0.01$). However, generally the rank order is the same: lack of patience, superficiality, the need for variety and activity, and then, surprisingly, sensitivity, a trait much appreciated by the other professionals, that is, by public opinion (cf. Table 4.5). Once more we are gaining insight into hidden occupational appeals and aversions. If the exercise of power is the hidden occupational appeal, then surely too much sensitivity is an obstacle.

In order to investigate the prestige attributed to occupational psychology in the three sample groups, subjects were asked to rate it on a 5–point scale, to name the factors that determine it, and to rate the influence of the occupation's prestige on their career choice.

In Table 4.6 it may be seen that occupational psychology is rated as being of medium prestige in public opinion, while its prestige is perceived as higher by people who work in this profession or intend to do so. There seems to be consensus regarding several components of occupational prestige: demand for it on the market, income, and education. Public opinion also stresses visible success, advancement, and power, while the overtly stated pride of occupational psychologists and students rests more on intrinsic dimensions, contribution to people's well-being and helping people, and also on their professional qualifications achieved by passing difficult selection procedures. These differentiating characteristics seem to account for the significantly higher influence that prestige was rated to have on the career of occupational psychologists. For clinical psychologists these figures may be even higher, since several subjects commented that clinical psychology is higher in prestige. Nevertheless, one should bear in mind that the factors of prestige mentioned above are the overtly declared ones and that there are others, which are concealed, whose influence could be much stronger.

Finally, the occupational image includes what, for the public opinion, appears to be the trade's negative features and difficulties (see Table 4.7). One may notice that the drawbacks known by psychologists (the need for rapid decisions, unreliable instruments, difficulty in finding jobs) are not seen as such by the others. They particularly emphasize low income, lack of public appreciation, and lack of feedback. The last two evaluations are shared by psychology students, who understandably are also worried by the lack of jobs, but less by the need to make rapid decisions on people's fate. "*Iuventus ventus*," said the philosopher of the Middle Ages (youth is impetuous like the wind).

The literature used to treat the problem of occupational images in a more specific manner, as the perception of job characteristics related to the meaning-

Table 4.6
Prestige of Occupational Psychology

Prestige characteristics	Total		1. Students		2. Psychologists		3. Professionals		Comparisons		
	x	SD	x	SD	x	SD	x	SD	1-2	1-3	2-3
A. Degree of prestige	3.6	.28	3.8	.36	3.7	.21	3.4	.24			
Influence of prestige on career choice	2.9	.27	3.2	.31	3.2	.23	2.5	.41		$t=2.61^{**}$	$t=2.77^{**}$
B. Demand, appreciation	27		8		10		9				
Income	26		8		10		8				
Education	21		8		7		6				
Difficult entry	14		6		5		3				
Professional qualifications	11		4		5		2				
Contribution to people	10		4		4		2				
Power	7		1		2		4				
Visible successes	6		0		0		6			$z=3.9^{*}$	$z=3.9^{*}$
Responsibility	5		2		1		2				
Advancement possibility	3		0		0		3			$z=2.08^{*}$	$z=2.08^{*}$
Other	11		1		4		6				
Total	141		42		48		51				
C. Interest	15		7		6		2				
Prestige	8		3		3		2				
No prestige	7		1		2		4				
Poor income	6		2		2		2				
Helping people	8		4		4		0			$z=2.59^{*}$	$z=2.59^{*}$
Intrinsic dimensions	23		11		9		3			$z=1.92^{**}$	
Extrinsic dimensions	24		7		9		8				

A = Evaluation of prestige; B = Factors on which prestige is based; C = Occupational image in projective questions
* p = 0.01; ** p = 0.05

Table 4.7
Difficulties and Negative Characteristics of Occupational Psychology

	Total	1. Students	2. Psychologists	3. Professionals	Z-comparisons		
					1-2	1-3	2-3
Rapid decisions	18	4	8	6	2*		
Lack of public appreciation	11	2	1	8	3.35*	3.76*	
Low income	9	3	1	5			2.16*
Lack of variety	5	2	1	2			
No jobs	5	3	2	0		2.08*	
Unreliable instruments	4	0	3	1	2.08*		
Long training, difficult entry	4	2	0	2			
Difficult empathy	4	2	1	1			
Burnout	3	1	2	0			
Other	9	2	6	1			
Total	80	23	28	29			

* p = 0.01
** p = 0.05

65

fulness of the job and to job satisfaction (Hackman and Oldham, 1976; Kulik, Oldham, and Hackman, 1987). In the view of these authors, three main job dimensions are linked to meaningfulness: skill variety, task identity, and task significance. There might be some doubt as to the usefulness of job-specific dimensions for the definition of the occupational image and also regarding the substitution for the concept of prestige of the narrower one of meaningfulness. Occupational image concerns the perception of a vocation and not of a particular job. Using the strictly circumscribed job-specific meaningfulness risks over-looking most important factors linked to a more dim and individualized sense of prestige and power that essentially influences vocational behavior.

In order to clarify this problem, research was conducted with 34 teachers and 26 applied computer programmers as to the perceived meaningfulness of their work and its influence on satisfaction. Satisfaction is generally considered an indicator of prestige, if measured in an occupational group and not individually (Robinson, 1969; Rainville, 1974; Weaver, 1977).

It was hypothesized that teachers would consider their work more meaningful, given its greater task significance (education of the young generation) and task identity (transmission of a well-defined body of knowledge) and the greater skill variety required for illustration, logical demonstration, eliciting active partici-pation, and transmitting values. Applied computer programming is of a more routine nature. It revolves around turning a general program into a collection of orders coded in the language of the computer with predetermined symbols. No values of high social appreciation are involved. It was assumed that, given the greater meaningfulness in teachers' work, teachers would be more satisfied, that is, would feel that their work has higher prestige than the work of applied programmers.

The subjects were administered a questionnaire on the dimensions of mean-ingfulness in their jobs, namely, the perceived complexity of their job, variety and difficulty of work tasks, overload and stress, logic and ability utilization, and the feedback received. Questions were rated on a 5-point scale, and their mean constituted the score of meaningfulness. For the measurement of work satisfaction, Smith, Kendal, and Hulin's (1969) Job Description Index was used. In order to guard against bias by an unequal number of relevant questions for the different job facets, raw satisfaction scores were divided by the number of items. Thus an index was obtained ranging from 0 to 1. The results are presented in Table 4.8.

It appears that teachers consider their work to be high in required skill variety, complexity, task significance, ability utilization, and self-expression and low in stress, overload, and boredom. Compared to teachers, programmers have lower ratings on all components, and the perceived meaningfulness of their job appears lower indeed. They are also less satisfied. However, while in programmers there are significant correlations between the component scores of job significance and the corresponding job facet satisfaction scores, this is not the case with teachers, where only ability utilization and the absence of stress and boredom

Table 4.8
Meaningfulness of Job and Satisfaction in Teachers and Computer Programmers

Components of meaningfulness dimensions	Teachers		Programmers		One-tailed t-test comparison		Correlation with job satisfaction	
	Mean	SD	Mean	SD	t	P	Programmers	Teachers
Skill variety	4.52	.70	3.38	1.41	3.77	0.001	0.25	0.08
Skill complexity	4.05	.73	3.53	1.27	1.86	—	0.49*	0.12
Task significance	4.41	.70	3.80	1.02	2.58	0.01	0.27	0.12
Ability utilization	3.97	.71	3.19	1.29	2.75	0.01	0.49*	0.39**
Self-expression	3.97	.93	3.26	1.18	2.48	0.02	0.56*	0.15
Feedback	3.73	.82	3.46	1.02	1.10	—	0.28	0.31
Overload	2.97	.99	2.96	1.21	0.03	—	-0.40**	-0.06
Emotional involvement	3.41	1.23	2.38	1.35	3.01	0.01	0.41**	-0.06
Boredom	2.58	1.10	2.96	1.14	1.16	—	-0.16	-0.32**
Bureaucracy	3.26	1.10	2.50	1.17	2.55	0.02	-0.43*	-0.01
Stress	3.41	1.13	2.80	.98	2.21	0.03	-0.48*	-0.44*
Qualitative overload	2.00	.85	2.53	1.30	1.82	—	-0.80*	-0.28
General meaningfulness	3.52	.43	3.06	.84	2.51	0.02		
Job satisfaction	0.84	.13	0.07	.07	3.17	0.002		

For all items DF = 25,33
* p = 0.01; ** p = 0.05

correlated with satisfaction. For the rest of the items the rating of meaningfulness in teachers' work does not correlate with the rating of satisfaction.

This means that the meaningfulness of work and job satisfaction refer to independent dimensions of the occupational image. Meaningfulness of work is not a substitute for the various content aspects of job satisfaction. It only partly accounts for the prestige of an occupation and for the satisfaction felt with various job facets. It follows that there are other job characteristics that are not manifest components of the occupational image but still influence its emotional impact. This problem is crucial because it underscores the issue of hidden characteristics in the occupational image. They eventually determine the perception of occupational prestige, whence the vocational choice and job satisfaction.

People choosing a vocation are first acquainted with it through its reflection image in public opinion. This reflection is not a true copy of the original. At the beginning of the century Binet (1911) demonstrated how facts were modified *bona fide* in subsequent accounts merely by being transmitted from one individual to another. As a result, essential facts are mixed with anecdotal, objective and verified information with mere impressions. We hypothesized therefore that the occupational appeal (its motivational valence) comprised both relevant and irrelevant information as far as successful performance of job duties is concerned. The pairing up between the relevant job information contained in the occupational image and the individual's interests and abilities is a necessary condition for staying in an occupation (Wanous, 1973; Warren, Winer, and Dailey, 1981). It follows that people active in a certain vocation would have traits that matched the institutionalized performance requirements; but according to our hypothesis, they would also have traits not related to the formally acknowledged job requirements, as they corresponded more to informal attributes.

It has been repeatedly pointed out that many applicants entering various jobs do so on the basis of nonscientific information (Lofquist and England, 1961; Allen and Keaveny, 1980; Taylor and Pryor, 1985). As irrelevant job traits are not contradicted by institutionalized criteria of vocational success, their possessors will not be "selected out." Notwithstanding, they strongly influence job behavior.

These hypotheses served as a basis for research studying both the manifest and the concealed content of occupational group images and their impact on vocational behavior. The focus of its content was the nursing occupation (Krau and Ziv, 1990).

Nursing is chosen as an occupation by young, predominantly female persons after finishing high school and also by "career changers." This fact is well known empirically and has also been established in several published studies (Haug and Sussman, 1967; Booth, McNally, and Berry, 1978). Consequently, the age factor does not influence the occupational appeal in this particular vocation, and there are common, widely publicized incentives that reinforce the occupational image as far as public opinion is concerned. These incentive image-characteristics attract candidates for nursing at the beginning and at the middle of their careers. It was assumed that the possibility of acting in accordance with the humanistic values of helping people was one such major appeal, and this value should have been particularly strong in people who chose nursing as a second career.

There is substantial empirical evidence that humanistic values are a very important feature of the public's image of nurses; one has only to mention the stories of the outstanding historical figure of Florence Nightingale who was known as the "Lady of the Lamp" because of her embodiment of the image of the "charitable nurse." The hypothesis was also in line with the findings of rigorous research attesting to the fact that humanistic values constituted a major reason for female students to choose medical school (Feather, 1982), and even more so for career changers choosing nursing as a second career (Haug and Sussman, 1967). However, in people switching to nursing after a lengthy history of vocational failure, the involvement with values in general and with intrinsic values in particular should have surrendered to a burnout-like indifference, as attested by the literature (Kafry and Pines, 1980). It was suggested, consequently, that career changers entering nursing did not constitute a homogeneous group, and one would have to consider the people who chose nursing for its intrinsic values after a more or less successful vocational record in a stable occupation separately from those who entered nursing after having failed repeatedly in different jobs. In the latter group burnout features should have been evident. On the other hand, some burnout should also have been evident in registered nurses because of the emotional stress of the profession.

In addition to humanistic values, other common appealing characteristics of nursing should stem from the adaptive environment (Holland, 1966) of this occupation. Holland (1973) classifies medicine as an Investigative-Social-Artistic occupation. Nursing certainly belongs to this domain, but nonetheless it is a vocation on its own and not only medicine. It was assumed that for nurses the social interest (helping people) would occupy the primary position in their orientation hierarchy, but there were grounds for some surprise at the presence of the Artistic orientation in vocations having nothing to do with the arts. One explanation would have been the need for emotional sensitivity, complementing the desire to help people. However, in accordance with the hypothesis of irrelevant vocational traits being mingled with relevant ones, there was a need to take into account all the implications of the Artistic adaptive orientation in the psychological profile of the nurse. In fact, this trait refers not only to the search for self-expression through artistic means, of which the nursing occupation offers very little, but also indicates emotionality, the relevant vocational trait, and a lack of conformity. It is in this last sense that Dupont, Bersier, and Müller (1987) found the artistic type among medical students. Nursing should, therefore, appeal to persons who, in addition to possessing the relevant vocational characteristics of emotionality and interest in helping people, will at the same time reject authority and demonstrate high intragroup solidarity. Objectively, resistance to authority does not impede nurses' vocational performance,

since paramedics provide specialized services and in many cases take on independent roles (cf. Birenbaum, 1974). Nonetheless, these irrelevant vocational
traits of authority rejection and group cohesion are prone to influence the occupational behavior of nurses. In this respect career changers with a previous
record of failure should be more conformist and have less "artistic" impulsivity.

Nurses' nonconformity and rejection of authority should also be linked to the
feature of prestige bestowed upon this profession by the public. In the prestige
ranking of Israeli society, nursing appears in the upper region of the upper-
middle quartile, with a prestige score of 64.18 out of 100 (Kraus, 1978). One
may conjecture that this relatively high prestige score is an effect of the link of
nursing to medicine and of its strong emotional appeal. However, it was considered likely that the prestige score of the occupation in itself acted as a vocationally irrelevant but very efficient cause of attraction. Registered nurses who
know their occupation from experience rather than hearsay should give their
vocation a lower prestige ranking, resulting in a lower preference based on the
value of prestige.

Prestige means comfortable working conditions and mainly power and/or a
high income (Mirande, 1968; Kraus, 1978; Curry and Walling, 1984). This explains why in the quoted research (Kraus, 1978) dentists are to be found at the
top of the prestige ladder. It was hypothesized that in addition to the relevant
vocational interests and abilities, nursing appealed to people having strong materialistic drives, as the latter are expressed in impulsive behavior dedicated to
the acquisition and the preservation of material property. Such drives should
have been especially strong in people making their first career choice and in
registered nurses looking back on a history of vocational success.

This hypothesis may shock the reader, but it should explain such astonishing
findings and events as nurses' negative attitudes toward aged patients (Campbell,
1971; Gillis, 1973), who generally are considered of low prestige (Rosencranz
and McNevin, 1969; Bengston, 1971); the indifference toward suffering and the
neglect of disabled patients during nurses' strikes, as in the highly publicized
Israeli ones in recent years, the real motive for which was the demand for
substantial pay rises and for more comfortable working conditions; and also the
strong demand echoed by Birenbaum (1974) for ending the subordinate status
of paramedics and recognizing them as members of an autonomous profession
with a legal monopoly for the performance of certain strategic aspects of health
work.

According to the hypotheses of the study, the research sample had to comprise
registered nurses and persons choosing the nursing occupation at the beginning
and in the midst of their working careers, that is, student nurses at their first
jobs and student nurses after a working record in other occupations. The registered nurses of the sample were employed in two large hospitals, and many
of them also had the task of tutoring the student nurses. The latter sample was
recruited from two nursing schools for registered nurses, one of them (mainly
frequented by women with children) with a four-year course of study and the

other with a three-year course. The content of the curriculum was the same in both schools and only the duration of studies was different, to facilitate the participation of mothers with children in the four-year course. To ensure the comparability of socialization periods, the subjects were drawn from the second and the third year of studies and divided in accordance with previous vocational socialization within an occupation, into four groups.

1. Seventy female students with an average age of 28.5 (SD = 7.90) years who entered nursing as their first occupation after their army service. Forty-three percent of this group were married and had been homemakers for several years. This percentage is high enough to control the variable of marital status vis-à-vis other groups where, understandably, the number of married women was higher as they were somewhat older.

2. Forty-two female students who chose nursing as a "second career" after a working record in another vocation such as teaching, laboratory work, or assisting a physician. One had been an engineer, and one an accountant. The mean age in this group was 31.6 (SD = 5.55) years.

3. Twenty-four female students who switched to nursing after multiple and quite lengthy trials in various jobs, mostly clerical, including computer data processing. The mean age of this group was 29.3 (SD = 4.24) years.

4. Forty-four registered nurses with an average age of 35.6 (SD = 5.93) years. Many of them had duties of instructing and tutoring the student nurses and as such represented a factor of occupational socialization.

In this context it should be underscored that despite the differences in age, all subjects belonged to what Super, Crites, Hummel, Moser, Overstreet, and Warnath (1957) described as the career stage of Establishment. Therefore all sample groups were largely comparable.

In accordance with the research hypotheses there was a need to analyze nurses' work values, interest profile, work motivation, personality traits related to their occupational life, vocational image, satisfaction, and biographical data. These analyses were performed as follows.

1. The instrument used for testing work values was the Values Scale of the Work Importance Study (WIS) elaborated by an international team. Slight modifications in wording have been made in each country to fit national particularities. The variant used in this study has been described in detail by Krau (1987). It is known as the "unshortened variant" and investigates 22 values, both intrinsic and extrinsic. The subject is asked to rate the importance of each statement on a 5–point scale.

2. To test nurses' interest profile a somewhat shortened version of Holland's (1973) self-directed search (SDS) inventory was applied. The instrument consists of three sections: activities, competencies, and occupations. As our subjects had already chosen their vocation, it was felt that the inclusion of the "occupations" section would blur the expression of the personal hierarchies of adjustive ori-

entations. Consequently, only the first two sections of the inventory were administered, ten items for each section that composes the validated Hebrew version of the instrument (Meir and Krau, 1983).

3. Work motivations were tested in three ways: (a) a direct question inquiring about the motives of choosing nursing as a vocation; (b) an open-ended projective question referring to the motives that lead people to choose a vocation ("When an employee is looking for a job or s/he has one already, what does s/he need to be satisfied?"). These questions were inserted in a biographical questionnaire, which also contained provisions to secure the necessary classification data (cf. item 7); and (c) the measurement of personality traits with the aid of a projective personality test (see item 4).

4. Relevant vocational personality traits were measured by the aid of the already-described projective personality test elaborated by Krau (Meir and Krau, 1983). It will be recalled that the test measures the following traits: behavior control, social extraversion, attitudes towards authority figures at the place of work, self-assertion, vocational involvement, the valuing of money, and control versus impulsivity of behavior in issues involving money.

5. The information pertinent to the vocational image of nurses has been obtained by asking our subjects: (a) what abilities and capacities are necessary to exercise the nursing vocation? (b) what are the difficulties a nurse encounters in her occupational activity? (c) what is the prestige of this occupation in the public eye? In order to know to which social strata the nursing profession appeals, information was obtained on the subject's socioeconomic level as expressed by the occupation of the husband or of the father (for nonmarried subjects). Lastly, the evaluation of relevant vocational concepts by the semantic differential method completed the information on this topic. The semantic differential list used the 12 qualifiers proposed by Osgood, May, and Miron (1975). The following concepts were investigated: Work, Nursing, My Previous Occupation, the Doctor. As known, in this method the concept-stimuli are rated on a 7–point scale for each qualifier pair. Scores are derived for the Evaluation, Potency, and Activity of each concept (Osgood, 1964; Osgood, May, and Miron, 1975).

6. The investigation of nurses' satisfaction was meant to complete the information on nurses' vocational image. The subjects rated on separate 5–point scales their overall life satisfaction and their satisfaction with their occupation, their family, and their personal functioning. The answers had to show how central was the satisfaction nurses derive from their vocation to the general framework of life satisfaction.

7. To complete the picture, some biographical data were collected, such as age, family status, number of children, previous jobs, and quitting motives.

As the research hypotheses referred to the presence of certain traits in the personality profile of people choosing nursing as an occupation, the main procedure lay in attesting to the presence of those features. Statistical tests of significance were applied in order to check the presumed differences between registered nurses and student nurses, between student nurses at their first occupational entry and career changers, between career changers with a previous vocational record of stability and those with a record of failure. Here are the results of the research.

VALUE PROFILE

Table 4.9 presents the work value profiles of the different sample groups, the rank order of value preferences, and the differential strength of the value involvement (value intensity). Differences appear (a) in the general value involvement of subjects belonging to different sample groups and (b) in the differential involvement (or lack of involvement) with certain values.

The data show a significantly lower general value involvement in the group with a history of lengthy unsuccessful occupational tryouts in comparison with the group of registered nurses ($t = 2.16$ significant at $p = 0.05$) and the group of student nurses in their first vocational experience ($t = 2.35$ significant at $p = 0.02$). This means that unsatisfying vocational experiences that lead to career changes reduce the general involvement with work values and that this group of people entering nursing does so with a burnout value profile.

The differential involvement with certain values is expressed in the shift of value-preference ranking from one sample group to another. Particularly interesting are the cases where certain values, such as Economic Security, Intellectual Stimulation, or Participation in Decision Making, are classified in entirely different quartiles. The last value seems to be only of medium importance for student nurses, who had no experience of working in an organization, but very important for the other groups.

As had been expected, the group that chose nursing after the experience of another, more-or-less stable vocation is more intrinsically motivated. Economic Security and Economic Rewards are less important for this group, and Intellectual Stimulation has a higher preference rank than in the other samples. In turn, this latter value is not important after lengthy trial periods. The more materialistic orientation of this group appears in the comparatively greater importance given to economic values (Security and Rewards).

A gradual process of "burning out" expressed in the change of value orientation is well exemplified in the rank-order modification of Altruism and Life Style (initiative in shaping one's life) and in the diminished attraction of Advancement in the group, which previously had lengthy unfruitful trial periods.

Important common value preferences exist across all sample groups. They concern the top preferences, as well as the least preferred and therefore rejected values. Thus, in all the sample groups, Physical Activity, Risk Taking, Authority, and Economic Rewards range among the least-preferred values. On the positive side, despite slight differences between the sample groups, the following values rank first in preference order: Ability Utilization, Supervisory Relations, Achievement, Economic Security (with the exception of the group of career

Table 4.9
Nurses' Value Profile

Work values	Total Sample			First Vocational Experience After High School			Switchers After Multiple Trials			"Career Changers"			Registered Nurses		
	x̄	σ	Rank	x̄	σ	Rank	x̄	σ	Rank	x̄	σ	Rank	x̄	σ	Rank
1. Ability utilization	23.79	1.68	1	23.57	2.00	1	23.12	1.45	2	24.42	0.72	1	24.18	1.19	2
2. Achievement	22.80	2.24	3	22.57	2.34	4.5	22.25	2.53	5	23.14	2.16	5	23.54	1.37	3
3. Advancement	20.02	3.51	13	20.68	3.38	1.3	16.50	3.39	16	19.85	3.31	12	20.72	5.59	12
4. Aesthetics	19.26	3.98	14	19.65	3.88	15.5	18.75	3.38	12	18.78	4.12	14	19.00	4.36	16
5. Altruism	22.20	2.36	9	22.57	2.46	4.5	21.75	2.94	7	21.64	1.54	8	22.09	2.19	10
6. Social interaction	20.77	3.26	11	21.17	3.22	12	21.50	1.80	8	19.00	3.70	13	21.27	2.79	11
7. Authority	17.54	3.67	20	17.71	3.84	20	14.87	3.65	20	18.35	3.08	17	17.90	2.90	20
8. Autonomy	20.48	3.18	12	21.20	2.69	11	18.00	4.66	14.5	20.5	3.28	11	20.00	1.90	14
9. Creativity	21.59	3.13	10	21.61	3.18	9	20.25	3.49	11	21.42	2.71	9	22.72	2.76	8.5
10. Economic rewards	18.02	3.53	18	18.58	3.31	19	16.12	4.31	17	17.07	3.86	20	18.90	1.97	18
11. Economic security	22.76	3.37	4	23.38	2.58	2	22.37	2.34	4	21.07	4.75	10	23.27	3.24	5.5
12. Environment	19.10	3.31	15	19.47	3.53	17	18.37	2.95	13	18.57	2.47	16	19.18	3.58	15
13. Intellect. stimul.	22.35	2.46	7	22.02	2.44	7	20.37	2.73	10	23.57	1.84	3	23.27	1.71	5.5
14. Life style	18.85	3.17	19	19.82	2.82	14	15.87	2.14	18	18.64	3.67	15	18.27	5.56	19
15. Particip. in decis.	22.55	2.71	5	21.58	3.11	10	23.50	1.87	1	23.57	1.59	4	23.54	1.77	4
16. Prestige	18.73	3.86	16	19.65	3.27	15.5	15.00	3.96	19	17.42	4.53	19	20.18	1.84	13
17. Responsibility	22.39	2.00	6	22.02	2.21	8	22.50	1.58	3	23.00	1.77	6	22.72	1.54	8.5
18. Risk taking	16.01	4.09	21	16.80	4.09	22	13.75	3.89	22	15.21	4.41	21	16.18	2.85	21
19. Spiritual values	22.22	2.32	8	22.25	2.25	6	21.12	2.14	9	22.07	2.52	7	23.09	2.02	7
20. Supervisory rel.	23.32	2.08	2	23.02	2.22	3	22.25	2.38	5	23.78	1.56	9	24.45	1.15	1
21. Variety	18.65	3.74	17	19.37	3.60	18	18.00	2.87	14.5	17.57	4.43	18	18.18	3.27	17
22. Physical activity	16.10	4.58	22	17.45	3.67	21	14.12	4.96	21	15.14	5.89	22	14.45	3.52	22
General value Involvement	20.43	2.33		20.73	1.96		19.10	3.19		20.17	2.80		20.77	2.76	

changers), and Participation in Decision Making. Student nurses without organizational experience give this latter value a lower rank; but taking into account
the preference for Supervisory Relations, nurses appear to have strong positive
attitudes toward an organizational climate built on participation.

The preferences for organizational ties and for teamwork are surely relevant
vocationally, as is a much higher preference given to Altruism in comparison
with an unselected population (cf. Krau, 1987). However, the rejection of Authority presages organizational trouble.

INTEREST PROFILE

Table 4.10 presents the data obtained with the administration of Holland's
S.D.S., that is, the general scores and those obtained separately for the sections
of "Activities" and "Competencies." As could be expected, the chief adaptive
orientation of nurses is the "Social" one (the "Supportive" social environment,
Holland, 1966), which mainly determined the choice of their vocation. However,
there are interesting differences in the second and the third places of the orientation hierarchies in the two sections of the inventory profile of Social-
Investigative-Realistic. This profile, the "formal" interest profile of nurses based
on job-relevant traits, closely follows the rank order of Competencies. A more
deeply rooted orientation profile appears (deeper because it is blurred by the
general profile) when examining the interest for Activities. Here the second place
is occupied by the Artistic adaptive orientation. Because it concerns Activities
that the subject likes to do or to learn (to see a theater performance, to paint,
to read popular literature, etc.) and not Competencies (I am capable of, or should
like to be a soloist in a choir, paint people, carve sculpture, etc.), this finding
is in line with the research hypothesis that the artistic interest in the context of
the medical profession means emotionality and nonconformity. This explanation
is reinforced also by the fact that the Conforming adaptive orientation occupies
the last place in the general profile and in the Activities profile of nurses' interests.

Breaking up the total sample into its composing groups does not bring significant changes in the configuration of the results, which means that whatever
the circumstances of vocational choice might be (first vocational choice or "second career"), nursing appeals to persons with a well-defined interest profile.
One is, of course, entitled to ask whether this interest profile could be the result
of occupational socialization within the nursing vocation during the subject's
apprenticeship, rather than one existing at the time the vocational choice was
made.

Our findings attest to the cumulative effect of vocational socialization, which
is superimposed upon the typical interest profile in persons choosing nursing as
an occupation. Vocational socialization produced a rise in the rank order of the
Enterprising orientation (in the Activities section of the S.D.S) in registered
nurses and in persons who functioned in another stable occupation, while in

Table 4.10
S.D.S.—Interest Profile of Nurses

	General Interest Profile						Activities						Competencies					
	Realist.	Invest.	Artist	Social	Enterpr.	Conform.	Realist.	Invest.	Artist	Social	Enterpr.	Conform.	Realist.	Invest.	Artist	Social	Enterpr.	Conform.
Total sample																		
x̄	6.88	7.35	5.66	8.51	5.94	5.10	6.23	6.35	6.77	8.23	6.13	5.23	7.54	8.33	4.55	8.80	5.76	4.97
σ	2.49	2.21	2.35	1.81	2.65	3.09	2.63	2.36	2.34	1.96	2.63	3.18	2.35	2.06	2.36	1.67	2.66	3.00
Rank order	3	2		1					2	1	3		3	2		1		
Registered Nurses																		
x̄	6.22	7.35	5.99	8.31	5.90	4.99	5.18	5.81	6.90	7.45	5.81	4.90	7.27	8.90	5.09	9.18	6.00	5.09
σ	2.08	1.91	2.05	1.75	2.55	2.63	1.99	2.32	2.19	1.77	2.24	2.77	2.17	1.50	1.92	1.74	2.86	2.50
Rank order	3	2		1				3.5	2	1	3.5		3	2		1		
First Career Choice																		
x̄	6.99	7.17	5.46	8.68	6.05	4.77	6.54	6.40	6.85	8.42	6.17	5.40	7.45	7.94	4.08	8.94	5.94	4.14
σ	2.57	2.43	2.43	1.81	2.84	3.18	2.69	2.52	2.53	2.01	2.90	3.19	2.46	2.34	2.57	1.62	2.78	3.17
Rank order	3	2		1			3		2	1			3	2		1		
After Another Vocation																		
x̄	6.67	7.74	5.82	8.42	6.14	5.21	6.00	6.85	6.64	8.42	6.71	4.57	7.35	8.64	5.00	8.42	5.57	5.85
σ	2.61	1.81	2.08	1.54	2.17	2.87	2.67	1.95	1.87	1.49	1.86	3.20	2.55	1.67	2.29	1.59	2.49	2.55
Rank order	3	2		1				2		1	3		3	1		2		
After Multiple Trials																		
x̄	7.68	7.43	5.81	8.24	5.18	6.49	6.75	6.12	6.50	8.12	5.37	6.12	8.62	8.75	5.12	8.37	5.00	6.87
σ	1.87	1.88	1.92	2.04	1.76	2.76	2.63	2.20	2.39	2.36	1.72	3.33	1.11	1.56	1.45	1.72	1.80	2.20
Rank order	2	3		1			2		3	1			2	1		3		

Reprinted with permission. Courtesy of Barmarick Publications.

Figure 4.1
Profile of Nurses' Personality Traits

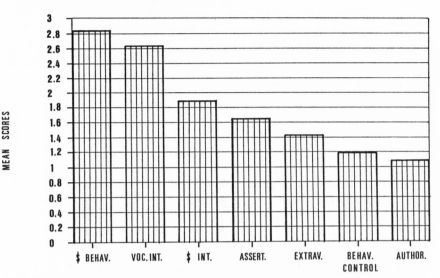

Note: Mean scores of the following traits (from the left to the right): Impulsivity vs. control of behavior involving money, Vocational interest, Valuing of money, Self-assertion, Social extraversion, Control of behavior (boldness-fear), Attitudes toward authority figures at the place of work. Scores of 2 and above are high, scores of 1 and below are low.

Reprinted with permission. Courtesy of Barmarick Publications.

individuals with a lengthy history of job and occupation changes it caused a significant burnout-like increase of the Conforming orientation in the general and in the partitioned interest measurements ($F_{ANOVA} = 2.85$ significant at $p = 0.05$) with a relative decrease in the rank order of the Artistic (i.e., nonconformist) adaptive orientation. This latter change also appears in persons who had worked previously in another stable vocation, but it does not appear in the group of registered nurses, the socialization model of the sample.

PERSONALITY TRAITS IN MEMBERS OF THE RESEARCH SAMPLE

Figure 4.1 presents the mean scores of the personality trait measurement performed with the aid of the projective personality test.

It may be seen that the intrinsic vocational interest is quite high, significantly higher than the attraction of money (*t*-test for correlated samples = 2.96, significant at $p = 0.01$), but in problems involving money the behavior is most impulsive with little restraint. It is even accurate to say that the profile apparent in Figure 4.1 is dominated on the "plus side" by this trait and on the "minus side" by a low, negativistic attitude toward authority figures at the place of work. Both these traits should have important organizational consequences, and their presence is not fortuitous: Both traits are the corollaries of the Artistic adaptive orientation apparent in persons to whom the vocation of nursing appeals. It is evident that the subjects chose the nursing occupation not with a main or with the only purpose of making money. Money as a vocational preference comes third, and only after the trait of vocational interest. This latter trait is strongest in persons who chose nursing as a second career, a finding already reported in the literature (Haug and Sussman, 1967). It will be recalled that in the rank order of value preferences, the most important work value was Ability Utilization, followed by Supervisory Relations and Achievement, which, for women, has a strong connotation of personal development (cf. Krau, 1989b). At any rate, the results mean that nursing appeals to persons inclined to display a strong vocational involvement (a relevant vocational trait!), but money is of great importance in the lives of nurses, and although they do not desire large financial gains (economic rewards as a value are rejected), they will react strongly should they feel that their rights to a fair remuneration are being threatened.

One could ask why the scores of Social Extraversion are not higher, given the importance of the social adaptive orientation in nurses. The point is that the latter is expressed not just in sociability, outgoingness, but also in group solidarity, which in the psychological profile of the figure appears precisely in the moderate values of self-assertion in relation to the group. This group solidarity of nurses again presages organizational trouble if seen in the context of the two already-mentioned dominant traits of the profile.

Nurses' nonconformity is underscored by their negative attitudes toward authority figures at the place of work, as the scores of 0 and 1 at this trait indicate negativistic attitudes. In a way, this result was to be expected because it is congruent with the high scores on the Artistic (viz. nonconformity) scale of the S.D.S. We may now say for sure that nonconformity in nurses is not so much the result of vocational socialization (although there certainly is peer pressure in this direction) as the expression of a basic personality profile to which nursing appeals.

WORK MOTIVATIONS

Table 4.11 presents the frequency of responses given by the subjects to the question of why they chose nursing as a vocation. First to draw attention is the high percentage of "Challenge to Achievement of Aspirations" answers in the group of career changers ($\chi^2 = 11.02$ significant at $p < .01$ after reductive correction for calculating in percentages) in comparison with the registered nurses. In the latter sample there is a higher percentage of subjects pointing out that they had already had a strong interest for this vocation in childhood ($\chi^2 = 6.88$ after correction significant at $p = 0.01$), but also a higher percentage stating that they chose nursing by chance ($\chi^2 = 14.63$ after correction significant at $p < 0.01$ for df. 2). The results mean that nursing appeals in the first place to

Table 4.11
**Motives As Indicated in Direct Questioning for Choosing Nursing As a Career
(percentage of answers)**

Motives	Registered Nurses	Student Nurses: Nursing as first career	Career Changers	After Multiple Trials
Desire to help people	27.2	38.7	35.2	30.2
Because of an experience in childhood (desire from childhood)	27.2	9.6	2.9	—
My studies promoted this choice	9.0	9.6	20.0	14.6
Challenge to achievement of aspirations	9.0	—	32.3	31.4
Advice of friends, specialists	9.0	3.2	—	—
I like this vocation	—	25.8	—	—
It corresponds to my interests and abilities	—	9.6	—	—
By chance	18.18	3.2	8.8	16.8

Reprinted with permission. Courtesy of Barmarick Publications.

people with strong intrinsic motivation and a strong specialized interest (this conclusion is supported by the high percentage of "Challenge to Achievement of Aspirations" and "I like this profession" answers), but yet the choices by chance are indicative of people who see in their occupation an opportunity to fulfill motives not linked to the content of work. Career changers choosing nursing appear more intrinsically oriented, and this finding is not new in the literature.

The projective question concerning work motivations sheds more light on the partly ambiguous findings above. Table 4.12 presents the frequency rank order of 12 motives that were consistently evoked. It will be recalled that this open question elicited several answers from each subject.

In the projective answers given without embellishments of social desirability, the intrinsic motive moves to the third place (in registered nurses who know their work from long years of practice, it moves even further), and in the first place appear the extrinsic motives of pay and working conditions, while the concomitant of social interaction remains second.

The projective work motivations given by nurses are supported also by the other findings of the research, especially by the significant rank correlation between motives and the separately assessed work values ($\rho = 0.38$ significant at p (0.01). Reference may be made also to the psychological roots of nurses' work motivations as they appear in the personality profile evinced by the projective personality test.

Table 4.12
Rank Order of Motives for Choosing a Vocation
(answers to a projective question)

Work motivations	Registered nurses	Student nurses: First career	After another "career"	After multiple trials	Total sample	Pooled work values in total sample	
						Rank	Pooled values
Supervisory Relations	9	6	7.5	8.5	7	1	Supervisory Relations
Ability utilization	3	7	9.2	4.3	6	2	Ability utilization
Interesting work	7	4.5	3.5	2.5	4	5	Intellectual Stimulation; Spiritual Value
Achievements and Satisfaction	5	4.5	5	7	5	4	Achievement; Altruism
Creativity	9	11.5	9.2	10.3	11.5	6	Creativity
Social interaction	2	2	3.5	2.5	2	7	Social interaction
Pay	1	1	1.5	1	1	3	Economic security
Autonomy	9	11.5	9.2	10.3	11.5	8	Autonomy; Life style
Consideration	5	9.5	7.5	8.5	8.5	12	Prestige
Advancement	11.5	9.5	6	4.3	8.5	10	Advancement
Variety	11.5	8	9.2	10.3	10	11	Variety
Working conditions	5	3	1.5	4.3	3	9	Environment

Reprinted with permission. Courtesy of Barmarick Publications.

NURSES' VOCATIONAL IMAGE AND SATISFACTION

Nurses' perception of their vocation is recorded in Table 4.13. The table shows that the ability perceived as most important for nursing is Understanding based on a supportive attitude. This trait is followed in order of importance by the integration of theoretical knowledge and practical skills. This evaluation of the necessary aptitudes for nursing corresponds with nurses' S-I-R adaptive orientation. Indeed, Holland (1966) assumed that the orientation profile was also based on the knowledge of one's abilities.

Looking at the table, it may be more accurate to state that interest orientation is related to self-evaluated abilities, because more than half of the student nurses entering their first job and even one-third of the registered nurses experience physical and emotional difficulties. To follow this line of thought, it could be stated that nursing appeals to people who think that they are high in understanding and supportive attitudes and in integrating theoretical knowledge with practical nursing skills. A proof for this statement is the fact that registered nurses and career changers who had occasion to test their abilities have significantly less emotional difficulties than student nurses entering their first job (χ^2 after correction for calculating in percentages $= 5.94$ significant at $p = 0.05$). Registered nurses complain more about the lack of consideration and of resources (equipment) and about task ambiguity. This means that status considerations are an important factor in the appeal of the nursing profession. In registered nurses this tendency is overtly expressed even in the ranking of work values (see Table 4.9) where Prestige climbs to a middle rank, while in an unselected population it generally figures among the rejected values (cf. Krau, 1987). Another proof for the status appeal of nursing in the public eye is the significantly higher percentage of student nurses at their first job entry who attribute to nursing a high or rising status in comparison with registered nurses (χ^2 after correction $= 13.45$ significant at $p < 0.01$). The former chose nursing merely on the basis of its appeal in public opinion; the latter made their choice on similar grounds but are now in full knowledge of occupational realities.

When speaking of prestige in public opinion, there is always a need to define the social stratum whose prestige image is involved. On the basis of the husband's occupation (or the father's for unmarried subjects), it appears that nursing appeals in nearly equal proportions to the stratum of type B professions (Roe, 1962) such as physicians, psychologists, or musicians (27.5 percent), to semiprofessionals such as technicians and teachers (30 percent), to skilled workers (including 38 shop owners) (25 percent), and then to semiskilled workers (10 percent). From these data, it may be concluded that nursing appeals mainly to the middle class and its image of prestige.

The perceived status of nursing was expressed also in the semantic differential ratings. It will be remembered that the subjects were asked to define the concepts of Work, Nurse, Doctor, and My Former Vocation (those who had one) by the method of semantic differential. Contrary to the expectation that the concept of

Table 4.13
Nurses' Vocational Image: Perceived Necessary Abilities, Difficulties in Practicing the Occupation, and Occupational Status (percentage of responses)

			Student nurses		
	Total sample	Registered nurses	First job	Career changers	After multiple trials
Definitions of vocational image	N = 180	N = 44	N = 70	N = 42	N = 24
PERCEIVED NECESSARY ABILITIES					
Understanding, supportive attitude	33.3	25.0	37.0	35.6	33.2
Integration of theoretical knowledge	26.6	29.5	28.5	21.6	24.6
Resistance to stress	5.5	11.8	1.4	4.8	4.8
Skills	22.2	24.8	20.0	23.6	24.6
Intelligence, thinking	7.7	9.0	10.0	4.8	4.8
Self-confidence; responsibility; order	4.4	–	3.0	9.6	8.1
DIFFICULTIES IN PRACTICING THE JOB					
Physical and emotional difficulties	41.1	32.0	52.8	35.4	33.3
Working hours	19.4	21.3	18.6	19.2	20.8
Lacking resources	5.5	13.7	–	6.8	4.2
Low image;lack of consideration	11.6	16.0	8.7	11.8	12.7
Task ambiguity	5.5	8.8	5.6	2.6	4.2
Difficulties in applying theoretical knowledge	8.8	6.9	5.6	14.0	12.7
Low pay	2.2	2.2	1.4	2.6	4.2
Patients with different mentalities	5.5	–	7.0	7.4	8.0

NURSES' PERCEIVED STATUS					
High	9.4	–	15.5	9.4	8.2
Rising	45.5	33.9	50.0	47.6	49.9
Declining	14.4	29.5	10.0	9.6	8.2
Low	22.7	27.1	20.0	23.6	20.8
Uncertain; changing	7.7	9.2	4.3	9.8	12.5

Doctor would be defined as brighter and more potent than nursing, no significant difference between the two appeared, either in Evaluation or in Potency. Obviously, nurses consider their vocation as being equally important, bright, and dynamic as that of the physician. Subjects for whom nursing constituted a second career see it significantly brighter in comparison with their first occupation ($t = 2.51$ significant at $p = 0.05$). Generally speaking, it seems that people entering the nursing profession expect it to be more dynamic than it really is, because Work is rated as being significantly more active than nursing (t for matched samples $= 2.17$ significant at $p = 0.05$); and as far as nursing itself is concerned, higher scores are given in the rating of its brightness (Evaluation) compared to its dynamics (Activity). The t-test for matched samples reaches 7.16 significant at $p = 0.001$.

This finding is upheld also by the difference between student nurses' satisfaction with their vocation (4.35 on a 5-point rating scale) and that of registered nurses (3.40). The t-test $= 2.71$ between these figures is significant on the 5 percent level. In the ratings of overall satisfaction, this difference disappears: student nurses rate their overall satisfaction with a mean score of 4.1 as compared to 3.9 in registered nurses (t-test is nonsignificant). The equalizing effect belongs to satisfaction with home, which received the highest scores. This also means that home ranks highest in centrality for nurses. However, it is characteristic that the difference between satisfaction with home (4.42) and satisfaction with vocation (4.13) is not significant. Nurses have a high image of their vocation and are strongly involved with it, despite its drawbacks.

The research has supported the hypothesis that the vocational appeal of an occupation does not extend only to the relevant occupational traits and that there is also hidden selection operating on irrelevant job traits, which give the vocational behavior of the entire group of practitioners a well-defined specificity.

In nurses, the hidden selection mainly concerns the "artistic" orientation, which apart from emotionality, also means lack of conformity. This trait also appeared in nurses' personality profiles as rejection of authority and as impulsivity attached to behavior involving money. The latter is another "informal" trait with far-reaching consequences for nurses' organizational behavior. In Israel we witnessed (long after these measurements had been taken) a confirmation of these statements in cruel and prolonged nurses' strikes involving the abandoning of hospital patients. These strikes were widely covered by the entire Israeli press, between January 1986 and November 1986. There were new strikes in the following years with a large one between October 1991 and January 1992. The real motive of the strikes was that nurses felt that their pay allowances did not correspond to the intensity of their average investments and discriminated against them as compared to other sectors of the economy.

In order to evaluate such phenomena correctly, one should bear in mind that nursing also appeals in an informally recognized manner to groups of people who, as a consequence of a burnout process, have a reduced general involvement with work values and that this burnout process, operating as a consequence of the stress of occupational life, first attacks values of high moral standard like Altruism.

The existence of an informal vocational appeal for which the organizational system has no corresponding accommodation lessens performance efficiency and provides a basis for frequent labor unrest. Organizations would be well advised to discover and uncover the real and the whole occupational appeal regarding the self-recruitment of employees into an occupation and to make it an object for consideration in regard to modification of the selection procedures and/or organizational settings, in case these procedures and settings contradict the practitioners' profile of vocational behavior.

To do so, the content of vocational images has to be clarified theoretically and practically. The investigations presented in this chapter have shown that for each vocation there is an image construed in public opinion and, in parallel, another by the individual who chooses the occupation. The content *categories* of these images are identical, but their concrete contents are not. The categories are occupational tasks, basic attitudes, abilities and skills required, difficulties one has to cope with, the returns, the meaningfulness and the evaluated prestige of the occupation, and the general mood of job satisfaction. The concrete contents of these categories are different in the two images, whereby both depart from the real and relevant occupational characteristics. Some of these exist in the real job, but are not to be found in the occupational image, and vice versa. The latter are vocationally irrelevant but receive emotional load in public opinion or in the eyes of certain groups or individuals.

The vocational image of people who have already chosen an occupation has the functions of self-presentation and of a yardstick for the evaluation of aspirational fulfillment. The teachers interviewed in the research spoke of multiple rewards and high satisfaction, but these declarations serving their self-presentation were contradicted by prolonged and ever-recurring teachers' strikes in this country. Compared to other professionals, psychologists rated their vocation as more prestigious and declared that prestige had influenced their career choice substantially. The other professionals reduced the magnitude of such perceived influence in their ratings. As far as their public self-presentation was concerned, this amounted to the phenomenon of "sour grapes." However, they too made their choice having considerations of occupational prestige in mind. These considerations were concealed, based as they were on characteristics that did not match the image of themselves that the subjects wanted to present. People's image of their own occupation has always the features of a stage-like self-presentation (Goffman, 1959), but at the same time, it also has other characteristics that are concealed from the public. These latter are not intended for overt display but actually they have a real influence on behavior.

All this should not diminish the role of occupational images in public opinion. They constitute the primary sources of occupational information and choice. They raise expectations both by their declared and by their concealed contents. Thus the interviewed professionals expected intellectual abilities to be the main criterion for promotions, and they were deeply disappointed if, in certain organizations, this was not so.

Vocational choice and vocational behavior in general are motivated by the emotion-laden elements of the vocational image. This emotional load stems from the linkage of particular elements of the vocational image with the end-state image of self-realization. Therefore we have stated that the choice of a career is a match of images. Now we are able to define this match more precisely as the linkage between particular elements of the two images. Every object or situation is perceived as a conglomerate, the meaning of which depends on the elements with the strongest physiological nervous stimulation (Krau, 1977b). Every modification in the mosaic of nervous arousal changes the meaning a situation has for the person. This is the origin of illusions in everyday life (Krau, 1962, 1977b). In the process of image comparison, emotionally loaded (and therefore aroused) elements in the end-state image of self-realization transmit their arousal to similar elements of the occupational image. The additional physiological arousal (expressing emotional load on the psychological level) causes these elements to appear as the occupation's key features, though objectively this may not be so. The result is an idiosyncratic perception of the occupation.

This process explains why more or less concealed irrelevant image elements are capable of having a stronger influence on behavior than overtly declared ones and why they determine how the entire occupation is perceived.

The gap between the social and the individual perception of occupations may be a frequent occurrence, yet it is desirable to avoid it in order to achieve organizational efficiency, as well as for the sake of a smooth progression toward accomplishing the goals of the person's self-realization. In this respect, organizational and individual counseling should prove helpful.

In order to protect the person from disillusion and continuous fights with management, who may see a particular job very differently, individual counseling should reveal the potential differences between the public and the individual image of the occupation that has been or is to be chosen. Clearly, counseling must not rely on phoney conventional occupational images, as it frequently does, but must discover their real, emotionally loaded components.

Then the counselor should evaluate whether the clients' occupational perceptions are realistic and conducive to the fulfillment of their aspirations.

There may be an argument about the admissible range of the counselor's intervention should there be a significant gap between images and reality. Surely, clients must neither be spurned nor deterred from the career they desire, but informed. As the ultimate decision rests with them, they have the right to know what presumably lies ahead.

5

The Motivational Steering of Careers toward Self-Realization

When speaking of motivational phenomena there always is a need to consider a push-pull dyad. The person is attracted by an object and driven toward it. Sometimes special concepts are used to designate one or the other of these aspects, like motives versus ideals. What is sure is that a self-regulatory goal-directed behavior (Kuhl, 1992) needs the organic combination of both aspects, and a successful combination depends primarily on the clarity of goals. Normally the latter become clear and spelled out only in adult life after establishment in a career. In the preparatory career stages the person's life-goal aspirations are contained in the end-state image of self-realization. The quality of this image deeply influences the subsequent course of events. The clearer and less contradictory it is, the smoother and less contradictory the person's career path will be. It is in this sense that Holland (1966) predicted the greatest career success to the modal type of a single and strong adaptive orientation.

In Chapter 3 it was shown that even in people who see their self-realization in a specific vocational activity the guiding end-state image is composed of work and nonwork elements. In order to permit a goal-directed striving and fulfillment, it is necessary not only that there should be no incompatibility between the elements of the image but also that there should be a hierarchical order of importance among them that allows for the elaboration of a plan and the focusing of the motivational process.

The chances of failure are high if the elements of the end-state image of self-realization are contradictory and cannot be achieved simultaneously and if the person has no clear notion of their hierarchy. The person may put the elements into the wrong order, so that the consequences of pursuing one element hinders the achievement of the others.

The theoretical reason why contradictory self-realization images result in life-career failure is that the solution of contradictions in aspirations requires compromises expressing the adjustment side of self-realization. However, the adjustment compromises should concern the nonsalient life areas only, in order to enhance a full realization of the person's dreams in the salient life domain. Compromises in the latter area endanger self-realization in its objective attainments and hence in producing an inner conviction that in the given circumstances nothing better could have been achieved. It is this conviction that lastly gives peace of mind and the feeling of self-actualization.

The life failure of three subjects described in Table 3.1 clearly points to contradictions in their guiding image that annihilated their chances of success and caused defeating compromises. Indeed, it should have been a matter of common sense that people living under a communist regime but dreaming above all of a decent life in the West should have strived to emigrate, refraining from anything that might have held them back, such as having a large family, which might have opposed or delayed emigration, or having a visible show-off job because of which they would have difficulty receiving an exit visa. If, on the contrary, the most important aspiration were vocational advancement, with emigration in the second place, the person would have to create a solid vocational position. This would have delayed emigration but ensured a favorable starting position for a new life. To mix up aims that pose contradictory demands plants the seeds of failure.

The following story is about **B.**, one of the members of the sample presented in Table 3.1, whose heterogeneous life aspirations included becoming a respected physician, emigrating to Israel, and living a well-off and comfortable life but in a religious style.

B. was from a religious Jewish background. His parents died during deportation by the Nazis. **B.** and his elder sister survived. After the war he returned to Romania, completed high school, and then wanted to realize his dream of studying medicine. His admission into medical school was first rejected because of his bourgeois background. **B.** did not choose another vocation but waited patiently until, after one year, he succeeded in passing his entrance examination. In 1950 his sister decided to leave for Israel (she actually left), and this event added weight to **B.**'s leaving motive. He applied for an exit visa, but his application was turned down. His whole life became a mere waiting for the proper opportunity to emigrate. As exit permits were more readily granted to bachelors and to people in unimportant positions, he remained a country doctor, refusing appointment offers in city hospitals, and he obstinately refused to get married. At a certain moment the girl he was dating wanted to compel him to propose to her by saying she was offered marriage by a common acquaintance. Although **B.** truly loved her, he declared that her choice was very clever and immediately sent to her suitor a telegram offering his congratulations, so that the girl could not draw back. Because of this ridiculous situation, **B.** exposed himself to very unpleasant jokes. Finally, in 1969 there came a time of passport and visa liberalization, and **B.** felt his time had come. He applied for the passport and the visa, and one year later, in 1970, he left the country.

In Israel he aspired to a hospital appointment, but got a job as a physician in social security. All his life he had been a country doctor, and in the eyes of Israeli health officials this experience did not warrant a hospital position. Before long he married a much younger woman. In time he was having some difficulties with her, and difficulties with his son, who took the religious inclinations of his father too literally; above all, he complained all the time about how much he must work to support his family and that the money was never sufficient. When his son grew up and wanted to dedicate his life to studying holy books in a Yeshivah, this plan seemed "too religious" even to his father and caused him much worry. Today **B.** is frustrated with his life, with his family, and with being a social security physician, and he has the feeling that all has gone astray. Such is the story of a life career in which mutually exclusive objectives were desired: professional advancement, emigration, a comfortable life, a young wife, and a religious lifestyle. Apparently, emigration and religion ranged first among his aims, yet the professional specialty was really important to him. His aspirations matched those of the group who saw their self-realization in a specific vocational activity, but at the same time he had strong aspirations that he could realize only in renouncing vocational advancement. Although he had the necessary aptitudes to attain his objectives taken separately, the endeavor to combine the incompatible in a wrong hierarchy led to downfall and the feeling of misery.

Krumboltz (1988) saw this phenomenon from the perspective of decision-making difficulties when he spoke of dysfunctional career beliefs in people who, for instance, would like to work in a certain occupation but feel they could not stand the training required for it. As a matter of fact, such dysfunctional beliefs reflect a contradictory guiding image containing aspirations that are incompatible in the existing conditions.

It appears that the problem does not lie only in a lack of internal contradictions in the end-state image of self-realization. Even a guiding image with internal compatibility may contradict the individual's abilities or the existing social and economic possibilities for the realization of that career aspiration. The problem has been raised many times, as a lack of realism in vocational aspirations. Analyzing the causes of failure, authors have referred to low intellectual capacities hindering correct discriminations and/or value beliefs extolling the universal accessibility of success, as it were, of the American dream (Paterson, 1957; Lofquist and England, 1961; Choubkine, 1966). Other authors mention ignorance regarding one's abilities (Arhangelski and Petrov, 1967) or psychological causes such as neuroticism, repeated failure, or a feeling of insecurity (Amerio, 1968), which all may heighten aspirations beyond any realistic chance of fulfillment.

Nevertheless, unduly high career aspirations do not necessarily lead to failure and maladjustment but may lead to acceptable compromises (Gottfredson and Becker, 1981; Gati, 1991). In order to preserve chances for fulfillment, the compromises must include only the nonsalient, nonessential features of the person's end-state image of self-realization; otherwise, a feeling of frustration and misery is inevitable. The ultimate locus of compromise appears in interests as cumulative results of social interaction (Hesketh, Elmslie, and Kaldor, 1990) and less in the most ancient factors of gender differences as Gottfredson's (1981) theory would hold, thus the problem has a pronounced individualized face related to the individual's history of socialization. It comes down to the question of which of these factors is closer to the very gist of the person's self-realization image. What we are interested in is not the compromises a person makes, but the ones the person accepts and can live with. If somebody dreamed of becoming a physician but, because of economic constraints, could not afford the lengthy studies and had to be content with being a paramedic, this compromise in itself does not preclude self-realization. If the guiding image of self-realization pointed to a specific activity of health care and if one achieves objective success in this field according to the standards of one's reference group, remaining adjusted and satisfied, such a compromise career is still to be considered self-realization. An accepted compromise that also leaves room for objective success is the expression of self-realization functioning in the framework of adjustment.

The evolution of aspirations based on the person's end-state image of self-realization has certain degrees of freedom. Paradoxically, they stem from the lack of precision in the guiding image, which allows for the nuancing and the adjustment of aspirations in the process of development. The flexibility of career behavior is enhanced by its motivational steering being performed by a collection of processes like ideals, aspirations, and interests that are connected but not directly equivalent.

Interests may coalesce with aspirations or not. The difference between them results from the fact that there may be activities or objects that interest us, as they attract our attention, but we do not aspire to them. Many people like detective stories but do not aspire to engage in the police force. Cooley (1967) went as far as saying that vocational interests are not linked to central aspects of the personality and that the remarkable stability of interests during periods of 20–30 years that has been recorded through retestings with the Strong test (SVIB) should rather be explained by stability in careers. Nevertheless, it has been established for a long time (Rubinstein, 1962) that there are also deep interests that pervade the basic tenure and traits of the personality, and they originate in the identification of the individual with the roles played by his significant other. The latter constitute the person's ideals. Objects and persons from the situational field are perceived as ideals if they contribute to the structuring and the development of the self-image projected into the future. The ideal is the individual's self-image in its future desired dimension. Essentially, ideals constitute the concretization of the person's values into a perceptive image. It is this integration of the image-ideal with values that provides the motivational process toward self-realization with deliberated goal directedness.

This is precisely the problem we have to answer: What ensures the goal directedness of the career behavior if, as it has been alleged, the end-state image of self-realization is often blurred and contains contradictory elements? The answer lies in the fusion of the guiding image with people's values, expressing the "objectives that one seeks to attain in order to satisfy needs" (Super, 1970) and with the salience of the various life domains.

Values constitute a cornerstone of substantive or content theories of motivation, which seek to explain what specific entities motivate people energizing and sustaining their behavior (Campbell, Dunnette, Lawler, and Weick, 1974). The problem is, first, whether values apart from expressing individual needs have a sufficient social anchorage in order to ensure the congruence of the developing process of self-realization with the norms of the social group of reference and, second, whether they are sufficiently stable to ensure the direction of a lifelong process of aspirational realization. The two questions have a joint corollary since, obviously, membership and reference group coincide in the first stages of development. Then the question arises of how their possible separation in later years is reflected in people's value profiles. We addressed these problems in a series of two investigations (Krau, 1987, 1989b). The planning of the research had been complicated by the presumed double origin of values in the individual's needs and in the process of enculturation. Some authors stress the needs aspect (Roe, 1966; Lofquist and Dawis, 1978); other authors stress the enculturation aspect (Rosenberg, 1957; Locke, 1976).

The tenor of our study was toward the conception of value enculturation. This choice was made, first, because this approach is better suited to a macroinvestigation of a social community and, second, because from a developmental point of view the transformations in values during adolescence are more normative (i.e., socioculturally determined) than ipsative in nature, that is reflecting the development in individual needs (Gribbones and Lohnes, 1965; Wijting, Arnold, and Conrad, 1978). The concept of value enculturation certainly does not neglect the motivating power of personal needs, because cultural norms are socially approved ways of satisfying individual needs.

In accordance with the concept of enculturation, I hypothesized that the source of work values is the subculture of the social group of affiliation, which has socioeconomic and cultural (national, religious) characteristics. The work value content of the source is transmitted by the agents of socialization, mainly the wider society (including the working environment and mass media), the family, and the school. The influence of the agents of socialization is age bound. Consequently, age and the activity of the socialization agents appear to moderate the involvement with the content message of the value sources.

I further hypothesized that the influence of the agents of socialization on work value formation would manifest itself "quantitatively" in the strength of value involvement and "qualitatively" in the hierarchy of value preferences and in the "principle" versus "specific" content of work values. The need to differentiate between the two aspects of work value content was felt already by Lofquist and Dawis (1978), who spoke of values as second-order needs, and by Pryor, who drew attention to the fact that second-order factors virtually never account for all the variance explained by the first-order factors. As conceptual entities, values, needs, and work ethics are not completely and simply inter-changeable (Pryor, 1982), just as work involvement and job involvement have proved not to be identical (Jans, 1982) despite their common ground. Beyond the preference for rewards stemming from the concrete aspects of a job, the individual has or aspires to, there is a general valuing of work as an important constituent of the work ethic. Work values comprise both these aspects.

In this study the "principle content" of work values referred to fundamental dimensions of work needs, both intrinsic and extrinsic, as the person does not have in mind the satisfaction derived from narrowly considered job facets. Con-versely, when thinking in terms of intrinsic or extrinsic rewards sought from specific facets of a certain work activity, the person manipulates the "specific content" of work values.

The distinction between the value contents is important, first, because it en-ables us to assess cultural differences regarding an orientation toward the fun-damental versus the immediate, practical aspects of life rewards (they may be intrinsic or extrinsic in nature), and second, because principle and specific value contents are likely to be formed under the influence of different agents of so-cialization. Therefore, through the analysis of value content we might be able to trace the influence of different socializing agents.

It seems appropriate to assume that in school the emphasis is mainly on transmitting the principle content of values, while schools also increase the gen-eral involvement with values: it is the contact with reality that inculcates their work-specific, practical content. This hypothesis was in line with several re-search findings dealing with the "normative climate" of the school and with its "certification effect." It means that norms in society govern the type of grad-uates various institutions are chartered to produce, and these norms are absorbed and transmitted by schools (Sewell, Hauser, and Featherman, 1976).

During adolescence the personality-shaping influence of school gradually de-creases (Cole, 1970; Pearson, 1958) as youth engages and strengthens contact with the occupational environment in the realization of the developmental task of vocational choice and of entry into the world of work (Ginzberg, Ginsburg, Axelrad, and Herma, 1963; Venables, 1968). To continue this line of thought, we should expect an increased involvement with values, especially with value principles, when school influence is stronger (i.e., generally until middle ado-lescence, and later only in the social strata where the contact with the occupa-tional world has been found to be delayed). These are the strata of high socioeconomic level (Maupeou-Leplatre, 1963; Venables, 1968). Paradoxically, we should expect in middle adolescence a lower general involvement with work values in individuals belonging to a low socioeconomic level, because they are neither firmly committed to school nor firmly engaged in contact with the work-ing environment (Hill, 1969; Jaide, 1966). Nevertheless, a growing involvement with work values may be expected of them toward late adolescence, when the strengthening link with the occupational world imposed on them promotes the increase of commitment to work values (Scharmann, 1966; Wollack, Goodale, Wijting, and Smith, 1971) in their specific, concrete content.

In the content area of value preferences (value hierarchies), I hypothesized that all agents of socialization will transmit values embedded in a culture content that is characteristic for the society as a whole; other transmitted values will characterize the narrower social group of affiliation. However, arguments might arise about the common values in a society torn apart by contradictions, as is the case in modern Western societies and especially in the Israeli society of today. Despite such a caveat, an investigation into the values of United States college students revealed a remarkable homogeneity, considering the variety of their backgrounds and their relatively unrestricted opportunities for freedom of thought and personal development (Jacob, 1965). In the Israeli context it was presumed that beyond all differences in nationality, religion, and socioeconomic stratification, there was a common ground of values at the level of the least common denominator in the aspirations and conceptions of all groups composing the Israeli society. It was presumed that this least common denominator comprises the basic values of a democratic society wishing to find a peaceful solution to its problems.

It was expected that another common trend in adolescents' value preferences would concern the preparation for future occupational life as pointed out by Zytowski (1970) and later in the investigations of Wijting et al. (1978) and Raven (1981). This common trend of preparation for future vocational activity should lead to value diversification in adolescents, paradoxically because of the dependence of vocational aspirations upon the "individual's position in society" (Linton, 1945), as determined by socioeconomic status and cultural tradition (national, religious).

Several authors (Stefflre, 1966; Kohn, 1969) have indicated that socioeconomic status has a powerful impact on value formation. It should therefore also carry this role in the Israeli society, characterized as it is by rather sharp socioeconomic contrasts. At a low socioeconomic status, work value preferences are expected to focus on economic security and good supervisory relations; in groups of high socioeconomic status, whose basic needs of security are satisfied, an orientation focus toward values characterizing higher-order needs is expected (e.g., intellectual stimulation, creativity). These values correspond to the kind of work that the subculture of this social stratum considers appropriate for its members.

The difference between urban and rural life constitutes a collateral influence of the socioeconomic status. In opposition with the individualistic achievement culture of the Israeli city, where values such as "achievement" and "advancement" are promoted, rural inhabitants emphasize independent, hard, diligent work ("autonomy," "physical work") and social relationships ("associates"). Such values follow from the very nature of agricultural work.

The second source of work values and of work value diversification was presumed to be the different cultural traditions (national, religious) of Israel's

Jewish, Muslim, and Christian populations. It was expected that in Arab youth there would be strong value preferences for values with a political affective connotation ("autonomy," "advancement"); groups near to Christian ecclesiastic tradition would be strongly oriented toward values that include spiritual and moral characteristics ("altruism," "esthetics," and "creativity"). No separate characteristic value preferences were expected in the Jewish subjects, as the common values of the democratic achievement society had to be attributed to the influence of the majority population.

Age, as a moderator variable and as a factor of value diversification, was expected to influence work value formation in adolescence less by the effect of maturation and more by the acquisition of life experience in connection with the start of an occupational career. In accordance with Wijting, Arnold, and Conrad (1978), and in opposition to Kapes and Strickler (1975), changes in value hierarchy were expected from middle to late adolescence, as school influence lessens and contacts with the working environment become established. From preferences for general principles (responsibility, participation in decision making), a shift toward late adolescence in the direction of value preferences related to job activity was expected.

The dependent variable of the study was the basic work value profile for the beginning of the working life (i.e., the moment of the youth's commitment to work entry). The age group of middle to late adolescence was chosen because this is the period in which the "final" crystallization of work values takes place in the sense defined above. Marginal youth were not included in the sample because they do not contribute to the mainstream development of work values in society, nor do they help explain this development. The independent variables were as follows: socioeconomic level, with its corollary of urban versus rural background; national-religious affiliation as value sources; and the moderating factors of age and of school, the latter being presumed to further the transmission of the principle content of work values. The other agents of socialization were not independently included. The reason for this is that the influence of the family has already declined in this period (Crow and Crow, 1965; Moore, 1976), and what is left of it coincides with the controlled variables of socioeconomic level and of national-religious traditions. It is also obvious that a person's or a group's socioeconomic level determines the working environment as a socializing agent.

The problem of measuring value dimensions has been a challenge for all researchers in this area. In Rokeach's (1973) view, the hierarchy dimension is representative for the value dimension and sufficient for its measurement. However, Katzell (1964) and Kapes and Strickler (1975) mention, in addition, the dimensions of magnitude (what level must be attained to satisfy a value) and intensity (what degree of satisfaction follows fulfillment). As the dimension of magnitude relates more to an ipsative approach and as this study used the normative approach, measurement is based on dimensions of work value intensity and hierarchy.

The broad research sample consisted of 913 high school students. Half of them were drawn from the twelfth grade, boys and girls in equal proportion, and the other half from boys and girls in the ninth grade. The sample was drawn from Jewish and Arab public schools and from Catholic monastic schools. The Jewish sample was further divided into groups from rural and urban areas; the urban group was divided into subgroups from high and low socioeconomic levels. The samples belonging to the Arab and to the Catholic monastic schools were not divided according to socioeconomic level, as there is not a strong differentiation in the respective populations. Their socioeconomic level is generally comparable to that of the Jewish rural sample (i.e., not too high but not low either). Values were not investigated separately for boys and girls because there are no attested significant value differences between adolescents according to sex in the chosen age period (Gribbones and Lohnes, 1965; Kapes and Strickler, 1975).

The sample was drawn from the following groups: Of the 464 students in the twelfth grade, 147 were Jewish urban, high socioeconomic level; 119 were Jewish urban, low socioeconomic level; 40 were Jewish, rural area; 57 were from a Catholic monastic school; and 101 were from an Arab school. Of the 449 ninth-grade students, 122 were Jewish urban, high socioeconomic level; 129 were Jewish urban, low socioeconomic level; 65 were Jewish, rural area; 53 were from a Catholic monastic school; and 80 were from an Arab school.

The instrument used for testing work values was the Values scale of the Work Importance Study (WIS) elaborated by an international team headed by Donald Super (United States). Slight modifications in item wording have been made by each national project director to fit national particularities. This applied also to this author, who was the Israeli national project director. The English variant used in this study has been published in Knasel, Super, and Kidd (1981). It is known as the "unshortened variant" and investigates 21 values, both intrinsic and extrinsic. The subject is asked to rate the felt importance of each statement on a 5–point scale.

The questionnaire makes it possible to investigate the "principle" and the "work-specific" content of the value phenomenon through rating five general, normative statements and five specific statements acknowledged as such by the international team of authors (see Knasel et al., 1981). In questions relating to Achievement Value, for example, "It is now or will be important for me to" (a) "do something that will result in lasting changes" or (b) "get the feeling that I have really achieved something" are general, normative statements and are referred to as the general, principle content of the value. The statements (c) "reach a high standard in my work" and (d) "have a job where quality counts" are specific items and are referred to as the specific, practical content of the value. The WIS instrument makes it possible to perform a combined measurement of value intensity and hierarchy. The instrument measures value hierarchy not through an ordinal scale, but through the metric scale of value intensity (for each value there are 10 statements rated on a 5–point scale, and the total score of the 10 statements is the subject's score on that value). The value intensity scores are the basis for the computation of the subject's value hierarchy. A value hierarchy for the entire sample group may then be computed from the arithmetical means of value scores throughout the sample.

The instrument was administered in Hebrew (after retranslation to English). In Israel, Hebrew is taught also in all minority schools and ninth-grade pupils have a good command of the language.

As far as the differences within the sample groups are concerned, the principle content of values appeared with a significantly greater intensity in comparison to the specific, job-bound value content in both age groups of the Catholic monastic school and at the low socioeconomic level of the Jewish urban sample in the ninth grade. As the general work value involvement of the latter sample is the lowest of all the sample groups, it is not the high interest in principles at a low socioeconomic level, but the weakness of contacts with the working environment that is the main source of the job-specific content of work values in this sample. The research hypothesis assumed that in this group the contact with school would also be weak, and indeed the score of involvement with the principle part of work values is again the lowest in this sample in comparison to all other sample groups.

Other significant differences in principle versus specific work value content within the sample groups of the monastic school, and of the rural sample, also confirm the assumed relationship between school and working environment in the transmission of work values. The heavy emphasis on involvement with principles in a monastic school explains the high scores on principles in that sample, whereas in a rural environment great importance is attached to involvement with the practical aspects of work, especially in the senior age group. It is well-known that adolescents living in rural areas participate in one form or another in the farm work of their families. And this is also the case in Israel.

In order to ascertain the differences in the intensity of work value involvement (general work value involvement, involvement with principles, and with the specific part of work values) among the sample groups, a multiple comparison of means was performed using the Newman-Keuls method based on the studentized range (see Tables 5.1 and 5.2). The pattern of differences was much the same in the complete work value scores and in the principle content of work values; therefore, the latter calculation is not presented. Mean comparisons of the specific part of work value scores are, however, given in Table 5.2, where there are some differences vis-à-vis the general pattern. The somewhat unusual appearance of the tables is due to the definite requirement of the method that comparisons be discontinued for any row at the first nonsignificant value. This rule prevents the making of inconsistent decisions by entering differences caused by chance (Ferguson, 1971).

The main difference between the sample groups in general value involvement (and also in the involvement with the principle content of work values) appears between both extremities of the socioeconomic level (high and low) and nearly all the sample groups. This finding points to the conclusion that the socioeco-

Table 5.1
Mean Comparisons of Complete Value Scores (Newman-Keuls Method)

	Low Socio- econ 9	Low Socio- econ 12	Jewish Rural 9	Monastic School 12	Jewish Rural 12	Arab School 12	Catholic Monastic School 9	Arab School 9	High Socio- econ 12	High Socio- econ 9
Low Socioeconomic 9		3.65*	3.86*	4.02*	4.51*	4.67	5.48	6.44	8.21	13.38
Low Socioeconomic 12									5.00*	10.32
Jewish Rural 9									4.45*	9.67
Catholic Monastic School 12										9.51
Jewish Rural 12										8.87
Arab School 12										8.70
Catholic Monastic School 9										7.90
Arab School 9										7.09
High Socioeconomic 12										5.32
High Socioeconomic 9										

Note: N for all groups = 21 values. Only significant differences are given. Q Criterion for 10 groups and df = 120. Numbers without * : p = .01; Numbers with * : p = 0.5.

Reprinted with permission. Copyright 1987 by Academic Press.

Table 5.2
Mean Comparisons of the Specific Part of Work Values (Newman-Keuls Method)

	Low Socio-economic	Jewish Rural	Catholic Monastic	Low Socio-economic	Catholic Monastic	Arab	High Socio-economic	Arab	Jewish Rural	High Socio-economic
	9	9	12	12	9	9	12	9	12	9
Low socioeconomic 9							6.08	6.95	8.26	9.78
Jewish rural 9								4.34*	6.30	7.82
Catholic monastic 12									5.43	6.95
Low socioeconomic 12									5.43	6.95
Catholic monastic 9									5.00**	6.52
Arab 12										5.86
High socioeconomic 12										
Arab 9										
Jewish rural 12										
High socioeconomic 9										

nomic and not the cultural factor plays the main role in determining the intensity of involvement with work values. As a matter of fact, it follows from Table 5.1 that increases in socioeconomic level produce increases in value involvement.

The mean comparisons of the specific part of work value scores confirm the emphasis on the practical content of work values in the senior age group of the rural sample. The significantly high scores of the high socioeconomic level group on the specific work value content is to be interpreted in the context of the nearly maximally strong general value involvement of that sample group. In this light the high rank position of the involvement with the specific content of work values may be considered artifactual and as reflecting the high overall and rather school-conditioned involvement with values at this age.

The rank order of preferences for work values in the different sample groups is given in Table 5.3. The differences between mean ranks of values were generally not large; the range of the 21 values is about 10 evaluation units.

In the ninth grade group of the Jewish sample groups, the work value pyramid is dominated by values attributed to working life by general public opinion and by school: supervisory relations and participation in decision making. In Israel the cooperative ideal is very strong in Zionist ideology and as such strongly supported by school. However, economic development goes in another direction. Although industrial democracy remains an important problem for the powerful General Trade Union, the general evolution of the society follows the capitalist pattern, fostering private initiative and private ownership. This explains why values close to behaviors inspired by a collectivist mode of thought do not appear among the top choices in the twelfth grade, when school influence weakens. The start of a socioeconomically oriented differentiation pointing to the direction in which work value preferences will evolve in the twelfth grade is apparent already in the ninth grade beneath the dominating rank positions of the school-inculcated values. Values such as intellectual stimulation, autonomy, and responsibility occupy a modest third and fourth place in the preference rank order of the ninth grade, but move to the top of the list in the twelfth grade.

There certainly could be an argument on how much of these changes in hierarchy of value preferences between the ninth and the twelfth grades are due to attrition and dropping out of school, but such a discussion would be beyond the point. This is a cross-sectional study of work values in youth entering work or vocational education. Some do it after the ninth grade (and then their work values are as described), and some after the twelfth grade, as they continued their studies in high school. The value hierarchy of this latter group is changed in comparison with the former, and from the macro point of view of a socio-cultural approach there is an evolution from the ninth to the twelfth grade.

Apart from the specific work linkage the value preference hierarchy seems to reflect also national and religious connotations of work, as assumed in the research hypothesis. The ninth-grade pupils' value preferences in the Catholic monastic school obviously reflect Christian work morale; in Arab schools the expressed work value preferences very transparently hint at the problem of na-

Table 5.3
Rank Order of Values in Research Samples

| Work values | 12th Grade | | | | | 9th Grade | | | | | Average societal work value profile | | Preference rank order | Consensus rank order |
| | Jewish | | | Catholic monastic school | Arab school | Jewish | | | Catholic monastic school | Arab school | | | | |
	High socio-economic level	Low socio-economic level	Jewish rural			High socio-economic level	Low socio-economic level	Jewish rural			$\bar{X}$	σ		
Ability utiliz.	7	11	10	7	6	13	4	4	8	5	7.50	3.02	7	8
Achievement	10	15	15	9	11	11	6	8	6	13	10.40	3.27	11	10
Advancement	3	10	5	5	4	5	17	13	2	2	6.60	10.0	4	21
Esthetics	11	13	11.5	6	15	4	15.5	18	5	16	11.50	4.96	13	16
Altruism	19	20	20	19	18	20	15.5	16	17	20	18.45	1.73	18	14
Associates	15	3	3.5	16	16	10	8	11	16	11	10.95	4.95	12	15
Authority	21	21	21	21	19	21	21	20	19	18	20.20	1.13	21	1
Autonomy	12	6	2	4	1	16	3	2	7	1	5.40	5.03	2	17
Creativity	4	7	14	1	3	8	13	12	1	8	7.10	4.81	5	14
Economic security	14	1	3.5	12	5	17	11	10	13	4	9.05	5.31	9	19
Environment	13	9	7	15	8	15	14	14	14	9	11.80	3.15	14	9
Intellect. stim.	1	5	6	3	7	3	5	6	4	17	5.70	4.34	3	13
Life style	18	17	17	11	9	14	10	9	11	6	12.20	4.07	16	12
Particip. decis.	9	16	16	8	12	1	2	7	12	14	9.70	5.31	10	18
Prestige	17	12	13	17	17	12	19	19	18	10	15.40	3.30	17	11
Responsibility	2	2	1	2	2	9	7	3	3	3	3.40	2.54	1	6
Risk taking	16	19	18	20	20	18	18	17	21	19	18.60	1.50	19	3
Spiritual values	6	8	9	10	10	7	9	5	10	7	8.10	1.79	8	5
Supervisory rel.	5	4	8	14	14	2	1	1	9	15	7.30	5.53	6	20
Variety	8	14	11.5	13	13	6	12	15	15	12	11.95	2.91	15	7
Physical activity	20	18	19	18	21	19	20	21	20	21	19.70	1.15	20	2

tional identity and rights. The heavy emotional load of declared value preferences in Arab schools is evinced by the fact that the same values appear also
in the twelfth grade. Here the very process of development in vocational attitudes seems to be strongly influenced by the problems that raised the national-
cultural factor to a particular importance.

In the other sample groups there is a definite evolution of the top value
preferences between the ninth and the twelfth grade. In the twelfth grade the
top preferences belong to values related to vocational life as it is lived in the
social environment of the subjects and represented in its subculture. In the Jewish high socioeconomic level and in the Catholic monastic school, where the
students are oriented toward urban life, these values are intellectual stimulation,
responsibility, advancement, and creativity. For the Jewish rural groups the
prominent values are responsibility, autonomy, social interaction, and economic
security. For obvious reasons the latter value occupies the first place at the low
socioeconomic level; it is followed by responsibility and social interaction.

To verify the hypothesis of the existence of a common value preference of
the whole society, despite all social and cultural differences, an average societal
work value profile of adolescents and the rank order of consensus in it was
computed (see Table 5.3), across all sample groups. The mean values of this
average profile were then arranged in rank order, to obtain a societal ''preference
rank order'' of work values. However, this latter ordering has a more theoretical
importance. The real commonality in values is expressed by the rank order of
consensus appearing in the table, that is, the degree to which the different values
are shared in common by the different sample groups.

The theoretical average value profile of the Israeli adolescent comprises the
values of responsibility, autonomy, intellectual stimulation, and advancement as
top preferences and authority, physical activity, and risk taking at the last places
of the value hierarchy. It seems that the commonality in value orientation lies
less in the common acceptance of certain values and more in the common rejection of what seems unacceptable for all. It appears from the first seven positions in the rank order of consensus that there is a nearly universal agreement
regarding the rejection of authority (as a work value), physical activity (contrary
to the research hypothesis), risk taking, and altruism; and there is a nearly general consensus to place spiritual values and variety in the middle of the value
hierarchy. As far as the positive side of the preference spectrum is concerned,
only the preference for the value of responsibility gains overall support.

The profile of value rejections in the research samples is characterized by a
remarkable stability across all samples and in both age groups. The rejection
profile of values is already formed at the age of the ninth grade, and there are
virtually no changes until school termination. It is appropriate to conclude that
these value rejections express the position of all factors of value sources and
are conveyed with steadiness by all agents of socialization.

Finally, it may be of interest to take a look at the values for which the
dispersion is largest (they appear in the last rank positions of consensus). The

figures indicate that a large rate of dispersion is generally attributable to the development that takes place between the ninth and the twelfth grade. Thus, supervisory relations and participation in decision making are values of top preference in the ninth grade but move to a less important place toward the end of high school. On the contrary, economic security and advancement move from a middle rank order position in the ninth grade to top priorities in the twelfth grade in the rural sample and at a low socioeconomic level, but remain in a low priority in the well-off sample groups. This brings to mind the underlying influence of growing knowledge and experience in the world of work in persons belonging to the less-privileged socioeconomic strata.

The research attests to the importance of the enculturation process in the crystallization of values. The data suggest that the source of value determination appears more so as the subculture of a socioeconomic environment that also integrates national and religious features.

The research upholds the existence of a common cultural (value) profile of the society as a whole, as initially presumed. However, in the light of the research findings, the common societal work value profile contains positive value preferences only in middle adolescence; in late adolescence it remains confined to the rejection of unacceptable values (the nonvalues).

The nature of the common societal value background warrants additional explanation. The rejection of authority does not mean only that people do not want to be bothered by a bully foreman, just as the top preference given to autonomy in Arab schools does not signify that the pupils' most cherished dream is to become self-employed grocers. It may therefore be appropriate to see in the rejection of authority and of risk taking a firm general plea for democracy and against risky experiences. Regrettably, the rejection profile also includes physical activity and altruism. Although not included in the research hypothesis, this situation seems in line with the conceptions of a strongly competitive achievement society entering the area of advanced technology.

Although the interpretation of these value rejections is my own, the rejections themselves have since been confirmed, both in a national cross-verification with the shortened 5-item WIS instrument (Krau, 1989b) and in the research reports of the international team presented at the twenty-first International Congress of Applied Psychology held in Jerusalem in 1986, mainly in the research performed in Portugal and Italy (Marques, 1986; Trentini, 1986), but partially also in other countries participating in the project. One has, therefore, to conclude that the phenomenon reveals a basic feature of the culture of the Western society, at least in our broad geographical area. It also appears that despite their somewhat limited extent, our research samples were representative of their respective subcultures and that the results are not due to chance. This last statement applies also to the results in the positive spectrum of value preferences.

The job-bound, specific value content is predominantly transmitted by the working environment. Together, school and the working environment appear as the main agents of work value transmission in adolescence. The evolution of their relationship determines the intensity of involvement with work values in general, and the involvement with value principles versus specific work-related content in ways presumed by the initial hypothesis.

In regard to the problem of evolution in adolescents' values, the main finding of the research was that the first to crystallize is the profile of value rejection. This profile is definitely formed toward the ninth grade in middle adolescence, and there is no further development until school termination. Thus the evolution of the normative work value profile between middle and late adolescence concerns only the positive aspect of value orientation; its main content appears in the diversification of preferences in accordance with the aspirations characteristic for the subculture of the social environment to which the subject belongs. Such is the sense of the process that starts with the common rejection of authority and the common acceptance of good supervisory relations and reaches a final diversification in the pursuit of creativity, intellectual stimulation, social interaction, and responsibility.

One should not conclude from this trend of development that young employees have no preferences for good supervisory relations and participation in decision making. These values have been found to occupy the top rank in the ninth grade (i.e., at a time when a nonnegligible part of adolescents enter vocational training and work). They do it with the value profile they have at the moment, just as students terminating high school enter vocational training and work with the value profile they have at the end of the twelfth grade. To establish this work entry profile was the task of the first study.

The second study concerned the transition in the salience of life domains and values as youth evolve from the role of student to that of adult job holder. It is obvious that the salience and the impact of life roles and theaters (Super, 1980) change as people move through the stages of their life cycles, and so do their attitudes toward the different life domains. It should be possible to describe and measure these changes of attitudes through the modifications in the value system of age cohorts, because values are explicit standards or designs for living and expressing the desirable for a certain group (Kluckhohn, 1962) and because the hierarchically organized system of values is a most characteristic feature of human persons and groups (Rokeach, 1973).

Since the publication of Erikson's (1963) theory, transitions are associated with crises. However, the meaning Erikson attached to the concept of crisis was a complex event of paramount importance (a critical event) for the development of the personality. It follows from the concept of development that the personality preserves a certain identity throughout all transformations. This had already been suggested by Künkel (1939), and later by Super, Starishevsky, Matlin, and Jordaan (1963) and Hall (1976). They have spoken of the translation of the self-image into occupational terms in order to create a career identity. In line with these theories we hypothesized that there is no gap in value profiles caused by the transition between school and work, but rather a process of value adjustment to a new role performed in a new theater with the preservation of a basic identity.

The hypothesis is in line with Rokeach's (1973) conception considering values as enduring phenomena, not completely stable or completely unstable. Any conception of values, he points out, must be able to account for the enduring character of values, as well as for their changing characteristics (Rokeach, 1973).

From this first hypothesis followed another: If it is true that there is a basic continuity in values throughout the stages of vocational development in adolescence and young adulthood, then it should be possible to trace the paths of social vocational mobility in a given society by the aid of value profile commonalities of people participating in institutions that represent the logical sequence of vocational development.

The rationale for this hypothesis lies in the fact that the basis of work values is acquired in early socialization (Rosenberg, 1957; Davis, 1965; Holland, 1976) but that their aim is to guide future behavior in future situations. It is an anticipatory socialization (Merton, 1957; Musgrave, 1972) in view of specific tasks through role socialization and of a certain generalized status in life through status socialization (Brim and Wheeler, 1966).

This is not to say that there will be no changes in a person's value profile after the early socialization has come to an end. As Brim and Wheeler (1966) observe, socialization experienced by people in childhood cannot prepare them for all the roles filled in later years. The necessities of vocational life impose an occupational socialization, which again will find its expression in the person's value system (Kohn, 1969; Mortimer and Lorence, 1979). However, occupational socialization applies to the foundation laid down by the process of early socialization.

Stability and change in the development of work values should characterize the individual as well as the social groups, since the essential phenomena of work value formation can be traced at both levels (Zytowski, 1970). The question is how to predict, on a group level, the areas of change and of stability in work values. We assumed that these areas are defined by the salience and the status of the different agents of socialization during the process of individual development.

The roles people perform during their life cycles are social roles that develop under the guidance of socialization agents. In each life stage, there is a salient social role that appears as a developmental task (Havighurst, 1964). It has to be assumed that the socialization agent introducing the person into a developmental task will be dominant for that period, and its dominance should be expressed in the value system of the age cohort. As the cohort moves to another life stage characterized by a different developmental task, another socialization agent will become dominant; and this change in dominance will produce modifications in the value system. In other words, the common and dominant influence of school should determine a certain commonality in value profiles of high school students regardless of differences in age and socioeconomic level. Similarly, the dominance of the world of work as a socialization agent should produce a certain closeness in the salience of life activities and in the values of adults regardless of occupational differences.

The dialectical character of the developmental process that appears in the change and at the same time in the preservation of identity demands that there be moderator factors controlling the process. It was hypothesized that, for the period under consideration, these factors were socioeconomic level and age-conditioned experience. It has been demonstrated in the previous research that with regard to work values these factors already include the influence of family and peer groups (Krau, 1987). Socioeconomic level is a broad factor of social influence, which also stands for cultural belongingness (Krau, 1987). It ensures the longitudinal preservation of sociocultural identity throughout all age groups while horizontally differentiating between the values of groups within the population. The second factor of age-conditioned experience fulfills the opposite role of horizontal unification of the value profile of age cohorts while also acting as a longitudinal differentiator. Thus the actual value profile of a social group appears as a combination of two identities: the longitudinal identity of social belongingness and the horizontal identity of the various age groups across the general population. Modification in age-related experience affects all members of the population, while changes in social identity produced by social mobility occur only in parts of it. It should be possible therefore to trace longitudinally the mobility path of cohorts by the aid of horizontally asserted value profiles in groups arranged in a sequential developmental order.

According to research hypotheses samples were drawn from groups belonging to high and low socioeconomic status at the main stations of the developmental process between the role of student and that of adult worker: (a) ninth-grade high school students from low socioeconomic level, N = 130; (b) ninth-grade high school students from high socioeconomic level, N = 124; (c) twelfth-grade high school students from high socioeconomic level, N = 123; (d) twelfth-grade high school students from low socioeconomic level, N = 125; (e) undergraduate students from various departments, N = 114; (f) youth in job search at private employment offices, N = 85; (g) white-collar employees in semiskilled jobs, N = 104; (h) blue-collar workers in semiskilled to skilled jobs, N = 80; (i) persons in professional or semiprofessional jobs that used to be occupied by former students of the specialties which belonged to sample (e) (e.g., psychologists, teachers), N = 45. The sample total was 930.

The socioeconomic level was established on the basis of the neighborhood in which the schools functioned. Such a division is typical for Israeli schools, and the samples are therefore representative for the main strata of the Israeli society. To enhance representativeness, the sample of undergraduate students was drawn from the departments most frequently indicated as college candidates' first choice: psychology, education, law, and economy. As far as private employment offices are concerned, they are very much part of the economic life in the country. As these offices mediate jobs for a certain fee, they are unlikely to be approached by individuals belonging to a low socioeconomic level.

The instrument used for investigating the salience of life domains and the work value profiles of research samples was the Salience Inventory (Participation Scale) and the Values Scale of the Work Importance Study (WIS). The American version has been published by Nevill and Super (1986a,b).

Both the American and the Israeli versions have the same source, the Values Scale published by Knasel, Super, and Kidd (1981). In the previous research, Krau (1987) pointed to the fact that the first 5 items reveal the principle content of values, while the last 5 items refer to the work-specific content. Although for research purposes this scale is quite appropriate, for reasons of parsimony the international team decided to elaborate a 5-item value scale in each country participating in the research. Of these 5 items, two had to refer to the general content of values and two specifically to work, while the last could refer to either general or work values. In practice the reduction to 5 items had to take into account the particularities of national culture, the factor analysis performed in each country (in order to ensure the consistency of the scale), and the practical purposes that this shortened scale had to serve. Consequently, there are certain differences between countries in the 5-item Value Scales. While the work orientation of the American WIS Value Scale is slightly over 50 percent, the Israeli version has a stronger work orientation and contains 73 percent work-specific items. The internal consistency (Cronbach α) for the Israeli 5–item Value Scale is (averaged across values) .78 for high school students, .74 for college students, .84 for blue-and white-collar employees, and .79 for the holders of professional and semiprofessional jobs. The reliability measurement using the test-retest procedure was performed with college students, as it has been in the United States, four months after the first testing, and the averaged correlation across values is $r = .69$. For the Salience Inventory the internal consistency averaged across domains is .83 in high school, .86 in college, and .88 in the adult samples. The test-retest score is .65 (in college).

Each item of the Value Scale is rated on a 5-point scale, and the sum total of the five items defining a certain value constitutes the subject's score on the value. From these individual scores a mean sample group score was computed for each value. The latter permitted the establishment of the sample group's value profile by arranging the values in rank order of preference.

Because the research hypothesis referred to the possibility of tracing group developmental paths through the investigation of their value profiles, the analysis aimed at establishing commonalities in value preferences along the vocational developmental path. To evidence the clustering of work value profiles, Spearman's rank order correlation was computed for the mean hierarchies of work value preferences in research sample groups, and the results were submitted to Guttman and Lingoe's Smallest Space Analysis (SSA), a general nonmetric method designed to find the minimal number of Euclidean dimensions for the description of a collection of variables (Guttman, 1968). The statistical significance of this method is indicated by the coefficient of alienation (Schlesinger and Guttman, 1969). Since at a coefficient of alienation of .141 a percentage of 98 percent of the variance is accounted for by the correlation (Guilford and Fruchter, 1973), a coefficient of .15 and below is generally accepted as indicating that the location of the variables in the space has statistical validity.

Smallest Space Analysis establishes commonalities but not causal links. Therefore, the data were subjected to path analysis. As Duncan (1971) points out, certain events and decisions commonly if not universally precede others, so that the status observed at the termination of a period of observation may logically be taken to depend on the initial status. In order to perform the path analysis, multiple correlations were computed between the value profile of every vocational development "station" and the value profiles of the variables following in logical and time sequence. The partial (pure) correlations of the "sending stations," as the determining variable with every subsequent developmental stage (the "receiving stations") constituted the path coefficients. In this study the statistical significance of the analysis rests upon the significance of the multiple correlation coefficient. This procedure was preferred to giving statistical values to residual variables up to the point where a complete determination of each "dependent" variable is reached (cf. Turner, 1964).

The tracing of modifications and identities in the development of group value profiles was completed by a content analysis. Since modifications in values, that is, in attitudes, had to find their expression above all in what is strongly desired or rejected, it was assumed that in the sample groups arranged in developmental order, the most and the last preferred values, would be good indicators of the phenomenon. Consequently, the value profiles with the values arranged in rank order were divided into quartiles. The method permitted the researchers (a) to establish the skewness of the value rating distributions by means of the median and the semi-interquartile range and (b) to detach the upper and the lower quartiles, composed of the five most- and the five least-preferred values, for qualitative analysis. The measurement of skewness of the rating distributions in sample groups was meant to give information on the evolution of the general attitude toward work values. A positive skewness would indicate a general positive attitude toward work values with the emotional emphasis on the spectrum of preferred values. A negative skewness would indicate the reverse phenomenon.

The Smallest Space Analysis of the value profiles yielded a well-defined three-dimensional space with a relatively low coefficient of alienation of 0.11, attesting to the statistical significance of the results. The first dimension of this space is by far the most informative, representing the transition in the dominant socialization agents: school versus the world of work. Projections 2 and 3 of the value space reproduce the dimensions of the mediating factors interacting at the high and at the low socioeconomic level. Since all this can be inferred from the position of the variables vis-à-vis the agents of socialization, only the first projection of the value space will be presented.

Figure 5.1 presents two salient clusters: The one to the right is the school

Figure 5.1
Smallest Space Analysis of Value Preferences

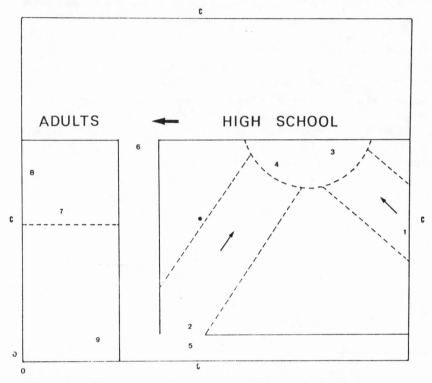

The dimension of dominant socialization agents: school vs. the world of work. (1) 9th-grade high socioeconomic level, (2) 9th-grade low socioeconomic level, (3) 12th grade high socioeconomic level, (4) 12th grade low socioeconomic level, (5) undergraduate students, (6) youth in private employment offices, (7) white-collar workers, (8) blue-collar workers, (9) professionals.

Reprinted by permission. Copyright 1989 by Academic Press.

cluster dominated as it is by educational institutions, and within it is a narrow well-defined subcluster reflecting the value commonality of the high socioeconomic level and pointing to the values of adults in professional jobs. Within the school cluster are high and low socioeconomic groups, the latter being marked by the closeness of the employment office for job mediation. College, the other "transitional" station, stands apart, as it is linked to the "corridor" of the high socioeconomic level and points to the values of adults in professional jobs. Within the school cluster, high and low socioeconomic levels evolve on separate lines; and between right (school) and left (work), university and employment office appear on the same "developmental meridian." The Smallest Space Analysis of values shows a clear-cut age differentiation (adults versus high school,

Figure 5.2
Path Analysis of Social Mobility through Vocational Development as Reflected in Value Commonalities

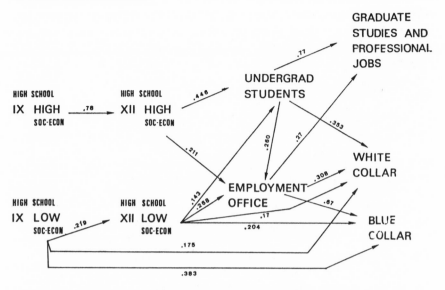

Reprinted by permission. Copyright 1989 by Academic Press.

and within high school the ninth versus the twelfth grade), that is, age-conditioned "vertical" differentiation along the lines of socioeconomic status. At the same time each status group evolves along distinct developmental lines, strongly suggesting the preservation of identity in an unbroken developmental pattern, as postulated by the researcher.

Smallest Space Analysis permitted the establishment of commonality clusters of values in the social space. However, the developmental link between the clusters is only suggested. Path analysis proves that work value commonality is indicative of a social-vocational developmental path (see Fig. 5.2) reflecting the "horizontal" status-conditioned differentiations within the age groups. The figures on the arrows between every two vocational developmental stations are pure (partial) correlations, excluding the other factors. They served as a basis for the computation of multiple correlations between each sending station and the receiving stations (see Table 5.4). The table shows that all correlations are statistically significant, but some of them account for a lower percentage of the variance of the social-vocational developmental path. This is not astonishing, because the universe of possible receiving stations (e.g., for school dropouts, persons who enter trade schools, self-employment, jobs of salesmen) is much larger than the possibilities sampled in this research. Nevertheless, the statistical significance of the correlations in the path analysis indicates that there is a

Table 5.4
**Multiple Correlations between the Vocational Sending Station and the
Receiving Stations (see Fig. 5.3)**

Sending Station	R	F	P	R^2 (r^2)
9th Grade high socioeconomic level	r = .78	–	.001	.60
9th Grade low socioeconomic level	.46	1.61	.05	.21
12th Grade high socioeconomic level	.48	1.90	.01	.23
12th Grade low socioeconomic level	.39	1.54	.05	.15
Undergraduate students	.88	3.05	.001	.77
Employment office	.70	2.40	.01	.49

Reprinted with permission. Copyright 1989 by Academic Press.

developmental link between the samples of sending and receiving stations and that work value commonality is an indicator of this link.

Turning now to the path analysis itself, one can see that the low socioeconomic level has a far more dispersed social-vocational developmental path in comparison with the high socioeconomic level, at least in the stages of adolescent and young adult vocational development.

However, not all the avenues and outcomes of vocational development have the same probability of incidence, as appears from the differences between the path coefficients leading from vocational ''sending stations'' to the ''receiving stations.'' It seems that only a minority of the low socioeconomic level's offspring pursue studies in senior high school, and afterward the majority end up in vocational positions occupied via a more direct path by those who did not continue their studies in senior high school. Nevertheless, it appears as an established fact that there is an upward social mobility path for the offspring of the low socioeconomic stratum, as there is a downward social-vocational mobility path for a minority of the high socioeconomic level's offspring. Only about 60 percent of the high socioeconomic level offspring ($0.77^2 = 0.59$) reach professional jobs, while a not negligible part end up in white-, and some even in blue-collar jobs. This means, further, that the conditions of career start are an important factor of influence on the process of career development, but certainly not the only one.

It has been documented so far that (a) common developmental stages and (b) common developmental paths determine the common character of the rank profile of values. The value commonality along developmental lines that permitted the establishment of paths of social mobility supports the suggested pattern of transition in values, wherein modifications are added to persisting core identities. However, the transition in work values between the status of high school student and adult job holder has important qualitative aspects that need to be clarified. Table 5.5 presents a cross-sectional picture of the upper and lower quartiles of work values in the transitional period investigated.

Table 5.5
Upper and Lower Quartiles of Work Values in Research Samples

9th Grade High Socioeconomic level	9th Grade Low Socioeconomic level	12th Grade High Socioeconomic level	12th Grade Low Socioeconomic level	Undergraduate Students	Youth at Employment Office	White Collar	Blue Collar	Professional
UPPER QUARTILE								
Economic Security Achievement	Economic Security Ability Utilization	Ability Utilization Achievement	Economic Security Achievement	Ability Utilization Achievement	Ability Utilization Creativity	Economic Security Supervisory Relations Autonomy	Economic Security Supervisory Relations	Ability Utilization Achievement
Supervisory Relations	Responsibility	Spiritual Values	Ability Utilization	Supervisory Relations	Achievement	Autonomy	Prestige	Supervisory Relations
Ability Utilization	Supervisory Relations	Economic Security	Supervisory Relations	Participation in Decisions	Economic Security	Economic Rewards	Autonomy	Intellectual Stimulation
Spiritual Values	Life Style	Autonomy	Participation in Decisions	Responsibility	Supervisory Relations	Prestige	Ability Utilization	Creativity
Q^a 1.51	0.67	1.63	1.40	1.25	1.23	1.54	1.60	1.65
SK^b 0.01	0.02	-0.38	0.22	0.06	0.04	0.40	0.00	0.32
LOWER QUARTILE								
Authority	Authority	Physical Activity	Risk Taking	Physical Activity	Risk Taking	Risk Taking	Risk Taking	Physical Activity
Risk Taking	Risk Taking	Authority	Authority	Risk Taking	Variety	Physical Activity	Variety	Risk Taking
Physical Activity	Environment	Aesthetics	Physical Activity	Altruism	Social Interaction	Altruism	Authority	Authority
Altruism	Physical Activity	Prestige	Prestige	Prestige	Altruism	Aesthetics	Altruism	Authority
Environment	Aesthetics	Risk Taking	Aesthetics	Aesthetics	Physical Activity	Variety	Physical Activity	Aesthetics

a. Semi-interquartile range
b. Skewness of distribution

Reprinted by permission. Copyright 1989 by Academic Press.

The coefficients of skewness in the distribution of value ratings indicate an even distribution in the ninth grade. Toward the end of high school, in the twelfth grade, the distribution becomes somewhat skewed: At the high socio-economic level there is a certain depreciation of work values expressed in the negative skewness of the distribution, while at the low socioeconomic level the tendency is to give more weight to preferred work values. This tendency gains momentum in adult white-collar and professional job holders, and can be recognized as one of the aspects of occupational socialization. The modification in values generally follows the emphasis in attitudes: It concerns more the upper quartile of preferences, where instead of Spiritual Values of Life Style fostered by school, new values like Supervisory Relations, Participation in Decision Making, Creativity, Intellectual Stimulation, or Prestige make their entry. The process of value modification starts with the groups for whom the proximity of work is a concrete issue. Such groups are the twelfth grade of the low socio-economic level and the college students of the high socioeconomic level. The "new" values emphasized by occupational socialization correspond to the aspirations and expectations of future career development. Intellectual Stimulation and Creativity appear in professionals, but not in white- or blue-collar workers. The leading motives of the latter, as expressed in their value preferences, are economic security (and rewards), good supervisory relations, and the wish for autonomy and prestige (what is called "consideration," in Maslowian terms).

The behavior of Ability Utilization may serve as a paradigm of the differential influence aspirations and career expectations have on value preferences. It appears from Table 5.5 that Ability Utilization is very important for professionals and generally for persons at the moment of work entry (in students and youth in job search). This applies even to the ninth grade of low socioeconomic level, as some of the pupils are constrained to leave school and seek a job. However, Ability Utilization is not a stringent problem for the high school students of the high socioeconomic level, who foreseeably will continue studying for some years, nor is it for white-collar employees in semiskilled jobs, who know they cannot get it. This value again seems to gain some importance in blue-collar workers who were partly working in skilled jobs.

The research has supported the hypothesis that the analysis of work value profiles performed in groups at key points of their vocational development indicates paths of social mobility. In the context of the present study this finding also meant that there is an unbroken transition in work values, that is, a transition in which despite vocation-stage-imposed modifications, basic identities are preserved as the various social groups move from junior high school to the role of adult worker. Modifications in the work value profiles are larger in the upward mobility path and are smaller when the subgroup evolves along the lines of its own socioeconomic status, high or low. However, a later position in the career evolution line always builds on the work values of the previous one. This finding may be interpreted as an extension of the "accentuation phenomenon" described in Sewell, Hauser, and Featherman (1976), which was concerned with the values of college youth.

As work values crystallize under the influence of early and occupational socialization, both these agents are under the influence of events occurring in the larger society such as economic boom or recession. Such events are to be taken into account when dealing with modifications in work values. In this research a general preference for Economic Security was expressed in all groups of high school students, regardless of their socioeconomic status. The finding apparently contradicts the results of the first research (Krau, 1987), where this value appeared as a top preference at the low socioeconomic level only. However, that previous research was conducted in years of relative economic well-being (1981–1982), while the present study was performed in the years 1985–1986, characterized by inflation reaching an annual rate of nearly 500 percent and then followed by fierce economic measures taken in order to deal with this situation. As a consequence, not only did redundancy figures reach very high levels but so did bankruptcies. It is not surprising that in this atmosphere there has been a general concern for economic security.

Such changes in values due to external circumstances do not affect the final goal of self-realization, which is sufficiently stable. What such value modifications do is to change behavior, including career behavior, which is modified precisely in order to achieve the final end-state of self-realization. If economic security, for instance, moves to a higher position in the value rank order, it is not to say that money will be people's only purpose, but rather that they have become convinced that they have to reckon more with economic problems. Apart from this, economic security is not the only value in a person's profile, and the other top values ensure the stability of a person's motivational directedness.

At this point the reader may want some proof that certain value profiles are more conducive to self-realization than others. Although the problem is obscured by the difference in aspirations of the three self-realization groups (see Chapter 3), some data are available from the investigation of 60 people reported in Chapter 3. It will be remembered that the subjects had to rate their self-realization on a 7-point scale and define what self-realization meant for them. In addition, they were administered the new 18-value WIS Values Scale. They also had to rate their satisfaction with their jobs on a 10-point scale and their general life satisfaction on a 9-point scale. The latter measurement was obtained by the aid of two questions:

Are you satisfied with your present situation? (please elaborate).

What do you think your chances are for success in the future?

The answers to these questions were classified into the categories of "satisfied," "dissatisfied," and "undecided" with regard both to the present situation

Table 5.6
Differences in Satisfaction between Self-Realization Levels

Group No.	Levels of self- realization	N	Mean work satisfaction	F ANOVA	Mean life satisfaction	F ANOVA
1	High self- realizers	28	8.67	7.675	8.39	14.35
2	Medium-level scores	28	7.64	p=0.001 Groups:	7.17	p=0.001 Groups:
3	Low self- realizers	4	8.67	1,2>3 (Scheffé)	3.25	1.2>3 (Scheffé)

and to the future. These categories were combined to yield a satisfaction score between 1 and 9 in which the greater weight was assigned to future outlook. Thus, for example, satisfied in the present but with a poor outlook on the future was given a score of 5, while dissatisfied at present but optimistic about future chances received a score of 6.

Results for all indices were computed for high self-realizers (self-realization scores of 6 and 7), medium-level scores of 4 and 5, and low self-realizers (scores 1–3). Understandably, there are few people in the last category ($N = 4$). However, the differences between this last group and the others are so large that a one-way ANOVA found them significantly different with regard to both life and work satisfaction (see Table 5.6). This finding was supported by correlations of $r = 0.422$, significant at $p = 0.001$, between self-realization scores and work satisfaction, and $r = 0.525$, significant at $p = 0.001$, between self-realization scores and general life satisfaction. A stepwise regression calculated on the multiple correlation of self-realization ratings with work and life satisfaction and also with the need for achievement (measured with an adaptation of the Mehrabian Risk Preference Scale) yielded an $R_{1.23} = 0.560$ in which life satisfaction is the most influential index determining self-realization ratings, with $r_{1.2} = 0.538$ as it explains 29 percent of the self-realization ratings. This result supports our theoretical position on self-realization on two important points. First, satisfaction with life is a condition for a positive appraisal of one's achieved self-realization; second, the two are not identical as Maslow's conception on "happy, healthy animals" would hold. One may be very satisfied but estimate that one has still a long way to go in order to fulfill one's aspirations, or contrarily, one may have achieved most important life aspirations but presently finds oneself in trouble. Tycoons like Robert Maxwell or ousted CEO Robert Stempel of General Motors sufficiently illustrate this case.

The differences in the value profiles of high-, medium-level and low self-realizers are presented in Figure 5.3. The figure shows that the value profiles of persons rating their self-realization at a high or a medium level are generally similar. Yet, high self-realizers have significantly higher scores in the values of

Figure 5.3
Value Profiles of People According to the Level of Their Self-Realization Ratings

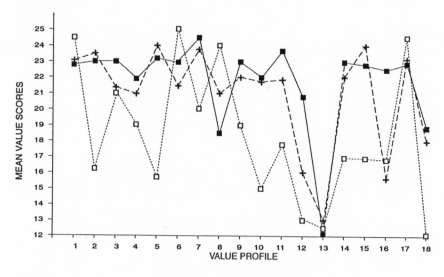

Legend

Values:
1. Economic rewards
2. Authority
3. Achievement
4. Creativity
5. Altruism
6. Ability utilization
7. Social interaction
8. Aesthetics
9. Autonomy
10. Participation in decision making
11. Prestige
12. Risk taking
13. Physical Activity
14. Intellectual Stimulation
15. Supervisory Relations
16. Life style
17. Responsibility
18. Variety

■ High self-realization scores
+ Medium-level scores
□ Low scores

achievement, prestige, risk taking, intellectual stimulation, and freedom of life-style. These values speak for themselves as a motivating force toward self-realization.

The big differences are again between these two groups taken together and the low self-realizers. Individuals belonging to the latter group are consistently lower in their general value involvement and its level is less uniform; they have value peaks higher than in high self-realizers (economic rewards, ability utilization, responsibility, and aesthetics) and lows like authority, creativity, intellectual stimulation, social interaction, altruism, risk taking, prestige, participation in decision making, and supervisory relations. Such a profile expresses high aspirations, but the value involvement with actions leading to their implementation is low. These people have a contradictory motivational basis that cannot sustain the implementation of their very high aspirations. Failure is a logical consequence.

The achievements of people rating themselves high on self-realization are also motivationally accounted for by their value involvement profile. Their lower commitment to economic rewards and responsibility (compared with the group of medium scores) suggests that they belong to the group of self-realization in a definite vocational activity. In all hitherto-considered research samples this group has been consistently higher in achieved self-realization, just as the "losers" are mainly from the group aspiring at self-realization in work career concomitants, whereby the occupational substance of the career is irrelevant to them. Needless to say, of the four "failures" of the sample, three belonged to this group, while the fourth sought the realization of his aspirations outside any vocational career (the division of this sample into the three groups of self-realization orientation has been discussed in Chapter 3).

If the general motivational steering toward self-realization is performed with the aid of values, the person's preference order of values expresses attitudes (Thurstone, 1960), which are already dispositions for action, as was stressed quite a long time ago by Allport (1937). While values are generalized behavior orientations, attitudes appear to be more situation specific. A high preference for the values of ability utilization or achievement will produce a corresponding implementation in the person's career only if accompanied by a positive attitude toward work and specifically toward one's job.

Here we come across an apparent contradiction. Either attitudes are instruments for implementing the person's values and as such are linked to a generalized life-plan implementation, or they are event specific, in which case they cannot direct behavior toward a prior established end-state of self-realization. The following research (Krau, 1983a) was aimed at clarifying the crystallization process and the scope of attitudes toward work at the entrance of major new career sequences, which represented stages on the road to implementation of the person's self-realization image.

In well-known studies Homans (1950) and Zaleznik, Christensen, and Roethlisberger (1958) stressed the importance of reward expectancies in the formation of attitudes toward work. Subsequently, however, the opinions became divided as to the factors and mechanisms producing changes in general work attitudes. In a study dealing with engineers' careers, Kopelman concluded that expectancies are the pivotal factor in determining job attitudes, but they always appear along with values. In his sample the expectancies-values couple tended to have a stable relationship over time, its modifications being linked to advancement in age (Kopelman, 1977). In contrast, Hayes (1973) and Flude (1977), investigating vocational trainees, found that the evaluation of work is closely linked to work experience and changes in accordance with the latter. Apart from the contradiction in these positions, the conclusions that follow are incongruent with the reality of organizational behavior, in which the motivation of people to work is not automatically shaped by working conditions nor exclusively determined by advancement in age.

To shed light on the formation of general attitudes towards work, some specific questions should be answered:

What expectations are included in the evaluation of work, not only at different stages in the same career pattern (Kopelman, 1977), but at different career transitions, at various ages, and in careers at different socioeconomic levels?

What is the link pattern, in the variety of situations mentioned above, among expectations, the evaluation of work, and personality traits motivating the modern search for life satisfaction?

It was hypothesized (Krau, 1983a) that a person's attitude toward work is formed in an anticipatory manner, before the career transition actually takes place. The changes in attitudes occur in view of new transition on the basis of expectations integrating available information on the labor market and job activities with the person's aspirations. The emerging expectations should be more than a probability statement of intervening events. They should express the affective valuation of this probability and lead to a "position" concerning the importance of work to the individual. The affective meaning of work together with the position adopted regarding its centrality are the presumed components of the general attitude toward work. This last assumption follows from the now classical acknowledgment that opinions are essential components of attitudes (Thurstone and Chave, 1929) and that attitudes are a guide for action (Allport, 1937), a predisposition to respond to situations that can be indexed by the measurement operation of the semantic differential (Osgood, Suci, and Tannenbaum, 1971). This assumption also follows from the acknowledged importance that work and occupational life have for the person's self-image (Super, Starishevsky, Matlin, and Jordaan, 1963).

The anticipatory formation of attitudes towards one's vocation has been described by Musgrave (1967), Kadushin (1969), and Flude (1977) as an *anticipatory socialization*, the term referring to the early identification of the individual with his vocation (mostly profession) as he progresses through his training course. Obviously, through this mediated contact with his future occupation, the individual obtains information that shapes his expectancies concerning the role his vocation will play in his life. It was assumed that the expectations extended from the vocational activity as such to all work-related factors (the place of work, the boss, work in general, career).

The expectations concerning work should be expressed according to the affective meaning these concepts have for the individual, not only by their evaluation dimension (Osgood et al., 1971) but in all three appraisal dimensions of "attitude objects": Evaluation, Potency, and Activity. These three dimensions of work-related concepts should correspond to distinct expectations that work is meant to fulfill.

The aspiration for an interesting job, which makes self-realization possible, is supported to find its expression in the Activity dimension of the affective meaning of work-related concepts. Therefore this dimension should be linked to measures of overall satisfaction.

It is obvious that career aspirations of people will be linked to jobs promising satisfaction. As a result, jobs considered as possible career paths should be viewed in a bright, positive light, and this appraisal would be expressed in the Evaluation dimension of the affective meaning of these jobs. The emphasis in this assumption is that the appraisal of work-related objects along the Evaluation dimension is linked to their capacity to fulfill career aspirations and hence is linked to measures of achievement motivation. This assumption was in line with the findings of Minor and Neel (1958), Burstein (1963), and Mischel (1968), who have pointed out that the perception of vocation and career becomes more positive as achievement motivation increases. In anticipatory attitudes toward work, developed at a time when the contact with the occupational world is mediated through school, mass media, or other social channels of information (e.g., in junior or senior high schools), the affective meaning of work-related concepts, along both dimensions of Activity and Evaluation, should be linked to measures of need for social approval and sensitivity to social desirability.

Finally, the appraisal of work and work-related concepts along the Potency dimension was assumed to express people's expectancies concerning the influence their future vocation is considered to have on their social advancement and the quality of their lives. Therefore, one should find a link between the Potency dimension of the affective meaning of work and the need for social approval.

Five samples with Israeli subjects of both sexes and of different ages and socioeconomic conditions were investigated as they approached a major transition in their careers. Two career paths were considered: the professional and the skilled worker. The samples were as follows:

1. Eighty-four junior high school students, 3 months before graduation, at the time when they were required to decide whether to continue high school studies or to go to a trade school and then begin work.

2. One hundred and eighteen senior high school students, 3 months before graduation, at the time when a final decision was due to be made concerning their future: whether to continue studying or to begin work. This sample was meant to be the link to the professional career path represented by the following two samples. Each of the school samples was composed of four classes with a nearly equal number of students. The classes were drawn randomly from schools located in urban and rural areas.

3. Eighty-six undergraduate university students, from the departments of psychology and economics, at the time they were to apply for admission to graduate school. They all volunteered to participate in the research.

4. Thirty-five engineers selected for higher executive positions in their organizations, who were sent to courses in management. Their mean age was 33.4 years, with a standard deviation of $SD = 6.14$. The range was between 26 and 48 years.

5. Eighty-eight trainees of a training center for industrial workers in a number of trades (lathe operators, grinders, electricians, motorcar mechanics). Their age ranged between 16 and 40 years, with the arithmetic mean at 25.8 years and with a standard deviation of SD = 5.93.

A 12-qualifier semantic differential list, that on which Osgood's cross-cultural research was based (Osgood, May, and Miron, 1975), was used to investigate the following concepts focusing on the meaning people attach to work and to their vocation: Work, Career, My Future Occupation, The Place of Work, and The Boss. High school students were not requested to define the last two concepts, as they had hardly any systematic information on these topics. As a term of comparison and in order to permit the assessment of work centrality, all subjects were also asked to define, according to the semantic differential technique, the concept of Amusement.

Tests were used to measure the motivational personality traits of achievement motivation and the need for social approval, both linked, according to the research hypotheses, to the formation of the affective meaning of work and work-related concepts.

As a measure of achievement motivation the German variant of the Mehrabian Risk Preference Scale (Mikula, Uray, and Schwinger, 1974) was used. It links the strength of the need to achieve with task difficulty, independent decision taking, and full task involvement. The internal consistency of this scale was .61 in a sample of students and .66 in a sample of soldiers. The test correlated .45 with the Orientation Inventory of Bass (1962) for students and .31 for soldiers. In the student sample a .42 correlation appeared also with the internal locus of control in Rotter's (1966) Internal-External Control scale. All these correlations were significant at the .01 level (Mikula et al., 1974). Administering this test to a sample of high school students, Krau found a significant correlation of .40 between test scores and the level of aspiration in choosing a work task that the subjects subsequently had to perform (Krau, 1982a).

The need to gain social approval and to present in one's activity an image of conforming to social demands was measured by the means of Crowne and Marlowe's test for social desirability (Crowne and Marlowe, 1960). The test is based on a content approach. The population of items is defined by behaviors that are culturally sanctioned and approved but are unlikely to occur. The internal consistency coefficient of this test is .88. Its correlation with the Edwards Social Desirability Scale oriented toward psychopathology (Edwards, 1957) is .35 significant at the .01 level (Crowne and Marlow, 1960). This test also proved to be a good measure of the need for approval in high school students, where test scores significantly correlated with the self-rating of abilities and with the effort the subject declared he would apply to a work task (Krau, 1982a).

Because the research hypothesis held that the Activity dimension of the semantic differential appraisal of work was linked to satisfaction expectations, subjects were asked to answer the questionnaire on satisfaction, which has already been discussed. It is scored on a 9-point scale wherein the greater weight is given to anticipated satisfaction in the future.

In the school samples the testing instruments mentioned hitherto were simultaneously administered by teachers and under the supervision of a psychologist. This arrangement was necessary because the testing took place during school time. The other research samples (undergraduate students and engineers sent to courses for executives) were tested in groups by psychologists at the place of their studies. It was possible to test all university students at the same time, as they volunteered to participate in the research. For ongoing executives, acquaintance with tests was part of their practice in organizational psychology.

Two things had to be made clear before any comparison between the attitudes toward work held by the research samples could be feasible. First, it had to be assured that the intragroup differences along sex and sociocultural backgrounds did not prevent a unitary outlook of the whole sample on the issues dealt with. Second, it had to be established whether the attitude objects of work-related concepts were understood in an identical fashion and referred to the same objective reality.

Accordingly, the heterogeneous samples were divided into subgroups: (a) the high school samples were divided along sex and along urban vs. rural backgrounds, and (b) the samples of students and of vocational trainees were split along occupational groups. For each of these subgroups the arithmetic means of semantic dimensional factor scores on work concepts were computed (Evaluation, Potency, and Activity), and scores were compared by means of the t-test.

To investigate the content of work-related concepts, every third subject in alphabetical order from each sample participated in a free-association experiment. The concepts defined by the semantic differential method were used in addition to others as word stimuli. Verbal reactions and reaction time were registered. In all samples this experiment was administered individually by psychologists in the subject's free time.

The relationships between Work, Career, and Amusement served to test the centrality of work in research samples. The generalized distance formula (Osgood et al., 1971) was used to index the affective distance between Work and Career and Work and Amusement. Then the arithmetic means of semantic differential factor scores were compared within each research group by a t-test for matched samples.

The t-test between mean affective meaning factor scores in the subgroups of the research samples did not reveal any significant difference. This is not astonishing, as the educational system is the same for boys and girls and cultural differences between urban and rural environment are small in Israel today. There is also no reason why the attitudes toward work should be different in students from the psychology and economic departments or in skilled lathe operators, grinders, and motorcar mechanics. Thus, comparison among the five research samples became possible regarding the affective meaning attached to work and to work-related concepts.

In the free-association experiment, differences appeared in the concept of Work and Career, mainly between high school and university students on the one hand and personnel working in industry and in trainees and executives on the other hand.

The main difference in the perception of Work is that for personnel in industry it is identified with one's job and one's life aspirations and evaluated in a positive light, while university students and partly high school students perceive Work mostly as compelled, boring, physical, factory routine, which evokes negative associations. In junior high school Work is generally linked to clichés reflecting what has been said by teachers or by school manuals. Senior high school students begin to have a more mature outlook.

The concept of Career is generally associated with achievement and success. However, for junior high school students and for trainees at the vocational training center it is more like a fairy tale, the story of great men, while university students and ongoing executives openly link the concept to their own achievement aspirations.

The different ways in which work was perceived did not prevent the comparison between samples, but this fact had to be taken into consideration while interpreting the particular differences that arose in the semantic differential definitions.

The most positive attitude toward work and career is held by ongoing executives, and it is not surprising that they have the highest expectations from their work, especially as far as interest and activity are concerned. Their work potency expectations are shared by nearly all other samples except senior high school students. The latter appear to have a drastic reduction in expectancies concerning the activity and potency of work as compared to the junior high school students, probably the effect of contradictory information coming from the labor market. As a matter of fact the largest amount of significant differences regarding the appraisal of work is to be found between high school students (junior and senior) and the other samples.

The research samples do not differ (except for the industrial trainees) as to the perception of their future occupation, and the general attitude is one of optimism.

Differences within the samples in rating Work and Future Occupation are significant in senior high school and in the vocational training center. High school students perceive their future occupation significantly more active ($t = 3.20$) and of greater potency ($t = 2.42$) as compared with work in general. As was already mentioned, in the free-association experiment, they do not identify the two. In vocational trainees the affective meaning ratings show the opposite direction, and work in general is perceived in a brighter light ($t = 3.12$) and also more active ($t = 2.15$) than the future occupation as the latter is known to subjects through practicing in workshops.

The (future) Place of Work is seen in a brighter light by undergraduate students in comparison with the trainees of the vocational training center, but no differences arose as to its potency or activity. More controversial is the perception of The Boss along all its characteristics; the highest evaluation is awarded by vocational trainees and the lowest by undergraduate students. This pattern appeared also in the rating of the potency of the concept of The Boss, but in factor scores of the activity dimension the executives rate the highest. While this last finding is fully understandable, the unusually high evaluation by vocational trainees as compared to undergraduate students needed an explanation. It was supposed that the difference reflects the social perception of the role of boss in an industrial milieu and among professionals. Accordingly, the ratings were correlated with the test measuring the need for social approval, and the score was .27 (significant at the .01 level) for vocational trainees and .25 for undergraduate students (significant at the .05 level). This means that the more students conform to social stereotypes the less positive is their attitude toward authority figures at the place of work.

The Evaluation and Activity scores of Career rank highest in executives, which might have been expected. The surprise is rather that Potency scores are significantly higher in undergraduate students. While executives have a realistic preview of their future careers, students only dream about it. The evidence is that there is a significant difference ($t = 2.33$) between the matched Potency ratings of Career and Future Occupation in undergraduate students.

According to the research hypothesis the affective meanings of work concepts, obtained through the semantic differential evaluations, express expectations developed during the encounter of personality-based aspirations and the field information of job preview. As far as the concept of career is concerned, a number of significant correlations appear between the evaluation dimension (positive, great, pleasant, bright) and achievement motivation. The higher the level of the latter, the more the individual, standing at a new opening of his career, will see it in a bright light, and vice versa. The same also holds true for work if this is identified with one's vocation. With undergraduate students this is not the case, and brightness is bestowed only on their future occupation and the place of work but not on work as such, which they understand as physical, unpleasant factory work. In trainees of the vocational training center, achievement motivation is associated with a positive evaluation of work in general and of their careers but not of their future jobs or the place of work.

Activity and potency of work and career are linked to satisfaction in undergraduate students, which apparently corresponds to social expectations, as the potency and activity dimensions of Work and Future Occupation have significant correlations with the need for approval. The tendency toward negative correlations in the appraisal of Career in high school students does not change this fact. High school students are known for their nonconformity and see in this context a career as active and work or career as having a more substantial influence, for the better, on one's fate. Nevertheless, the resistance to conformism is in itself a social expectation and is subject to the need for approval by social environments.

Table 5.7
The Affective Distance between Work, Career, and Amusement at Various
Career Transitions

| | D–distance for | |
Sample	Work–Career	Work–Amusement
Junior high school	0.108	2.212
Senior high school	0.708	0.749
Undergraduate students	0.597	1.240
Executive training program	0.180	1.113
Training center for industry	0.266	0.768

Nonconformity of undergraduate students surrounds the ideal figure of the boss: powerful and dynamic. They project themselves into this position as the correlations with achievement motivation indicate. On the contrary, the boss's figure elicits no achievement motivation in vocational trainees. His dynamism appears to be a source of satisfaction, but public opinion in the trainees' milieu does not expect bosses to be characterized by this feature.

The link between the affective meaning of work, future occupation, place of work, career, and motivational factors in trainees of the vocational training center is also very peculiar. The Activity dimension yields no significant correlation with any of the motivational factors or with satisfaction: Apparently there are no crystallized individual and social expectations regarding the existence of such a dimension in their work. However, it seems that, contrary to social expectations, they hope the boss will provide dynamism and ''activity'' in their work and thus allow for satisfaction to emerge.

Work potency appears to be an important characteristic for the vocational trainees, and indeed they undertook the training courses to improve their material and social positions. However, this latter event is expected only by the less-conforming and less-conventional individuals. This attitude is not expressed in the rating of careers, which appears as the embodiment of an ideal working life linked to achievement motivation.

As a matter of fact the work potency appraisal in itself may be a good measure of work centrality for the individual. More information on the topic was obtained by relating the appraisal of Work to that of Career and Amusement. This was achieved by computing the generalized distance formula (Osgood et al., 1971), based on the square root of the summed squares of differences between the scores of two concepts, on all affective meaning dimensions (Evaluation, Potency, and Activity). The results appear in Table 5.7.

It may be seen that Work and Career are closest for junior high school students and executives, while the distance between Work and Amusement is very large. The next rank in work centrality is occupied by the trainees of the vocational training center. All samples considered Work as having greater potency, and the differences are significant at the $p = .01$ level. As far as the Activity dimension is concerned, the findings showed that high school students ranked Amusement higher ($t = 3.60$) while for executives Work was more active ($t = 1.98$), an additional proof of their high work centrality.

The attitude toward work emerged from this study as a function of expectations, which refer to a situation evaluated in light of the person's aspirations. For new attitudes toward work to appear, there must be new expectations (for better or worse) on the basis of an entirely new situation or of new aspirations. This is the case in career transitions, and it follows that changes in work attitudes mainly occur then. Therefore, authors who investigated employees who were stable in their careers saw a remarkable stability in their attitudes toward work, with transformations only at the rate of advancement in age, while others whose subjects underwent vocational training observed newly formed attitudes in connection with the next stage of their careers and concluded that every work experience is automatically reflected in a change of attitudes. The mechanism of anticipatory attitude formation does not warrant the conclusion that every modification in working conditions changes general attitudes towards work, but attitudes do change when a transition to an entirely new situation elicits new expectations.

Age per se was not found to exert a major influence on the formation of attitudes toward work. Persons of various ages but with similar expectations regarding their career advancement and vocational status appeared to have similar attitudes as they approached the same career transition. In this respect the samples of vocational trainees and of ongoing executives are very instructive because both of them are characterized by a considerable dispersion in the age of their members, ranging from work entry to mid-career, and in a number of cases even until the age beyond mid-career. The finding underscores the role of the common career path as a unifying factor of work perception.

It appears, therefore, that attitudes and the subsequent behaviors they command are very much produced by the anticipation of the future, rather than by the past (Rotter, Chance, and Phares, 1972). In this sense Raynor (1974) is right when he says that individual actions gain their meaning by being instrumental for the achievement of the person's broader and more fundamental aims. These aims are reflected in the person's aspiration for self-realization and guided by his/her fundamental profile of value preferences. We may, therefore, safely conclude that values are the key indicator of career goal directedness, and they also have sufficient stability to sustain it via the attitudes pointing toward specific career actions.

It is interesting to note that the motivational impact for advancement toward self-realization is usually provided by the individual's membership group and not by his reference group, although the self-realization criteria of the person reflect the norms of the latter. In cases where membership group and reference group do not coincide, the latter rarely exercises an active facilitation and, more often than not, is indifferent or even hostile to the individual's vying for membership and to his aspirations for advancement. It is quite another matter with the social membership environment, which has a very strong motivational impact, because it induces either a striving for upward social mobility or an attitude of indifference. Rosenberg (1957) and later Werts (1968) pointed out that the parents' socioeconomic level influences expectations and thus the choice of occupational level by their children. It should seem, however, more accurate to speak of the aspirations of social strata and not of their actual socioeconomic level as motivational factors of influence on children's careers.

Common sense ascribes social activism to the middle class and apathy to the lower social strata, as several research data substantiate this image (Wolfbein, 1967; Goodman, Salipante, and Paransky, 1973). However, there are data contradicting such a conception. Stacey (1968) pointed out that in Britain the nonskilled and semiskilled strata have good chances for upward social mobility while for the nonmanual working population there appears a definite probability of social descent. In formerly communist Romania, Krau et al. (1969) compared the grades at the entry examination and in the first years of trade school for lathe operators for 234 youths from urban and 771 from rural origin. They found significant differences in favor of rural youths regarding the entrance into the desired trade ($\chi^2 = 7.85$ significant at $p = 0.02$), higher school marks ($t = 3.26$ significant at $p = 0.01$), and in a significantly higher percentage the rurals motivated their choice with the necessity to build themselves a better future ($\chi^2 = 27.91$ significant at $p = 0.001$). Of 45 rural parents interviewed at their offspring's school entrance examination, only one expressed the wish that their son return to his home village after finishing school. One of the fathers said, "No parent wishes that his children stay home as peasants." Added the mother of another student, "Only people who are incapable of sending their children to the city schools or to learn there a trade say they want them to return, because in the countryside life is much more difficult" (Krau, Aluas, Latis, and Jurcau, 1969). The research concluded that although youth from urban environment had far better conditions to succeed with less effort, they were less motivated to apply it. In formerly communist Romania the reason for this situation was the fact that the offspring of the urban working class enjoyed all kinds of favors simply by belonging to the working class, while the peasantry was literally near to starvation, and frustration ran high. Also, in France twenty years ago it was recorded that rurals used to develop a stronger motivation to enter the teaching profession compared with the urban population (Corruble, 1971). One may conclude that the stronger the frustration felt in a social class, the more strongly they will motivate their children to realize themselves through upward social mobility. However, this is true only if certain expectations of success are maintained. In their absence social groups experiencing only failure will lose hope and develop indifference and passivity as to the realization of a career (Mury, 1965; Wolfbein, 1967) or, on the contrary, develop violence as a means of need gratification and expression of frustration. The spread of rioting and criminality in cities with large masses of underprivileged are indicators of this situation.

It may be appropriate, therefore, to differentiate between aspirations and expectations, as proposed by Kuvelesky and Bealer (1966). While aspirations reflect the orientation toward a desired goal, expectations refer to the estimated probability of reaching an objective, which may be desired or not. It so happens that for the offspring of the well-off middle class there is a good probability to maintain the socioeconomic level of their family, but they do not always aspire to this status, as their chosen reference group may belong to a lower stratum. Therefore downward social mobility becomes a reality for some of them (Krau, 1989b).

It is quite another question whether the family's dynamism concerning upward social mobility incites toward realistic career aspirations and jobs congruent with their children's personality type and capabilities. In this respect the already-mentioned study of Krau et al. (1969) found that frequently parents do not base their advice on the objective assessment of their children's aptitudes and expressed interests; consequently, the prediction value of parents' guidance (as opposed to guidance by teachers, peers, friends) is at the limits of negative significance ($\chi^2 = 4.56$ significant at $p = .10$) pointing toward vocational failure in the future. It follows that the motivational impact of the family on children's careers is a complex phenomenon dependent on (a) the economic and social motivation displayed by its social membership group, (b) the willingness and the capacity to make an objective assessment of their children's aptitudes and interests, and (c) the nature of the "dyad relationship" (Palmer and Cochran, 1988) between parents and children. Only in a primary partnership dyad can a maximal positive influence of parents be expected. It is understood, however, that the aim of such influence must be the formation of the child's independent evaluation of his life goals and capacities, not to shift the parents' own ambitions on their children, as was pointed out by Jung (1954). They want the best for their offspring, which always is what they themselves had neglected and which amounts to loading children with ambitions that are never fulfilled.

Research originating in the Adlerian conception of compensation for the feeling of inferiority has evinced the motivational strength of unsatisfied needs and ambitions in childhood (Roe, 1966; Savickas, 1989). This is an indirect and deviated influence of the family on the motivational steering toward self-realization, but a psychological process does not need to be justified morally. Precisely from a psychological point of view such compensatory aspirations may have the advantage of introducing a hierarchy into the collection of elements of the self-realization guiding image, thus promoting an approach of planning and stepwise implementation. On the other hand, the strength of the "complex of inferiority" hinders the acknowledgment of success and the emergence of satisfaction, both vital to self-realization.

The achievement of self-realization requires a person to define one's own goals, to commit oneself to them, and to planfully realize them. These are the assumptions of the agency theory of Fryer (1986). According to this theory, people try to make sense of what goes on and to act in accordance with their values and purposes and in the light of estimations of possible scenarios and outcomes. Purposes and values are not implemented automatically. There are certain instrumental ingredients that must be appropriated and career scenarios must be planfully realized. This is the subject of the next chapter.

6

The Instrumental Ingredients of Career Goal Implementation

So far it has been made clear that people's career choices and direction of subsequent career behavior depend upon their end-state image of self-realization. The implementation of life plans depends on the strength of the motivational process sustaining and driving the goal-directed activity, on commanding the skills necessary to take the right decisions, and on successfully performing the activities implied by the goal image. Last but not least, the implementation also depends on what has been termed the "context of careers" (Jepsen, 1992), the texture of external conditions in the social environment. The latter may also be instrumental in attaining cherished goals.

In considering the motivational process from an instrumental point of view, there is need to differentiate between efficient and inefficient aspirations, the latter being a simple exercise in dreaming. The test is whether people do what is necessary to fulfill their aspirations, for example, for adolescents to make good progress in school subjects related to the vocation for which they have a strong interest.

Some twenty years ago Haldane (1974) spoke of motivated skills that enable the individual to achieve success and plan for the transformation of skills into future career development and satisfaction. In accepting this concept I would like to see in it two ideas complementing each other: (a) the necessary instrumental skill coverage for the person's aspirations and (b) the need of a strong motivational coverage of skills, the use of which should lead to the attainment of career goals linked to self-realization. The two links do not function automatically. There may be strongly motivated, yet unrealistic aspirations that lack skill coverage, but also aspirations that are unrealistic because they lack the necessary motivational strength even in the presence of corresponding skills.

Although the motivational factor is a powerful ingredient of career development towards self-realization, the process draws heavily upon factors offering the means for attaining the goals that individuals have set for themselves. These "means" are (a) personal: vocational aptitudes and social abilities, vocational knowledge and skills, and a positive attitude toward work and authority figures at the place of work and (b) social: a given labor market, existing occupations and their structure, career paths in organizations if the person chooses an organizational career, and the career start. These factors are interdependent. Aptitudes and skills present a complicated picture of intertwining between the person's natural endowment and the social environment, while economic opportunities depend both on the subject's aptitudes and skills to constitute an instrument for career accomplishment. Although the instrumental factors of the career have an objective existence, they fulfill their role of tools for career realization only in so far as the individual perceives them as such and makes appropriate use of them. It is an illustration of the principle of unity between conscience and activity, as advocated long ago by Wallon (1955) and Rubinstein (1962).

Research on celebrities used to emphasize their personality traits as the basic conditions of their success. One may get the impression that vocational achievements depend nearly exclusively on the orientation of interests, on character independence, and on the capacity of concentration (Fürstenberg, 1969). The error lies not in the emphasis on the importance of personality traits in vocational performances, but in separating vocational abilities from personality traits. Since the latter contribute to the success of vocational performances, they should be included among the components of vocational aptitudes. One may even go one step further and include here also physiological traits and functions that are linked to the successful accomplishment of occupational activities. Parmentier-Beloux (1963) pointed out that in selection procedures for manual activities ailments of a medical nature used to appear in about 20 percent of the applicants. In some occupations such physiological characteristics may be of paramount importance. Teplov and Gurevitch (1966) reported very good results in the selection of personnel for hydroenergetic plants with a selection procedure based on comparing the typological properties of the applicants' nervous systems with the requirements of the vocational activity in critical moments or under stress (e.g., the breakdown of an installation).

It follows that vocational aptitudes comprise all the potentials necessary for the successful performance of vocational activities: (a) the psychometric abilities of cognitive or motoric nature, (b) personality traits of temperament and character, and (c) physiological and anatomical characteristics (in some occupations a certain building of the body is required). Up to a definite degree there is the possibility of mutual compensation among aptitude components, and within these limits the lack of aptitudes as such can be compensated for by a superior development of other career adjustment ingredients, such as motivation, knowledge, and skill. In a research with 575 trainees for lathe operators and casters, 28.5 percent of the persons lacking aptitude succeeded in making a satisfactory

Table 6.1
Psychological Examination of Lathe Operators

Abilities Correlations (Pearson)	Mechanical understanding	Attention	Movement accuracy	Surface touch	Reaction speed	Motor coordina- tion	Physical force
With the exceeding of nominal salary (mean of 6 months)	.44 P = .01	-.18	.02	.24 P = .03	.10	.28 P = .02	.37 P = .01
With mean income (mean of 6 months)	.44 P = .01	-.18	.05	.39 P = .01	.08	.36 P = .01	.40 P = .01

adjustment as deficient components were compensated by a superior development of others (Krau 1970, 1977a).

The longitudinal research with lathe operator apprentices was preceded by an experimental investigation of the vocationally relevant psychological qualification for that occupation (Krau, 1970). We had to avoid the practice of using reliable instruments in the examination of various traits, but to deduce the necessity of these traits in the job description from the analysis of work conditions. Thus, testing would apply to aptitudes and traits that might not be decisive in carrying the job, while others, on which occupational success depends essentially, would be overlooked.

Investigations started in Romania in 1966 with a psychological job analysis. The searchers first observed the various job activities, then questionnaires were distributed to 40 engineers, supervisors, and front-rank lathe operators. Work movements were registered by the method of time studies and motion pictures.

In a further stage, the hypothetical job description drawn from the observation material was submitted to an experimental control by means of a battery of tests specially set up for this purpose. The battery was applied to a sample of 82 lathe operators working in several metallurgic plants. The dependent variable of adjustment at the job was based on three criterion measurements: average income over 6 months, evaluation by supervisors, and the exceeding of the nominal salary as a result of additional production performances. The last criterion proved to be the most appropriate. Supervisors' evaluations mainly referred to personality traits and hardly at all to abilities that considerably influence performance. Thus, while mechanical understanding correlated $r = .44$ with the objective of performance (exceeding of nominal salary), it had no correlation with supervisor evaluation ($r = .02$).

The average income was under the strong influence of seniority through wage categories, while the exceeding of the nominal salary reflected ability in a better approximation, as it also included other possible criteria such as work attendance, quality of work, and the absence of accidents. Therefore this criterion was best suited to measure a complex organizational behavior subject to systemic influences.

The results of the examinations, presented in Table 6.1, show the following abilities as relevant for the worker specification of the lathe operator (at that time neither computer nor numerically controlled): mechanical understanding, differentiation of surface smoothness, motor coordination, and physical force in extension movements simulating lathe operations. These tests gave a significant multiple correlation of $R_{1(234)} = .56$ with the criterion of exceeding the basic salary.

Personality traits were measured by a projective sentence completion test elaborated by Krau (Krau, 1967; Meir and Krau, 1983). The test measures the following traits: self-assertion, social extraversion, attitudes toward authority figures at the place of work, vocational involvement, the valuing of money, impulsiveness in matters concerning money, consumer tendencies as opposed to thrift, and the control of behavior in a continuum of audacity-deliberation-fearfulness.

For each trait measured by the test there are two basic items. For scoring purposes the answers given to each sentence are evaluated vis-à-vis a list of examples corresponding to one of three typical attitudes and scored from 0 to 2 points. For example, an item measuring attitudes toward figures of authority at the place of employment is the following: "Sometimes the supervisor . . . ;" and there are three typical attitudes: (a) full acceptance of supervisors, emotional identification with them (e.g., takes measures, teaches, helps, makes a man out of you)—2 points; (b) no identification with requests made by supervisors but still an attitude of goodwill and fairness (e.g., comes to the bench and supervises, does the job, some are good, others nervous)—1 point; (c) supervisors are blamed for being malicious; only emotionally loaded and unpleasant experiences with them are recorded (e.g., is unfit, has no idea of how work should be done, bothers you all the time)—0 points. In the case of ambiguous answers, auxiliary and control items help assign the right score. The arithmetical sum of the two items characterizing a certain trait form, on a 5-point scale from 0 to 4, the scoring of that trait: e.g., $0 + 1 = 1$; $2 + 2 = 4$. This is an interval scale, the degree digits having no metric meaning.

The original validation of the test was carried out in Romania by means of peer rating (Krau, 1967). In Israel the test was adapted and revalidated with samples of 65 university students, 124 twelfth-grade high school students, 118 vocational trainees, and 66 employees (36 in white-collar jobs and 30 industrial workers). In order to ensure construct validity, behavior samples were elaborated in a pilot experiment for each degree of the traits to be measured, and then each subject was rated by two to three (in case of differences between the two) peers. Here are examples of behavior samples, for attitudes toward figures of authority at the place of employment:

> Always showing acquiescence with the supervisors (manager, teacher, headmaster), the person works diligently, always supports the supervisors (manager, etc.), justifying all their demands (4 points).

The person is not at all enthusiastic about the supervisors (managers, etc.) and feels that they are not on the same side as the employees (students), but recognizes that they too have a job to do. Therefore, the person honestly performs all duties, so as not to give them too difficult a time (2 points).

The person's attitude expresses revolt and contempt toward the supervisors (managers, etc.). The person accuses them of being parasites and incapable. They are always wrong, and the person does not make any attempt to come to terms with them (0 points).

The peer judges were asked to determine, for each personality trait measured, which behavior sample best describes the rated subject. The closest two (out of three) ratings were averaged, and then trait ratings were correlated with the test measures of the traits. Correlations ranged between .38 at self-assertion up to .58 at the control of emotional reaction. All correlations were significant at the .01 level. To obtain a general validation for the whole test, the correlations of trait scores with ratings were transformed into Fisher's z coefficient (in order to avoid biasing by large r coefficients), then averaged, and transformed back to a corresponding r. A validation coefficient of $r = .485$ was obtained, again significant at the .01 level.

Processing of the personality test data was based on the calculation of the chi-square coefficient for frequency differences in the various personality traits between good and poor lathe operators. The results showed that the former are more balanced in their social relations, in valuing money, and in their intrinsic involvement with their vocation. It seems that poor lathe operators are either excessively motivated by the drive to make money and so neglect quality requirements or, on the contrary, they have craftsmanship preoccupations that appear to be detrimental to mass production. Good lathe operators are also confident in their social relations, while among poor operators there are both more secluded and more extraverted people. While secludedness impedes the worker's integration within a team, excessive extraversion leads to social contacts during work time and thus hampers production.

Training has a differential influence on these abilities, as may be seen in the differences between the correlations of the criterion of exceeding the basic salary, which emphasizes aptitudes, and the criterion of mean income, which is influenced by seniority and work experience (see Table 6.1). In the worker specification of the lathe operator, longer work experience mainly improves motor coordination and differentiation of surface asperities, but not practical intelligence (mechanical understanding), physical strength, or the required personality traits.

Let us now return to the problem of aptitude component compensation. The selection strategy used in the research was based on two principles: (a) the possibility of compensation in nonvital components of the vocational aptitude and (b) the rejection of applicants with deficiencies in vital components. Aptitude components were considered vital if their absence or low-level development caused the worker to be maladjusted on the job, no matter how high the worker was in other aptitude components. In this particular investigation the lack of physical force proved to be an absolute "inaptitude" for lathe operators, unconditionally leading to vocational failure. As to the other aptitude components, the selection strategy allowed for compensation for an undeveloped component by the superior development of another one. Applicants with two uncompensated aptitude components were rejected (Krau, 1970). However, in a career perspective the lack of aptitudes in itself may be compensated by a superior development of motivational factors and knowledge acquisition.

Adjustment to the requirements of the job, let alone career achievements, do not depend on abilities alone. It is knowledge and job skills that ensure a high level of work performance, with all its material and social consequences. The examination of this factor from the point of view of prediction and then of vocational guidance or employee selection once more raises the problem of abilities, but this time in relation to skill acquisition. Correct guidance and selection procedures for apprentices should avoid the fallacy of unilaterally considering that job performance abilities already include learning abilities. The two are different (Krau, 1971), and only their junction offers a valid basis for prediction.

With the aid of specialists we elaborated occupational knowledge and skill tests for lathe operators and casters, whereby each item was correlated separately with the adjustment on the job of the former apprentices 10 months after production entry. The results showed that the global test score did not correlate with the adjustment on the job, but in each plant particular test items were significantly linked with the criterion, depending on the specific production tasks and level of technology.

Another peculiarity of the predictive validity of the vocational knowledge and skill test appeared when used in a 5- and 10-year follow-up. The items expressing practical know-how were significantly related to adjustment on the job but not to career advancement, while items of theoretical knowledge predicted career promotions but the adjustment to a particular job less well (Krau, 1977a). Therefore, the psychological analysis of the individual's investment in the job will have to consider the skill variable under the double aspects of: (a) knowledge related to school curricula based on scientific argumentation and referring to the vocation in its entirety and (b) knowledge and skills referring only to operations performed with the technology of a given plant. We shall call the latter practical knowledge, and they correspond to what Leplat (1965) defined as the acquisition of a trade in a narrow sense within a particular enterprise. In the same sense, Myers and Davids (1993) recently spoke of the acquisition of tacit skills developed through direct experience rather than through formal training. These skills have a more reduced range than those taught in trade schools, and their scientific basis is not used to improve the performance of the equipment or of work methods.

Occupational knowledge and skills constitute one of the most important career ingredients. In the research that will be reported in the next chapter, it will be shown that this factor alone accounts for nearly one-third of the variance (28.3%) of the process of successful career development.

In the former USSR, Aganbegian, Osipov, and Shubkin (1966) computed the "preparation time" for being promoted into a higher wage category in different industrial branches. They concluded that this time interval inversely correlated with the degree of qualification. At equal degrees of qualification the preparation time depended on the employees' personality characteristics, on their health and physical resistance, on their work experience in other organizations, and the like.

Nevertheless, it seems that in the presentation of these results a certain artifact is produced by the assumption that aptitudes and knowledge (skills) are independent factors. As a matter of fact they are related. Skill is acquired and applied by the aid of aptitudes. Acquired knowledge (on the basis of learning ablities only) remains sterile, from an occupational point of view, in the absence of aptitudes required by the vocational activities, and the latter need the skills necessary to correctly perform what is required. Therefore, both should be considered indispensable instruments for the realization of a career without emphasizing the primacy of one of them. The problem is to be able to get an education that ensures a maximal development and utilization of the person's aptitudes. From a societal point of view people should stay in school until they reach the degree of education enabling them to make maximal use of their aptitudes, and school education should be related to real life, contributing to people's adjustment to the world of work and to their self-realization.

The methodological facet of the question refers to the link between general and specific vocational education. General education improves people's vocational versatility and their chances for upward mobility, and it also prepares them for a healthy occupation of their leisure time. When speaking of self-realization, this aspect ought not to be neglected. At any rate, a successful career or just a satisfactory adjustment requires more than only narrow occupational skills. Wolfbein (1967) refers to Super in describing the paradigm of people moving to a bigger city. For this activity, the most important skills are related to solving the problems of housing, transport, and so on, without which they will not be able to maintain or perhaps even find a job.

Some years ago Herr (1984) introduced the concept of general employability skills as a vital connection between the preparation for work and actual employment, apart from occupation-specific and task-specific skills. General employability skills comprise effective work competencies (attitudes, values), work context skills (regularity of attendance, peer and supervisory relations) and self-management skills (decision making, reality testing, etc.). The point is that although such skills are vital for a successful career and also for efficient performance on the job, they are rarely deliberately taught. Bingham (1986) points out that, by and large, programs designed to prepare young people for employment are reasonably thorough in treating occupation-specific skills, but less complete, less carefully articulated with respect to how they address general employability skills.

This insistence on the importance of general education brings into focus the problem of the not utilized "redundant knowledge," or overqualification. Rumberger (1982) observed that between 25 percent and 30 percent of U.S. college graduates are overqualified for their jobs. This is so because the educational rate is growing in parallel with a reduction in the requirement level of many jobs as a consequence of new technologies. Yet, overqualification does not necessarily mean low satisfaction, since such jobs may provide gratification of concomitants or needs in other areas of life: nice people to work with, pleasant place to live, and the like (King and Hautaluoma, 1987).

If there are doubts as to the immediate usefulness of education, the point of view of self-realization restores its original importance. Louise Fitzgerald (1986) pointed out that education has never been defined only in terms of its relationship to work and that therefore one might be overqualified for a certain job but not overeducated. She also speculated that possibly a majority of workers did not derive their self-identity or their major life satisfaction from jobs.

We should like to add that general education also has mind-shaping influences that increase people's discriminative powers, the quality of their life judgments, and their versatility. It gives them the opportunity to remain abreast of new developments in order to finally obtain the advancement they aspire to, even if their present jobs discourage the use of deeper knowledge. They will be better prepared to use life opportunities and to correctly decide on which aspects they may compromise and on which they must not.

This is not to say that the absence of formal general education makes self-realization impossible. It is not a necessary condition, because time and again life itself is the teacher. Nevertheless, general education is a helping condition, and the higher people's aspirations, the more they may benefit from it.

At the confluence between personal and societal instruments of career realization lies the vocationally relevant biographical background (Krau et al., 1969). This variable comprises of several factors that condition the preparation for a vocational life: (a) in the cognitive domain appears the social background supplying vocational information outside the official and specialized educational channels (city inhabitants are advantaged); (b) in the emotional domain the preparation for a career is favored by developing emotional ties with the intended vocation, by the presence of a vocational ideal, the interest for vocationally relevant school matters and by guidance or advice received from friends, teachers, acquaintances; and (c) in the conative domain the social background maintains a lasting mobilizing tension (in the historic-geographic conditions in which the research was conducted the rural environment deployed a stronger activism). A positive predictive value is also attached to having chosen one's vocation independently. Frequently parents are guided by considerations of prestige and less by the need to find the best occupational match for their children's interests and abilities.

Among the instruments for achieving adjustment at the place of work and through it self-realization there is one which seems naive and banal, but has deep roots in the personality and far-reaching consequences: It is a negative attitude toward authority figures at the place of work. In a longitudinal research with 198 lathe operator apprentices (see Chapter 7), there was a group of 16 young workers (8% of the total sample, and 38% of the maladjusted workers) in which the only hint as to what might have caused this situation was a negative attitude toward authority figures at the place of work (measured by the projective personality test). However, the test results seemed confusing, because only some of the people with negative attitudes were maladjusted. A careful scanning of all available data gave the following curious solution: Negative attitudes toward authority figures at the place of work led to maladjustment only if the subject characterized his father in denigrating terms or came from a disintegrated family. It follows that in a number of cases the negative attitudes toward the place of work that causes maladjustment may not be induced by events in the employing organization but reflect a deeply rooted personality disturbance that seriously hinders adjustment and self-realization. The difference between this and the other factors influencing career adjustment is that the impact of attitudes toward authority figures is felt only one-sidedly: the more negative they are, the stronger is the obstacle they represent for career realization, but high degrees of positiveness do not increase the individual's chances for adjustment. The meaning of a positive attitude toward authority figures simply is that from this point of view there is no threat to adjustment and aspirational realization.

The relationship of "malign" negative attitudes with family influences raises the question why, for both genders, the dominant impact belongs to the father, and whether this finding still holds today after all the transformations in family life in recent decades.

When speaking of the child's later career development, the father's presence in the process of child rearing has an especially weighty importance, and not only in the classical family structure described by Parsons and Bales (1955). He elaborated on a structural-functional theory on families in which the father is concerned with tasks termed as instrumental, while the mother's role centers on emotions and can be termed as expressive. In this family structure the father provides a role model of vocational behavior and the guidance necessary to materialize it. Obviously, it is extremely difficult to introduce the world of work to a youngster who has never seen his father steadily working. Research data attested to significant differences in IQ and juvenile delinquency between adolescents from families with and without fathers (Wolfbein, 1967).

At any rate, it is not the division of roles within the family that is important for the child's future career development, but the model of a father which conforms to sociocultural norms. His absence or his deviance from the cultural pattern has a deep destructive influence, as does the mother's absence as a loving caretaker. This is true even today when speaking of the "new father" increasingly nurturing and involved with the caretaking of children and housework

(Lewis and O'Brien, 1987). Careers remain a matter of primary concern for men, and men involved with their jobs would not let parental and household commitments interfere with their work. The newly existing condition of role-reversed families did not change these basic trends. Role-reversed families have shown tensions between parents because mothers resent fathers deciding about household matters and also their ever-increasing contact with children. Therefore, a majority of role-reversed families are reverting back to a more traditional pattern (Lewis and O'Brien, 1987). For the healthy development of the child's personality it is of utmost importance to be brought up in a family where the father is present and actively participates in the child's education.

The research of Palmer and Cochran (1988) attests to the fact that most parents maintain a relationship of an "observational dyad" with their children. They focus some attention on their children's career development, but they are not actively involved and do not provide the real partnership of a "joint activity dyad" and even less a "primary dyad" requiring reciprocity and balance of power. The authors state that parents may appear as efficient agents of their children's career development only if the latter is the result of a family plan with parents' contribution of resources, finances, advice, and personal support. In this case the parental family truly fulfills its role as a social instrument for the child's self-realization through vocational career.

The formation of the father's image in the child's mind is not a mechanical process, nor is its evolution uniform in all people. Bauer, Wetta, et al. (1965) point out that the father's image crystallizes according to (a) the contacts established between the person and his father (is he interested in his child or indifferent even if physically present in the family); (b) the evaluation of the father's personality, his value; (c) his vocational and cultural qualities; (d) the father's aspirations regarding the fate of his children.

The identification process of the child may amount to taking over the father's features and behavior as an ideal or sometimes merely to showing concern for the father's position in the world, which the child intends to defend by other means. In a series of cases I observed the identification with a "good," "quiet" father dominated by the mother in the family and by external circumstances in his vocational life. The adolescent's entire personality profile stood under the overwhelming impression of this father image, which he, however, did not copy, but he manifested attitudes of rebellion all the time, as if his sole aspiration were to render justice to his father.

It follows that negative attitudes toward authority figures at the place of work may appear as a consequence of identification with a father who has such attitudes, but also with a subdued one whom the child wants to "revenge." It also may be the consequence of despising the father and of identifying with a youth gang leader who holds such attitudes. Even so, the final crystallization of negative attitudes occurs in connection with frustrating events in which the person is involved. In some cases in our high school student samples, we witnessed positive attitudes towards the school while the father was depreciatingly characterized, but we also saw negative attitudes towards the school while the father was positively evaluated (e.g., as "severe"). This last phenomenon appeared also in workers and meant that this negative attitude was caused by certain concrete circumstances and as such could be compensated and improved. The combination of frustrating events with attitudes held toward a negatively evaluated father makes such attitudes "malignant" and destructive for the person's career.

It remains to explain why the characterization of a father as "good" is a negative career predictor, while a father characterized as "severe" or "tough" would be a positive one. To clarify this point, we performed, in the middle of the 1970s, a free-association experiment with 50 university students of both genders. As a matter of fact it was a contribution to Osgood's intended enlarged International Psycholinguistic Atlas, and our purpose was to verify the meaning of the qualifier pairs used in the semantic-differential method with a group of Romanian-speaking subjects. The results showed that adjectives like "good," "tender," and "soft" had a connotation of femininity and were associated with mother, cat, China porcelain, bird, and delicate girl. If used in a feminine context these adjectives have a positive emotional connotation as attested to by the Evaluation ratings in the semantic differential. If attributed to a man, the connotation becomes negative. Western culture, and also that in the former Eastern bloc, favors strength, power, and masculinity. In our association experiment "severe" and "tough" were associated with worker, friend, father, and good teacher and got a highly positive evaluation rating. (In the semantic differential method each concept is rated in the dimensions of Evaluation, Potency, and Activity). Indeed, a few years later Hofstede (1980) identified masculinity as an important component of culture.

In order to get more precise data on parental influence on children's careers in the conditions of Israeli contemporary society, we recently conducted a research with 40 parents and their offspring (23 boys and 17 girls). The research concerned the relationship between children's careers and three variable areas of the parental family: (a) parents' occupation level, (b) emotional ties of children to their parents, and (c) the influence of the latter on children's vocational choice. It is understood that the contemporary Israeli society is very much achievement-oriented and therefore parental influence may definitely favor children's career advancement.

It was presumed that children would aspire to occupations of higher levels than their fathers, except in cases where fathers' occupations were in the upper levels in Ann Roe's classification (1962), in which case children would aspire to an occupation of the same level. It was further presumed that parents' influence on children's vocational choice would depend on the psychological climate within the parental family and on the relationship between parents and children. Higher education of fathers was presumed to strengthen this relationship. Normal relationships with the children would presumably be harmed in disorganized families or by fathers' neurotic character.

It was presumed that the stronger the emotional ties between parents and offspring, the closer their occupations would be in terms of the distance between the occupational fields. To measure the field distance, a division of occupations into eight fields was used, which constitutes the basis for the "Ramak" test of occupational choice (Meir and Krau, 1983) based on Holland's SDS: Business, Organization, General-Cultural, Arts and Entertainment, Outdoor, Science, and Technology. These fields are arranged in a circle (cf. the RIASEC circle of Holland), and therefore Technology is close to Science and to Business.

All subjects (fathers, mothers, and offspring) were administered Krau's aforementioned projective personality test and an adaptation of Woodsworth's Neuroticism Inventory, on which the more articulated MMPI is based. Finally, the offspring were asked to rate the emotional attachment they felt towards their parents on a 5-point scale and to answer questions about their overall career satisfaction.

The following questions measuring overall satisfaction were built into a larger autobiographical questionnaire: "Are you satisfied with the vocation you chose? (please elaborate). If you are not, what makes you feel dissatisfied? What do you think your chances are of being satisfied in the future?" The answers to these questions were classified into categories of "satisfied," "dissatisfied," or "undecided" with regard both to the present and the future. In order to score the questionnaire, the categories were combined to yield a satisfaction score from 1 to 9 points wherein the greater weight was assigned to the future outlook. This method was based on the assumption that quite independently from their present satisfaction or dissatisfaction, the subjects could see good or poor chances for being satisfied in the future. They could also declare that they are not able to make up their minds. The score assigned the greater weight to the future outlook because the person's attitude towards a vocation and the entire motivation to strive for career goals depend on the meaningfulness of the person's endeavors in the perspective of the future.

In the encoding of occupational levels, the professional-managerial level was not divided into level 1 and 2 as done by Roe, because the Israeli economy does not warrant a differentiation in its upper income stratum. As such, the following levels were considered: professional-managerial, semi-professional, skilled, semi-skilled, and unskilled.

The results showed that only four offspring out of 40 entered an occupation that was not higher than their fathers' occupation of levels 3–5 or was lower than their fathers' occupation of levels 1, 2. This gives an observed proportion of 0.90 significant at $p = .002$ at a one-tailed binomial test confirming the research hypothesis. As to the occupational level 2 of semiprofessionals, four offspring out of 12 subjects belonging to such families (33%) entered occupations on the second and not on the first level. However, they received an education enabling them to work on jobs of the first, professional-managerial level. Although data were also gathered on mothers' occupations, they did not indicate reliable relationships, and in 35 percent of the cases mothers' occupations ranked lower than fathers'. Therefore the criterion of comparison appears to be the father, whose occupational level the offspring strives to excel. This is not to say that mothers have no influence on their offspring's career. Even if the comparison in vocational choice is made with the occupational level to which the father belongs, the mother may appear as the children's significant other, shaping children's interests and influencing their choice of a career domain. This usually happens in the case of atypical interpersonal family constellations with dominant mothers and weak fathers, as the child is emotionally attached only to its mother. Still, the father's occupational area and level remain the challenge and standard of comparison for the child's vocational choice, as the formation of attitudes toward authority figures essentially also remains linked to the figure of the father.

It appeared in the research that the stronger the children's attachment to their parents, the closer the vocation chosen by them was to the field of their father's job. Offspring's rating of their emotional attachment to their parents correlated negatively with the distance between the field chosen by them (in the Ramak model of occupational divisions) and their father's job ($r = .31$ significant at $p = .05$). The correlation was nonsignificant with mothers' occupations ($r = -.16$), again confirming that the family factor, for comparisons for children's vocational choice, is the father. Since the research sample comprised boys and girls in nearly equal proportion, this finding refers to both genders, of course with all limitations imposed by a sample of limited size. It was also found that fathers' education significantly correlated with perceiving parents' influence on the offspring's vocational choice as encouraging ($r = .4$ significant at $p < 0.05$).

Since the parental family appears as an instrument for enhancing career development toward self-realization, one of the problems in this research was whether there was any link between the parents' personality and offspring's later life satisfaction, as expressed by satisfaction with their present situation and confidence in the future.

The results showed that the offspring were satisfied with their career development in those cases in which test measurements had presented their fathers as having a healthy personality, free of neuroticism. A point-biserial correlation between the absence of neuroticism in fathers and general satisfaction in offspring gave the significant result of $r_{p.bis} = .51$ significant at $p = 0.01$. However, the situation changed when fathers' attitudes toward authority figures at the place of work were considered. Then the emerging correlation with offspring's overall career satisfaction was negative, $r = -.63$ significant at $p = .01$.

In order to understand this very complex phenomenon, let us bear in mind that generally the offspring sought to obtain an occupation ranking higher than that of their fathers, which means that the latter were not at all placid and satisfied with their own occupation, but incited their children to seek a better and higher-ranking one. Of course, there is the looming question of how a personality trait linked to maladjustment, like negative attitudes toward authority figures, can have a positive influence on the career of an offspring. However, as the person advances in age and gains seniority at work, the virulence of negative attitudes recedes. At that time job duties require less effort and motivation. For some people, in and after mid-career, advancement at the place of work seems to have lost all instrumentality for life-goal attainment as the latter refers to work concomitants and satisfactions in other areas of life. Hostility toward management may still exist, but the individual has learned to keep apart feelings and the performance of duties at the job. In examinations we performed with older lathe operators, negative attitudes toward superiors were not linked to maladjustment in production activity. This is precisely the situation with fathers reaching the moment when their children grow up and enter the world of work. The memories of their frustrations have lost the maladjustment-prone edge and merely incite their offspring to seek advancement beyond their own occupational status. This outdistancing of the father leads to the feeling of achievement and satisfaction in the offspring.

Having said this, there is need to underline that in the research fathers' attitudes were related only to offspring's declared satisfaction with their career choice and not with any objective measure of adjustment. At career start these two measures do not necessarily coincide. Moreover, career advancement beyond the starting point requires independence and a sort of disengagement from the parental family. Today this point is well documented (Sheehy, 1976; Levinson, Darrow, Klein, Levinson, and McKee, 1978). Nonetheless, family influence can be beneficial in the realization of life plans, especially at career starts.

A second conclusion regarding the conversion of negative attitudes from a maladjustment-causing trait to a mere innocuous feeling in older years concerns the necessity to reject the widespread opinion that ability is reduced with age. The inferiority in job ability of older people is more of a prejudice. Vocational aptitudes include also job-relevant personality traits, and the criterion of effective adjustment presupposes the possibility of compensation between all aptitude components. Figure 6.1 presents the distribution of degrees of occupational ability in 198 lathe operator apprentices of the above-mentioned research and in 60 lathe operators above the age of 40. The curve is definitely normal for the apprentices, but somewhat positively skewed for the operators above 40. Should there have been a decrease in ability, the curve would have been skewed negatively. Of course, the curve also reflects the departure of incapable or maladjusted workers who presumably tried their luck elsewhere.

A more direct influence of the parental family on its offspring's career development is shown in the help given at the career start of the offspring. In a certain sense, career starts are linked to the socioeconomic level of the parental family and to the psychological climate within the family, which ensure help, open discussion, and advice or withhold them. More than 50 years ago Eckert and Marshall (1938) pointed out that the greater part of first jobs are obtained through personal connections of the fathers, and this situation has not changed much even today. Simpson (1962) pointed out that children who succeeded in entering college received more moral and material support, parental advice, and

Figure 6.1
Distribution of Occupational Ability Degrees in Apprentices and in Workers above the Age of 40

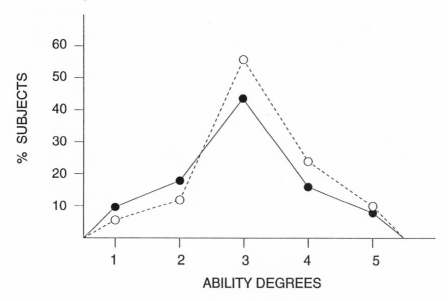

orientation than children who did not. It is not surprising, therefore, that the large sample of adolescents interviewed by Noeth, Engen, and Noeth (1984) rated their family as the most influential factor in their vocational choice.

From the data presented so far it emerges that a family with healthy personalities and healthy relationships between family members greatly enhances its offspring's career starts, while a socioeconomically inactive environment or a family burdened with disturbed personalities or inappropriate relationships constitutes a considerable stumbling block to its offspring's realization of their life goals. This conclusion is also in line with those of social research. Wolfbein (1967) noted that in the lower social strata there are many people whose only legacy to their children is the same one of poverty and deprivation that they received from their own parents.

It remains true that people with outstanding talent will finally achieve their aspirations but, let us be sincere, it matters at which age this is done. The later aspirations are fulfilled, the more the long, frustrating efforts applied to reach the desired position will wear people down and diminish their creative efforts, when conditions would already have allowed their unimpeded development.

In the early 1970s a Romanian journalist interviewed Nobel Prize winners in order to discover "their secret" (Roman, 1971). Beyond the usual commonplaces of hard work, love of science, and the like, one thing stood out in these biographies: Nearly all of them attained a university professorship before the age of 35. Their spectacular scientific achievements came 10–15 years later, prepared during those most fruitful years in which their initiative was at its highest level, combined with knowledge and experience amid the most favorable settings of freedom for research and freedom from material distress. One cannot help but speculate how things would have turned out had they reached their positions at the age of 50 or more. Some would have become famous even so— and Pavlov, who was forced to live in obscure conditions until the age of 49, is a vivid example—but it is hard to generalize, and the question of career starts stands with all its pungent sharpness.

It is clear, therefore, that the actual deployment of a career rests not only on the instruments of the individual's endowment and investment but also on the instruments offered to him by society: the situation of the labor market, the contemporary structure of occupations, organizational career paths, and the career start. The latter itself is very much an external variable. However, the point is that these external variables are not just added, agglutinated to the personal factors, but there occurs an integration sui generis. The situation of the labor market and the structure of occupations are generally considered as variables included in the process of transmitting occupational information, but this information has to be analyzed and evaluated, mentally and emotionally "appropriated." Labor market conditions contribute to the crystallization of vocational plans and their realization, through a selection effect in the sense of "selecting oneself into an occupation" (Krech, Crutchfield, and Ballachey, 1962). Furthermore, an existing structure of occupations appeals to a definite aptitude profile, eliciting an emotionally loaded motivated activity toward acquiring skills and performing the vocational tasks on the required level.

The integration between personal and external variables is best exemplified by the much publicized phenomenon of mentoring. If in 1978 the title of Collins and Scott's article "Everyone Who Makes It Has a Mentor" (Collins and Scott, 1978) was only an attention-getting headline, in our postmodern world of global turbulent fields with no direction and the crumbling of classical work values (Globerson and Krau, 1993), this adage becomes more and more a reality.

The phenomenon was generally defined as the relationship between mentors and protégés (Phillips-Jones, 1982), between senior and junior colleagues, but Kram (1985) pointed out that peer relationships may fulfill the same functions. These functions are twofold: (a) career functions that serve to aid advancement up the hierarchy in an organization and (b) psychosocial functions contributing to the enhancement of the person's self-worth both inside and outside the organization (Kram, 1986). Important in Kram's work is also the psychological aspect of the analysis, proving that mentoring is a gratifying experience for both parties because it contributes to their ego-development. We see here a continuation of the phenomenon of the significant other—the significant adult of the childhood.

The developmental process does not cease in childhood. There is a continuation of the psychological mechanisms of development, but with a changed content. In the previous chapters evidence was presented that vocational choices are being made through individuals' identification with their need gratifier. Essentially the same occurs in the mentoring relationships, but the needs and their expression have changed, as have the modi of gratification. The crux of the matter is that in childhood the directions of choice, including the selection of significant people, are widely open, while in adulthood they are limited, and in order to achieve advancement a particular mentor has to be found. If such a mentor is not available, the whole process of career development may be halted. We may, therefore, consider the mentor as a societal career ingredient who has to be mentally and emotionally "appropriated" by the individual, making sure that the relationship includes the psychosocial functions of mutual comfort in order to be gratifying for both sides.

From all that has been discussed, there emerges a general model of career development (see Figure 6.2). The basic ingredients of the career (motivational factors, personal and societal instruments for the implementation of aspirations) are developing in the process of vocational socialization and achieve task directedness and content specificity. The model sketches the possibilities of reciprocal compensations within the components of the same ingredient compartment (between aptitudes and skills) and between the components of various compartments (e.g., strong aspirations and interests may compensate for certain weaknesses in ability or in skill or for a tough labor market or a disadvantaged socioeconomic background). A successful career in which the life aspirations are realized will rely on a match among the three compartments of career ingredients: the motivational and the instrumental career factors, the two personal ingredients (motivational and instrumental), and the societal factor. Although life aspirations are not exclusively career bound, career adjustment is a basic precondition for aspirational realization in other life domains. The difference between careers embodying the main content of self-realization and careers merely sustaining the efforts made in other life domains lies in the level of the desired achievements and not in the need for vocational socialization, for compensating one's weaknesses and for finding an optimal match between the motivational and the instrumental career ingredients, thus ensuring adjustment to the requirements of one's work activity.

Self-realization through vocational careers is a unique and complex process, integrating the personality and the environment existing in a definite historical moment and evolving with it. People live in society and can realize themselves only through the means offered and permitted by society. However, these means are only a form vested on the content of their self-realization. It is precisely the lack of clarity in details of the end-state image of self-realization that permits a plurality of possible forms at the final realization status, while the degree of correspondence between the content of the initial image and its eventual embodiment heavily depends upon personality characteristics. Economic, social, or political difficulties may alter or hamper the realization of careers in people with dull aptitudes, especially in those for which the vocational career as such, or at

Figure 6.2
The General Model of Career Development and Prediction

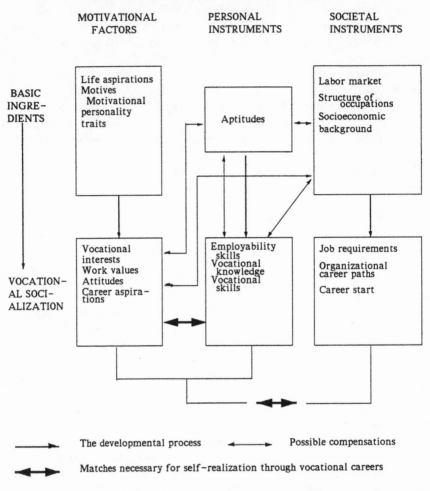

least a certain vocational activity, is not essentially linked to their end-state image of self-realization; not so in people for whom their vocation represents the main vehicle for attaining their life goals. One may think of Shakespeare, Abraham Lincoln, or Henry Ford, and it is in this sense that there is truth in Carlyle's adage that heroes make history—of course, only in the direction of society's objective development. *Mutatis mutandis*, on a much more modest scale, well-endowed and strongly motivated people make their own history.

7

The Planning, Implementation, and Prediction of Careers

The desire to control one's career and to realize one's life aspiration through it rests on two interwoven conditions: the possibility to plan for and to predict the course of one's life career. The first of these tasks is today widely acknowledged. Savickas and Super (1993) see as one of the objectives of the Growth stage to develop a sense of control over one's vocational future, resulting in the willingness to shoulder the responsibility for it. However, planning, let alone prediction, requires more than an emotional and volitional attitude component, and the difficulties that stand in the way of such an endeavor are tremendous. They stem from the multitude of factors involved from the anxiety produced by the responsibility of having to plan for one's entire life (Krumboltz, 1993) and from the lack of predictability in events. In the previous chapters we tried to clarify the key ingredients of a vocational career and the laws by which their action can be described. We shall now continue the analysis of the patterns of linkage between the career ingredients, so as to obtain a model allowing for the prediction of the process of career development. To do so, the relationship between aspirations and performance first, has to be clarified on the molecular level.

Although experimental research in the field of goal-directed behavior succeeded in establishing firm links between motivation and level of aspiration, the link between motivational strength and level of performance proved to be essentially nonmonotonic (Atkinson, 1977), leaving open the question of why high levels of motivation materialize in a corresponding level of aspiration but not in performance. The differential link of motivation vis-à-vis level of aspiration and performance could well mean that different motivational variables are involved in the two phenomena and are not due only to the moderating effects of aptitude. The problem was investigated by Krau (1982a), who hypothesized that level of aspiration and implementation were different action stages and were thus governed by different motivational variables.

The idea of action stages is not new. Even in the classical period of psychology, authors were concerned with the transition from cognition to action. A promising approach is rooted in the description of action stages as the individual passes from intention to execution (Rubinstein, 1962; Woodworth, 1958) through unified behavioral structures (Wallon, 1955), viewing the whole process as one of control and command (Miller, Galanter, and Pribram, 1967; Piaget, 1967). For Miller et al. (1967) behavior is organized hierarchically; and its basic unit, the Test-Operate-Test-Exit (TOTE) appears to be the feedback loop itself. The molar control instance is the *plan*, a construct relying on Bartlett's concept of *schema*, an active organization of past experiences (Bartlett, 1932). If behavior is a hierarchical organization of TOTE units, it should follow that every stage of action has its own TOTE unit and thus has its own feedback loop with its own controls. One may assume that at every stage these controls are different; hence, the weight of motivation changes, as do the motivational control components, as the individual moves from one stage of action to another.

To prove the latter statement, one will have to consider the behavioral act not only from the holistic viewpoint of a relationship between initial stimulus and final response but also as a temporal sequence in which each phase has its own input factors and results. It should follow that any measures taken from the various variables that intervene in the course of action will be related more closely to the input and output variables of the proper action stage.

The following hypothesis concerned the number and nature of the stages constituting the temporal sequence of action. There are obviously two stages: a preparatory phase and an executory one, as in William James's (1890) classical paradigm of getting up in the morning. It suits every action in which the implementation plans are well known and firmly acquired. But what if the action the subject wants to perform is not a routine one and no ready execution plans are available? In this situation, an additional stage should be assumed on the basis of the image (cf. Miller et al., 1967), the value-loaded strategy outline of the activity by which the person elaborates an action plan and mobilizes his or her energy resources to fulfill it. The scene of this phase is the intellectual level, and its content fits the comparing, structuring, and organizing activity of formal propositional thinking in Piaget's theory (Inhelder and Piaget, 1958). It is a mental experimentation of future actions. Consequently, three action stages will be postulated: (a) goal setting, (b) preparation for implementation, and (c) actual implementation.

According to Atkinson (1977) and Weiner and Kukla (1970), it was assumed that the controls' repertoire of the stages of motivated activity in a worklike setting consisted of motivational variables, aptitudes, knowledge, and skills. In the field of motivation, a most important variable is, of course, need for achievement, associated mainly with intrinsic work motivation (Jung, 1978). Because extrinsic factors are of great significance in real-life activities that develop in a social field of relationships and norms, it seemed that one had to consider two more variables: the need for approval (for creating a positive self-image for the public) and the general attitude toward work and authority figures at the place of employment.

The need for approval appears to generate a motivated and purposeful behavior of conformism to social stereotypes that are acceptable to acknowledge about oneself (Crowne, 1979). In work or competitive life situations, this factor plays the part of a major motivator. Many important studies on work motivation emphasize the striving to obtain the approval of peers and management (Herzberg, Mausner, and Snyderman, 1959; Saleh and Hyde, 1969; Vroom, 1964).

The general attitude towards work and authority figures at the place of work is an important moderator of other motivational factors. Negativistic attitudes were found to cause poor performance at work, even in the presence of motivating factors (Krau, 1970).

All in all, an attempt was made to study the relationships between motivation and other behavior variables in the process of action developing from intention to accomplishment. The field of activity chosen was a manual work activity in a real-life situation.

The research design had four goals: (a) to investigate a real-life activity in a nonroutine condition, so that there were no readily available "plans" that could be applied automatically; (b) to investigate a real-life activity that centers around a choice, thus allowing subjects to make a real choice and then to implement it in practice; (c) to administer complex psychological testing in order to arrive at a reliable picture of the interrelated factors of the motivation phenomenon; and (d) to include not only the choice as such but to trace the relationships among the various factors assessed in the process of choice up to their implementation in task execution.

An activity that seemed to correspond to these requirements was production work by boys in a junior high school. It is a manual work activity in a real-life situation, but it has not yet become routine. Thus, action plans for every new work piece have to be newly elaborated, and above all, there is the possibility of enabling subjects to choose tasks and levels of tasks, an impossible condition to apply when conducting research in industry.

The research was conducted in the year 1976 in Romania over a period of 6 months and comprised a total of 60 eighth-grade pupils. Under the educational system in force, all subjects attended vocational training once a week. As the school program included locksmith work in the school shop for the sixth and seventh grades, at the beginning of the experiment all subjects had 2 years of experience in studying technology and working in the school workshop.

The experimental variable was the possibility of choosing and manufacturing artistic locksmith pieces with obvious usefulness, mainly furniture. To facilitate the choice, subjects were presented with pictures of objects, technical drawings, and a description of the technological process. At the disposal of the subjects was a total of 24 objects selected and rated by two specialists into three categories: objects that the subjects (considering their work experience and an average dexterity) could finish in less than 25 work hours (easy work pieces), objects with a medium degree of difficulty (25–40 hours), and objects on which, in the specialists' evaluation, subjects would have to work more than 40 hours in order to perform complicated operations (difficult pieces). Subjects who finished their first work piece before the end of the school term had to choose and produce another piece in a fashion identical to the first choice. This procedure made it possible to trace the dynamics of motivation in an activity in which sequences belong together but are not related to each other instrumentally, as in behaviors to which Atkinson and Raynor's (1974) findings apply. Because the research hypothesis focused on the sequential character of action stages, with time as a control variable, the different measurements were taken at various moments of the objectively developing action. The various instruments were administered according to the objective phase of the experiment.

In the stage of *acquaintance with the task and autonomous goal setting*, after choosing an item for manufacturing the subjects rated the difficulty of the chosen task on an 11-point scale. They then were administered a variant of the Mehrabian Risk Preference Scale (Mikula, Uray, and Schwinger, 1974) and also Crowne and Marlowe's test for social desirability (Crowne and Marlowe, 1960). The appraised difficulty of the work pieces, evaluated by specialists, was used as an objective yardstick of this behavior stage.

One week later the subjects made their requests for raw materials and the necessary tools in accordance with written plans, as they entered the *stage of preparation for implementing the chosen task*. At this point they were asked to evaluate separately their own ability and the abilities of their classmates to accomplish the chosen task, on an 11-point scale, and to make an estimate of the results they expected to obtain, using the system of 10 school marks. They also made an appraisal of the effort they intended to apply (on an 11-point scale).

In the stage of *actual task implementation* all subjects were tested for aptitudes for the locksmith trade (the norms had been established earlier) and for attitudes toward work and authority figures at the place of work. To this purpose Krau's projective personality test (Krau, 1967) was used. The supervisor-instructor rated the subjects' full use of time and their weekly progress in percentages of execution of the work piece and recorded all critical positive and negative incidents. At the end of the school term, subjects' performances were evaluated on a 10-point scale corresponding to the system of school marks.

The analysis of the data had to show whether the variables measured at a certain moment of the developing action (when they were supposedly active) are related more closely to one another in comparison to variables measured at other action stages. The problem was approached by computing the intercorrelations of all study variables and by submitting them to Guttman and Lingoe's smallest space analysis (SSA) (Guttman, 1968), a general nonmetric method designed to find the minimal number of Euclidean dimensions for the description of a collection of variables.

The rationale for using this method is that it goes beyond the intercorrelational matrix. It constitutes the space of the considered variables, revealing synoptically the link patterns that exist between them. The closer two variables are in that space, the stronger the link is. The link can be thought of as a cause-and-effect link, as a reciprocal influence, or as a common influence by a third variable, in the same way one would interpret the correlation coefficients on which the SSA rests.

The SSA performed on the study variables constituted the action space; its facets (dimension factors along which the clustering of the variables occurred) reflected the stages of action within the link pattern that existed between variables.

The SSA yielded a coefficient of alienation of .24 for two dimensions and .14 for three dimensions, proving that three dimensions are necessary to link the variables together. Figures 7.1, 7.2, and 7.3 are two-dimensional projections of the three-dimensionally constituted space after principal axes rotation. They reveal distinct dimension factors in the three particular facets of the action space.

The dimension factor linking the variables in Figure 7.1 must be considered active during the goal-setting stage. On the right, there is a motivational cluster with achievement motivation linked mainly to rated task difficulty. Need for approval serves as the connection link between the motivational cluster and rated abilities and, to some extent, the real effort. At this stage, real effort seems more distant to the other variables.

All variables pertinent to material implementation (intended effort, aptitudes, real task difficulty, task-relevant skills, and attitudes toward work) are clustered in the lower-left quadrant. It it interesting to note that at this stage of goal setting, the transition from intention (the motivational cluster) to implementation is mediated by the general attitudes toward work, as the specific task to be implemented is a work task.

The dimension factor arrangement in Figure 7.2 may be considered to act at the moment of the preparation for implementation of the chosen goal. There is a well-defined strong cluster now, composed of real task difficulty and task-relevant skills, together forming hard situational data that must be taken into account. However, at this stage, they are linked to rated abilities and rated effort. This cluster stands in front of the motivational cluster and a grouping of other variables relevant for the final execution (real effort, real aptitudes, and attitudes toward work).

The real effort displayed stands between the rated effort, the real aptitudes, and self-presentation (need for approval). This last variable is somewhat closer to the determination of the real effort than is achievement motivation. Attitudes toward work are now more remote; the decision to implement the intention has already been made, but the real execution has not yet begun. Nonetheless, work attitudes are in link with aptitudes, indicating that the final use of aptitudes will depend on them.

The last dimension factor of the variable links consists of the execution stage (see Figure 7.3). It is a dimension of great complexity. The extreme variables of Figure 7.3 (achievement motivation, real aptitudes, attitudes toward work,

Figure 7.1
Smallest Space Analysis: Dimension Factor Diagram of Links Between Action Variables at the Moment of Goal Setting

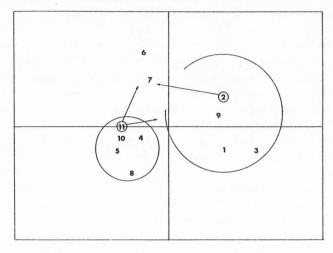

1 = achievement motivation, 2 = need for approval (self-presentation), 3 = rated task difficulty, 4 = real task difficulty, 5 = intended (rated) effort, 6 = actual (real) effort, 7 = rated ability, 8 = real aptitudes, 9 = estimated results, 10 = task-relevant skills, and 11 = general attitudes toward work.

Figure 7.2
Smallest Space Analysis: Dimension Factor Diagram of Links between Action Variables at the Moment of Preparation for Implementation

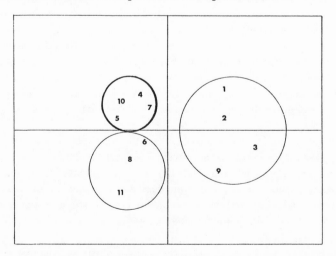

(For the full names of the action variables represented by numerals, see the caption for Figure 7.1.)

Figure 7.3
Smallest Space Analysis: Dimension Factor Diagram of Links between Action Variables at the Moment of Execution

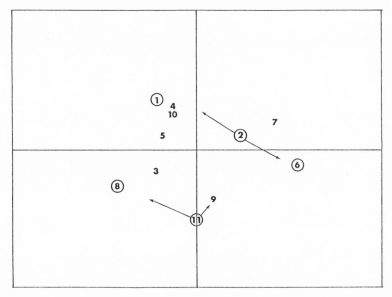

(For the full names of the action variables represented by numerals, see the caption for Figure 7.1.)

and actual effort) may be considered the situational data: They influence the task execution but they are far less under the influence of other variables.

Achievement motivation is not linked to the actual effort that subjects display in task execution (see also Table 7.1). However achievement motivation in the execution stage is linked to real task difficulty, task-relevant skills, and also to the intended effort (i.e., to variables that prepare for the final outcomes). Attitudes toward work return to a moderating role. They stand between aptitudes and the estimation of results. The use made of the individual's aptitudes will depend on rated task difficulty and rated effort as much as it will depend on attitudes and the cluster dominated by the variable measured through the test of social desirability. Because of its central position in mediating the whole transition from intention and aptitude mobilization to final implementation, one should take a closer look at the meaning of this test.

High scores on the Crowne-Marlowe test should reflect the tendency to report a highly positive self-image, but it cannot be ruled out that such a presentation is not a genuine self-image. The link between self-presentation and self-image has been emphasized by Goffman (1959) and Mangham (1978), who pointed out that in the social drama of everyday life, self-image expresses the appraisal made of the person by the public significant to him for the given interaction. In

Table 7.1

Results of Analysis of Variance for the Factors Involved in Aspiration Level, Motivation, and Need for Approval

	RESULTS					
Index	Motivation	Need for approval	Interaction of levels	Joint factorial	Residual	General
Sum of squares	42.7	9.3	1.8	53.8	45.9	99.7
df	2	2	4	8	51	59
Mean square	21.3	4.6	.45	6.7	.9	
F	23.6^{**}	5.1^{*}	.4	7.4^{**}		

$^{*}p = .05$ $^{**}p = .01$

that context, low test scores on the Crowne-Marlowe test appear to indicate a feeling of insecurity stemming from low self-regard, perhaps as a result of social rejection.

The motivational factor measured by the Crowne-Marlowe test should therefore reveal more than social desirability. It is certainly rooted in the need for favorable self-presentation, but it is also linked to the structure of self-concept formed and maintained by social demand. This force does not correlate directly with achievement motivation, but shares with it the control of the motivational aspects of the different action stages. The space diagrams presented in the SSA clearly defined the functioning of the two motivational factors in task execution but not in setting the level of aspiration. Their functioning in the setting of the level of aspiration is, however, essential to understanding the motivational regulation of action. Therefore, the choice gradient of the task (low, medium, and high estimated task difficulty) was plotted in a two-way analysis of variance against the levels of achievement motivation and need for approval (self-presentation and self-concept in light of social demands). The results appear in Table 7.1.

As may be seen, the most significant factor defining the level of aspiration is the achievement motivation factor; the joined action of achievement motivation and need for approval is also highly significant. The influence of self-presentation alone (need for approval) is significant only at the .05 level. It should follow that in a considerable proportion of cases, achievement motivation alone determines aspirational goal setting.

As a single factor, self-presentation has a substantially smaller influence on the level of aspiration than does achievement motivation. Apart from some idiosyncratic cases that will be discussed, the combined action of the two factors occurs when there is no discrepancy between them; in gradation relationships of high to low (between achievement motivation and socially mirrored self-concept), choice follows the motivation factor except in cases where the self-concept is very low. In relationships of extreme to medium values of either factor, choice follows the superior term.

To explain the causal links of choices that did not conform to the established pattern, I assumed that they were influenced by the additional factor of general attitudes toward work. Negativistic attitudes express the disturbance of the person's normal relationship with the environment. It is therefore not surprising that such a negativistic attitude should distort the normal way of relating to tasks by affecting their choice, their evaluation, or the relationship between subjective and objective task difficulty.

As far as choice is concerned, the level of aspiration pattern appeared in a distorted form whenever an individual manifested negativistic attitudes as measured by the test. In this respect, correlations are categoric ($\varphi = .51, p < .01$). There are, however, some grounds to predict (although with less certainty) the direction of the deviation by introducing the variable of knowledge and skill, as measured by the initial assessment of skills. It appears that the normally existing relationship will be distorted in the direction of choosing an easier task when the subject has poor knowledge and skill. The correlation between the direction of deviation and the quality of initial skill and knowledge is $\varphi = .358$ ($p < .07$).

The results substantiated the hypothesis that different motivational variables exercise control functions in the feedback loops of three stages of action that characterize the transition from intention to the act itself. In goal setting, an evaluated situation is tested chiefly against the more internally determined achievement motivation, whereas the socially rooted need for favorable self-presentation (in many cases a socially mirrored self-concept) is the more dominant motivational variable at the time of preparation for implementation. The stage of task execution is controlled in principle by the skill and knowledge necessary to perform the task. The motivational feedback loop is represented mainly by attitudes toward work, which correlate highly with the effort actually displayed. Attitudes play a moderator role in the other action stages; negativistic attitudes distort the perception of the task and/or the perception of task-related abilities.

The research applied to an activity for which no readily elaborated plan of action was available. Subjects set their goal aspirations according to the height of their achievement motivation, but to pass to the implementation stage they had to forge a plan of action. This mentally elaborated plan referred to an imagined action and not to a real one they had experienced. Thus, intervening variables like task difficulty or aptitudes had to be substituted for by their subjective evaluation. It is not surprising that the mental state of an imagined action in a social environment with merely evaluated abilities was controlled motivationally, chiefly by the wish for a favorable self-image with others. The output variable of this stage of mental planning was the effort the individual intended to apply to implement his chosen level of aspiration (chosen in accordance with his achievement motivation).

The output variable in the stage of task execution was the effort actually displayed, but it too correlated significantly with the factor of self-presentation (need for approval). This factor represents the main motivation feedback variable of the stage of preparation for task implementation. At the same time, it shares with achievement motivation the control of the goal-setting stage. Thus, the implicit linkage of achievement motivation with the final performance becomes quite evident.

If we rise from the molecular level of manufacturing a work piece to the molar level of career-choice planning and implementation, the analogy is striking. Not only will the process of career development include the same stages of goal setting, preparation for implementation, and actual implementation, but the structure of stages and their command-and-control variables will be the same as those that appeared at the molecular level. In both cases the action has not been previously experienced, and there is need for a mental preparation, a mentally elaborated plan in order to implement aspirations. In this context planning coincides with what Baron (1993) recently termed as thinking about what to desire and thinking as a part of the theory of action.

In performing a concrete task, the height of aspiration level is primarily defined by the person's achievement motivation, but the latter is related to the intended effort and not to the actually displayed one. Neither does the motivational goal setting appear to be related to the objective task difficulty, but to its subjective evaluation obtained by projecting the self-perceived abilities onto the evaluated task. The use the individual will make of his abilities depends upon the evaluation of task difficulty and of his intended effort. Individuals with good aptitudes may not use their full potential and fail in realizing their aspirations if task difficulty and intended effort are inadvertently defined. Negativistic attitudes toward the task and the persons who are in charge of it distort the whole process of task choice and implementation, as do poor abilities and skills in planning and performing.

At this point we ought to underline a psychological difference with important consequences between a concrete work task and the process of career development. While in the former the construction of a plan is relatively simple and overlooks all action stages from the beginning up to the end, the complexity of work careers may deter people from even thinking of an all-encompassing plan. This does not mean they have none. Usually life plans exist on an imagery level, but are not acknowledged as such. The end-state image of self-realization is a life plan, but it is not conceptually analyzed, clarified, ordered, and hierarchized.

In Russian psychology Galperin (1957) created a school of thought teaching that mental actions reflect and internalize external actions with objects. Consequently, concepts and images are the "infolded" pattern of formerly unfolded material actions with objects. Krau (1971) pointed out that planfulness in performing practical actions with objects is controlled by a superior type of images expressing the sequence of operations by which the object had been produced. He named them *constructive images*, which enable the person to reason and act on a rational goal-directed level. Behavior is regulated also by images that are not constructive but exist on a perceptive-active level only: There is no anticipation of events, and the individual merely reacts to occurrences and situational characteristics by using acquired action stereotypes (Krau, 1971).

In neurophysiology Anohin (1963) spoke of a "situational acceptor," a fourth link of the nervous reflex bow that acknowledges the feedback of an action, rejects it, or imposes corrections. In the area of career and life plans the end-state images of self-realization have the role of such a situational acceptor. They constitute the body of acceptance or rejection vis-à-vis events, actions, and intentions. End-state self-realization images have (or at least they should have) the quality both of constructive images and of a situational acceptor. As such, they not only are a body of acceptance-rejection but also contain an action plan by which the desired end state may be achieved. The following research will prove that persons whose self-realization images indicate planfulness achieve higher levels of self-realization.

In 1987 research was conducted with 55 persons aged between 25 and 60 (mean age 36.4 years), 36 men and 19 women of different occupations: 39.3 percent engineers, 14.3 percent technicians, 14.3 percent in managerial positions, 16 percent professionals, and 16 percent in clerical and manual jobs. They were asked to define what self-realization meant for them and then to rate their self-realization on a 7-point scale. In the data processing the scores 1–4 were considered low and the scores 5–7 as high. Then the definitions were also divided into two groups: one indicating the planful implementation of aspirations, the other without such elements. Here is an example of "planful implementation": "the realization of capacities and aspirations in the personal and interpersonal domains."

Such definitions stress the presence of deliberately chosen aims and of planful efforts in order to achieve them. These features do not appear in the other groups of definitions, which mainly emphasize the outcomes of pleasure and fun, such as "To do what you like to do with pleasure, to have a pleasurable occupation, to live in a loving and beloved family." The computational data are presented in Table 7.2, and they show a clear tendency for definitions comprising elements of planfulness to belong to persons with higher scores of self-realization. (The χ^2 coefficient is 10.85 significant at $p = 0.01$.) It is the difference between seeking a planful realization of one's aspirations, the way a constructive image of the self-realization end-state would enable one to perform, or merely accepting or rejecting offers and events brought by the waves of life.

In order to receive more information on persons rating themselves at different degrees of self-realization, all participations in the research had also been administered Krau's projective personality test (Krau, 1967, 1981a) assessing various personality traits, and also the Mehrabian Risk Preference Scale in the variant of Mikula, Uray, and Schwinger (1974) for the measurement of achieve-

Table 7.2
Planfulness and Achieved Self-Realization

	Definitions refer to plans	Definitions refer to pleasure	Total
High self-realization scores	19	12	31
Low self-realization scores	4	20	24

ment motivation. It was hypothesized that personality traits motivating towards the achievement of aspirations would mainly characterize individuals with high self-realization achievements. The hypothesis was confirmed: self-assertion correlated $r = 0.28$ (significant at $p = 0.05$) with self-realization scores, achievement motivation correlated $r = 0.26$ (significant at $p = 0.05$) and courage $r = 0.28$ (significant at $p = 0.05$). Finally, there was a high correlation of $r = 0.57$ significant at $p = 0.01$ between self-realization scores and the rating of satisfaction with one's work on a 10–point scale. This correlation is higher as the previously mentioned links with achievement motivation or self-assertion. Indeed, some people who are not self-assertive or driven by achievement motivation may also consider themselves self-realized. Be the content of self-realization as it may, one has to come to terms with one's work in order to feel realized.

Our conclusion so far that planning increases the chances for self-realization raises the very important question of what can be planned. It seems a contradiction in terms to plan for unforeseeable events in a time span ranging from 10 to 30 years ahead. We have also seen that the self-realization image refers to an end-state, and even in its constructive form it is not a detailed action plan, because the intermediary stages have not been directly experienced by the person. What can be planfully realized is the choice of a career and its general sense of development in accordance with the aspiration hierarchy established in the end-state image of self-realization.

Literature has repeatedly analyzed the problem of career stages and patterns. Career stages described by Bühler (1933), Super, Crites, Hummel, Moser, Overstreet, and Warnath (1957), or Hall (1976) deal with the developmental tasks throughout a vocational career without considering the problem of specific aspirations and orientations. The same may be told of the career patterns put forward by Super (1954). They describe variations and timings in the periods of vocational stability: the stable career, the conventional career wherein stability is reached only after a lengthy period of trials, the unstable career, and the multiple-trial career. Even in the somewhat earlier studies of Miller and Form (1951) dealing with types of career orientations on the basis of the relationship between aspirations and adjustment, the focus was on the link between job security, hope, and ambition versus uncertainty and indecision. All these variables were related to the expectations of parents or relatives and not to the combinations of objective and subjective career ingredients that result in specific ways of aspiration formation and realization. It is the merit of Crites (1969) to have linked the probem of job satisfactoriness to that of career success and satisfaction, but he has not formulated theories of his own on this subject.

As a matter of fact a model of career patterns should be related to career stages but yet should have enough generality so that it may also include the development of "second careers," which people enter because of unfavorable occurrences on the labor market or emigration. According to Lawler (1971) career models should be based on salient variables inherent in work adjustment. It should indicate which stimulus conditions will create problems, describe the mechanisms by which problems may be alleviated, and formulate hypotheses that may be empirically tested. In his career model of immigrants, Krau (1982b) enlarged this framework, pointing out that immigrants' problems consist not only of adjustment to the company they work for but at the same time adapting to a new society. The proposed career model of immigrants included the following stages: crystallization, vocational retraining, job entry and trial, establishment, and maintenance. The justification of these stages lay in the specificity of the behavior displayed vis-à-vis the problem-creating conditions that appear along the path of career reconstruction. The career stages described in the model are generally common to all mid-career changers, people who suffer from disability, and so on. The model (see Table 7.3) assumed certain key variables predicting the success of the coping behavior in each stage expressed by the mastery of the skills necessary to the adaptation process (vocational knowledge, skills to comply with unfamiliar environment, the reduction of cognitive dissonance over status incongruence, etc.).

Psychologically, the main problem in the first stages (crystallization and vocational retraining altogether) is the perceived cognitive dissonance over past and present status incongruence. The behavioral strategies adopted to cope with this problem and the personality variables involved in them have been described elsewhere (Krau, 1981a). It has been pointed out that the strategies center around the adjustment of the self-image to the experienced status incongruence. Some reduce the self-image to fit the objective situation, while others choose to deny the objectively existing predicament and do not reduce or may even heighten the self-image.

However, a change in the self-image in itself is not enough to cope with concrete vocational problems. It was assumed that in the crystallization stage the career task was the need to learn the new language and to gather information about possible work opportunities. Consequently, we should look at this stage for the coping behaviors of learning and of help seeking.

In the stage of vocational retraining, the feeling of status incongruence, producing cognitive dissonance, remains a major problem and may still cause changes in self-assertion. The concrete vocational task facing the subject is skill

Table 7.3
The Career Development Model of Immigrants

Career stage	Problem creating condition	Coping behavior	Variables tested as success predictors	Measures	Stage criterion measure
Crystallization	Language difficulties. Lack of information on labor market and on job requirements. Cognitive dissonance over status incongruence.	Learning. Help-seeking behaviors. Reducing cognitive dissonance.	Learning achievement. Bid to be admitted to training program. General attitude toward work. Interest in new occupation. Self-assertion (lowered vs. unchanged).	Language examination. Admission to retraining program. Personality test. Vocational interest test. Personality test.	Governmental examination of lower accountancy degree.
Vocational retraining	Cognitive dissonance over status incongruence. Need to accept also unfamiliar occupation. Lack of skill in new occupation.	Reducing cognitive dissonance. Emotional acceptance of new occupation. Acquisition of occupational knowledge and skills.	Self-assertion. General attitude toward work. Vocational involvement. Valuing of money. Learning aptitudes. Vocational aptitudes. Acquisition of initial skill in new occupation.	Personality test. Personality test. Personality test. Personality test. Domino test. Turse Clerical Aptitude Test. Lower accountancy degree examination.	Governmental examination for high accountancy degree.
Job entry and trial	Competition on the labor market. Short employment interviews and tests.	Competitive behavior. Efficiency in test situation and display of vocational knowledge and skills.	Boldness. Social skills. Vocational knowledge and skills. Vocational aptitudes.	Personality test. Personality test. High degree accountancy examination. Domino test. Truss Clerical Aptitude Test.	Location of employment.

Establishment	Job requirements. New work community. Need for enculturation. Need for economic security.	Conforming to requirements. Openness to social contacts and new values. Effort to achieve a permanent income.	Vocational aptitudes. Vocational knowledge and skills. Vocational involvement. Social skills. Valuing of money. Positive attitude toward work. Location of employment.	Domino Test. Turse Clerical Aptitude Test. High degree accountancy examination. Personality Test. Personality Test. Location of employment.	Vocational achievement (adjustment to the job).
Maintenance	Job requirements. Need to heighten living standard and position in community.	Conforming to job requirements. Effort to catch up economic community standards. Effort to assert oneself in the community.	(Vocational skills). Vocational involvement. Valuing of money. Social skills. Self-assertion.	(Vocational achievement). Personality Test. Personality Test. Personality Test.	Adjustment to the job.

Reprinted with permission. Copyright 1982 by Academic Press.

acquisition in a new, unfamiliar occupation; to cope with this task, the person will have to develop a positive general attitude toward work and emotional acceptance of the new occupation. Starting from the skills acquired in language, as well as in the area of solving elementary vocational problems in the previous career stage, the immigrant will have to achieve progress in vocational skill acquisition until a fully qualifying level is reached for the job requirement in the new country. This latter state is linked to some forms of vocational aptitudes.

It was assumed that cognitive dissonance recedes in the forthcoming career stages, as the individual moves toward a practical solution for it. Self-image will no longer be the gist of adaptation strategies. In the stage of job entry and trial the main problem will be the strong competition for work entry, which requires a competitive behavior, relying on boldness and social and vocational skills to deal successfully with employment interviews and testing.

Subjects who succeed have a chance to enter the establishment stage, a crucial point in their new careers, presenting them with a variety of the most complicated problem-creating situations, both in the field of the vocation and in the larger, social integration. Now, coping behavior must include achievements on the job, so it will have to display vocational skills (based on a certain profile of aptitudes and the vocational knowledge assessed at the termination of vocational retraining), a positive attitude toward work, and involvement with their occupations, motivating them to industriousness and to compliance with job requirements. At the same time, in order to be accepted by peers at the place of work and by the community at large, they will have to display openness to social contacts and to acquire new social values. Therefore, beyond the purely vocational skills, successful adaptation will require some sort of social extraversion and social learning.

Existing career models link the maintenance stage to reaching a certain age (45). As already stated, this age link to career stages is not always feasible for immigrants. Many of them are in their late thirties or forties when they arrive, and they are faced with having to cope with career stages that fit younger workers. Therefore, the time of passing career stages will be somewhat contracted, and a more rapid slipping into maintenance should appear, especially in the case of recent immigration and unfamiliarity with the new social and vocational environment that makes steady advancement look like an unreal perspective. For that reason, it was assumed that the transition to the maintenance stage began when the former immigrants, who are close to or over forty, acquired tenure at the job and succeeded in overcoming the main difficulties in the field of social adaptation and enculturation.

In accordance with the career development outlined by Super et al. (1957), it was assumed that keen competitive risk taking would no longer be of relevance for coping with the problems of this stage. However, the effort to catch up to community standards, as far as economic and social positions are concerned, should require the strong action of work motivators (vocational involvement and/or the valuing of money) and of course vocational skills but also self-assertion and again social skills.

Immigrants' careers emphatically raise the psychological and social problems linked with the loss of stability and the impossibility of planning ahead. Besides, in modern times instability has become a way of life. Recently, career stability has come under attack altogether, because of the economic tendencies to downsize organizational staff and to rely more on a temporary workforce. There are voices questioning even the usefulness of the career concept. Under such conditions the whole issue of career planning may seem ludicrous.

In our view, and we are relying in this respect also on the views of Super and Hall, an interrupted or an unstable career remains a career nonetheless. While the new economically induced instability may pile up new difficulties in the way of life-goal achievement, it makes life projects even more necessary, if anything at all is to be achieved. Precisely the career model of immigrants shows how careers must be reconstructed in spite of severe economic, social, and psychological problems. The career model of immigrants demonstrates how the stability of goals functions as a lifelong career plan, initiating the coping mechanisms necessary to fend off the threat that adverse occurrences pose to people's life projects.

Of course, projects have to be flexible, but it is flexibility within the person's image of self-realization. The initially blurred character of this image allows for such flexibility. In no case should flexibility amount to renouncing life goals and the planning for them. It is the life project that preserves the individual's psychological health in face of threats of chaotic instability and the specter of destitution. Success in the fight against poverty and crime lies in the inoculation of life projects that can be implemented.

Careers will continue to exist, and career planning remains a necessary instrument for realizing life aspirations; but instead of planning one's career in a single organization (or business), one will have to take into consideration changing jobs, businesses, and even vocational specialties, as long as new ones do not contradict the person's life project for self-realization.

Whether stable or not, the prototype of careers is the organizational career. Milkovich, Anderson, and Greenhalgh (1976) defined the organizational career primarily as a structural property of the organization, a patterned sequence of positions through which organizational members move in an order set by rules and policies. Conceived as such, the organization offers a canvas on which career moves may be performed. Wellbank, Hall, Morgan, and Hamner (1978) and Vardi (1980) insisted that the direction of rational career paths from the point of view of the organization are by no means only upward but also lateral and even downward. Previously, Schein (1968) had described the direction of organizational career mobility as hierarchical (upward), functional (lateral), and radial (advancement toward the center of power).

The problem is that the career has two faces. It takes place in an organization and abides by the latter's regulations, but it belongs to an individual and is performed by that individual in accordance with the person's specific motivations and capabilities. Whereas organizational socialization remains a key feature of organizational careers, the person's position in an organization is best thought of as a negotiated one, and the individual's location in the organization is never accomplished definitively (van Maanen, 1978). One may choose not to accept an offered position, to manage one's own advancement by striving and lobbying, or to leave the organization, if one can better achieve one's aspirations in another place of work. The attainment of self-realization would require the grasp of the best possible opportunities always.

Can such moves be planfully performed? Are they? From a ten-year longitudinal study (Krau, 1977, 1981b) we reached the conclusion that a majority of people have a sort of planning for the general conduct of their career, allowing for prediction to be made by counselors within a reasonable range of accuracy. Most recently in the investigation of career certainty, Schulenberg, Vondracek, and Kim (1993) also pointed out that their subjects, high school students, seemed to have a career plan in mind, as well as some sense of how to proceed with the plan. The plan may not be well formed, yet it strives to orient educational and occupational decisions.

As already mentioned, 575 lathe operator apprentices in 1967 were administered psychological tests as part of trade school entrance requirements. A group of 110 apprentices was followed up during their stay in trade school, and later for from 5 up to 8 years in production. For some of the subjects the follow-up period was ten years, as after a short training in the trade school they entered production and continued trade school concurrently with evening courses. The psychological examination comprised testing of interests, vocational abilities, personality traits, vocational information, and later occupational knowledge, skill, and vocationally relevant family characteristics (Krau, 1977, 1981c). The vocational ability profiles had been established experimentally in testing earlier representative samples of workers (Krau, 1970).

A first tentative outscreening for lack of aptitudes took place at trade school entrance. Subjects who failed to pass the vocational aptitude testing were recommended not to enter lathe operator training, but the psychologists' recommendation was not mandatory and some chose to ignore it. A subsequent, not entirely vocationally relevant knowledge examination had a "normalizing" effect on the distribution of aptitude grades in the sample. A second outscreening took place at trade school termination. This time, trainees who had failed absolutely to acquire the minimal necessary knowledge had to leave the courses. The effects of the two selections were that in broad lines all subjects (the 110 who remained) had the minimal requirements to work as lathe operators, and they all were hired by two metal plants, which sponsored the courses.

To determine vocational aptitudes and adjustment to the job, an industrial criterion of work adjustment was used, consisting of objective efficiency indicators (average fulfillment of production norms during a period of 6 months) and supervisor's ratings for discipline. The two indicators were combined on a 10–point scale to a single adjustment score.

The following measurements of career ingredients were obtained (Krau, 1977; 1981b):

Vocational Aptitudes. The general aptitude score of lathe operators was based on tests correlating with the industrial criterion for work adjustment: mechanical reasoning (Differential Aptitude Test), manual coordination (measured by Lahy's device), physical force (measured with a dynamometer), and the differentiation of surface asperity through touch (measured with a Moede tactometer). Included were also the personality traits of moderation in social extraversion, the work values of vocational involvement, and the valuing of money. These were measured with Krau's projective personality test (Krau, 1967).

A composite 5–degree aptitude score was based on the relationship between critical negative and compensating positive test scores of the variable measurements. At the psychometric tests critical negative scores were those that fell in the three lower stanines, but in the computation of the overall aptitude degree such negative scores would be compensated for by aptitude components falling into the three upper stanines. At the personality traits the critical negative and positive test scores were assessed by means of significant chi-square frequency distribution differences between satisfactory and unsatisfactory workers. The minimum overall-aptitude degree of 1 was assigned when two critical negative-variable scores remained uncompensated by positive ones. The maximum overall aptitude degree of 5 was assigned when a subject had three positive variable scores without any critical negative result.

Attitudes toward Authority Figures and the Place of Work. The already-described projective personality test of Krau (1967, 1981) was used to measure workers' attitudes. Scores range from 0 to 4, wherein the scores 0 and 1 express negative attitudes.

Vocational Mastery. A knowledge test in lathe technology elaborated with the aid of specialists was used to measure vocational mastery. Scores were given separately for theoretical and for practical occupational knowledge (on previously determined plant-specific items). Both measurements were standardized into 5–point scales.

Active Vocational Interests. Worker's interests were measured by a Book Catalog test devised by Krau (cf. Meir and Krau, 1983). The test was designed mainly as an instrument for the appraisal of employees as candidates for promotion. The idea of the test was to measure the motivational coverage of expressed vocational preferences in order to examine the emotional involvement behind them. The measurement used the method of expressing literary preferences. It follows from the principle discovered by Strong (1960) that people involved with a certain vocation tend to have common interests not only in connection with their job but also regarding school subjects, books, sports, and hobbies. Other studies show that the reading of literature linked with one's vocation correlates significantly with career ambitions and the attitude toward the updating of knowledge (Rubin and Morgan, 1967; Tausky and Dubin, 1965).

The test had the form of a book catalog, as described long ago by Baumgarten (1928), but some important modifications were introduced. Firstly, it was an objective personality test (Anastasi, 1964), the real purpose of which was not revealed to the subjects. They were told that in order to help public libraries in keeping their book stock updated in accordance with the public's demand, a reader survey would be conducted. They were requested to designate, out of a list presented to them, five titles that should be acquired by public libraries in general, so that "you too may use them." They were also asked to reject five titles that "you do not want to read or to see in a library." By this method it was possible not only to define areas of interest but also to determine the intensity of rejection of certain fields.

The test presented the subject with a list of widely known books. The variant for persons with a high school background comprised 37 book titles referring to 15 fields of human activity: economics and business, technology, mathematics, physics, chemistry, biology and medical sciences, psychology, education, sociology and politics, law and administration, history, geography, the arts and literature, religion, and sports. Each field was represented by three book titles with several titles representing two fields. There was a variant of 23 titles of a more popular character, for persons with only a junior high school education, like our subjects.

Pilot studies with students and persons in various occupations established interests profiles for 32 occupations, that is, which book titles people engaged in these occupations are likely to choose. Vocational interest profiles were not always identical with an interest in one single field; for example, book choices of teachers of literature fell in the field of education as well as literature, and the interest profile of accountants included the economy and the application of mathematics to business and industry.

The scoring of the test was on a 4-point scale (from 0 to 3) and took into account the ratio between choices and rejections within each occupational interest field. The maximal score of 3 was assigned when choices exceeded by at least three the rejections in the vocational interest field (or when three positive choices appeared without rejecting any relevant title). The minimal score of zero was assigned when rejections of the evaluated interest area exceeded choices or when they appeared without any positive choice.

The validation of the test was based on the construct of vocational interest as a motivating force determining the initiation of a vocational activity, an extra effort in it, or also the discontinuation of an emotionally rejected vocational activity. Thus, an active vocational interest would be reflected in the application for courses or jobs and mainly in the extra effort the individual would apply to some fields in order to get promoted. The reverse of vocational interest, amounting to an emotional rejection of a certain activity, would be expressed in terminating it after a short period of participation. Three validation criteria were used: (a) school degree coverage of vocational interest, (b) the initiating of vocational activity, and (c) the termination of a vocational activity as a result of failure (e.g., dropping out from training courses before any examination is taken).

Relevant Biographical Background. The role of the parental family in the implementation of career aspirations has already been discussed. In this research a questionnaire was administered inquiring about the size of the parental family, the emotional ties within it, including dominances, and the family's influence on the subject's vocational choice. A specific question asked for a characterization of the father.

Several Stages of Follow-Up. First, during a two-year period in trade school (for some subjects three years), school progress was assessed every year. The assessment comprised the general mean of school marks, the mean score obtained in technological school matters (equipment and operating technology, technological mechanics, the technology of materials, electrotechnics, and mathematics) and the degrees obtained in practical training. For evaluations in this latter area the critical incidence technique was used for activities like asking the instructor for information, the scanning of the technical drawing, the quality of performance, initiative, and also discipline infringements.

After leaving school, another follow-up was conducted one year after production entry. Objective efficiency indicators were registered for each subject, which were rated by their supervisor for the discipline shown at work. The two indicators were combined into a composite adjustment score on a 10-point scale. This procedure was repeated after a 4-year period and then again after another 3 years. As some of the apprentices had entered production after an intensive short course, their follow-up actually encompassed a time interval of 10 years in production.

Before turning to the analysis of outcomes, let it be remembered that the whole sample had been subjected to ability testing at school entry and for prediction purposes had been divided into a group with abilities, a group without occupationally relevant abilities, and a third group with negativistic attitudes toward authority figures at the place of work. It was hypothesized that the group with abilities would have better results in school and later on in production than the other two.

As far as the general mean of school marks is concerned, the differences among these three groups were not really significant, and the reason was that the trade school curriculum did not consist only of occupationally relevant matters. However, in this last area the differences significantly favored the group with vocational abilities. In technological disciplines the mean difference was significant with $t = 1.63$ ($p = 0.10$) in the first year and raised to $t = 2.58$ ($p = 0.01$) in the second year (the third year had only practical training). In the practicum the difference in favor of the group with vocational abilities was high from the beginning with a coefficient of $t = 2.38$ ($p = 0.02$) in the first year raising further to $t = 2.50$ ($p = 0.01$) in the third year.

Table 7.4
Centroid Factors after Rotation (one year after production entry)

No.	Variable	I	II	III	IV	V	h^2
1.	Initial adjustment to the job	.690	.550	.375	.000	-.005	918
2.	Vocational abilities	.390	.540	.315	.460	.130	556
3.	Attitudes toward authority figures	-.010	.460	.000	-.125	.090	234
4.	Vocational knowledge	.590	-.225	.000	.360	.005	741
5.	Vocational know-how	.750	.005	.210	.000	-.240	678
6.	Promotional aspirations	.230	.230	-.370	.030	.190	225
7.	Relevant biographical background	.630	-.040	-.110	.250	.000	522
	% of explained variance	28.3	12.5	6.2	6.1	2.2	55.3

In the follow-up one year after production entry the measurements of all independent variables were correlated with a normalized composed 10–point score of adjustment to the job. It consisted of objective efficiency indicators: average exceeding of nominal salary or average fulfillment of production norms during a period of six months (it depended upon the evaluation and wage system in the employing organizations) and supervisors' ratings for discipline.

Although all independent variables had a significant correlation with the dependent variable of adjustment to the job, correlations differed largely, indicating that the measurement of present satisfactoriness on the job might not be the only and final variable of reference, especially if a long-term adjustment was considered. It was hypothesized therefore that a factor analysis rather than a simple correlation matrix would describe the variables of adjustment to work more accurately, because the influence of different psychological factors would already be manifest at this early stage of the vocational career. Table 7.4 presents five orthogonal centroid factors after rotation, derived by the Thurstone method.

The table shows an idiosyncratic behavior of the last two factors, which heavily draw on abilities, vocational knowledge, and vocationally relevant biographical background but have a negative load on attitudes toward authority figures at the place of work and no load on the initial adjustment to the job. It seems that these factors are pointing toward a career development that is beyond the scrupulous fulfillment of job requirements and the obedience shown to the foreman. Their relatively weak action may be explained by the fact that one year after production entry their influence is in an embryonic stage and is not affecting all subjects.

It had to be hypothesized therefore that a follow-up at a more distant point of time would evince two types of vocational careers: one aimed at upward mobility and the other at building a comfortable position without hierarchical advancement and the changes in lifestyle that they entail. In order to build a verifiable profile of the two career types, we leaned on the action of factors II–III versus IV–V, as they emerged from the analysis presented in Table 7.4. Here is our interpretation of all five factors:

Factor I appears as a general factor of vocational abilities and skills enabling career adjustment. It explains 28.3 percent of the total career adjustment variance and has a strong load both on initial adjustment and on promotional aspirations, on theoretical vocational knowledge and on practical know-how. This factor could be characterized as acting in the direction of general vocational adjustment (in either career type) rather than total maladjustment and vocational unfitness.

Factor II is a motivational factor already specifically directed at building material and social comfort around the person's present career position. The factor has a strong load on initial adjustment to the job, on positive attitudes toward authority figures at the place of work, and on abilities but a strong negative load on theoretical vocational knowledge. There appears a load even on promotional aspirations; evidently the person would not refuse them. Nonetheless, the load on present adjustment is stronger, and there is resistance to learning.

Factor III completes the picture of individuals who do not strive for promotions. It is the key factor for describing the performer qualities of this career type. The factor has a strong negative load on promotional aspirations while having a high positive load on initial adjustment and abilities related to know-how on the job.

Factor IV describes the performer qualities of the career type striving for vocational upward mobility. It has a strong load on abilities and on theoretical vocational knowledge but not on initial adjustment to the job or on job skills (know-how). Most significantly, the loading on authority figures at the place of work is negative. The factor has a strong load on the vocationally relevant biographical background, which plays an important role in upward mobility careers.

Factor V attaches additional psychological emphasis to the picture outlined by the previous factor: The load on adjustment to the present job is negative and there is a strong negative load on skills of know-how on the job. The highest and virtually only loads of this factor are on promotional aspirations and on vocational abilities.

The new fact revealed by this research is the existence of a two-type career orientation based on the presence or the absence of aspirations for hierarchical promotions and the aptitudes and skills necessary to materialize them. Through this typology the vocational career appears related to the end-state image of self-realization. To be sure of this conclusion the experimental sample was followed up over periods of 5 and 10 years in production in addition to a control sample of another 88 young lathe operators. This control sample had also passed the already-described psychological examination before their admission to trade school in 1966. In the follow-up all subjects were divided into two groups: the first group comprised the persons who had obtained some hierarchical promotion during the first five years (appointed as foremen, sent to courses for supervisors, admitted to the military academy, etc.), and 35 percent of the total sample entered their group. The second group consisted of persons who did not change their hierarchical status during this period.

We called the two types of career *ascent* and *horizontal*. According to the data of the factor analysis, it was presumed that persons striving for hierarchical promotions, the **ascent career type**, would be characterized by:

1. High school degrees in the vocationally relevant theoretical matters, a good theoretical knowledge in vocational matters.

2. High promotional aspirations and a positive attitude toward authority figures at the place of work (perhaps less positive than the other career type, yet a negativistic attitude is a sign of maladjustment and will constitute an obstacle for a person being considered for promotion).

3. High vocational ability scores.

4. Modest scores in present satisfactoriness at the job but still rated generally satisfactory (otherwise, again, there would be no promotion possibility).

5. Biographical background relevant for upward social mobility.

In defining the last characteristics we relied on Lipset and Bendix (1953) and on Fürstenberg (1969), who stated that upward social mobility from lower socioeconomic levels is furthered by loose links with the person's primary environment. Using the data we had on our subjects we computed a composite score of links with the primary social environment based on: (a) size of the parental family; (b) cohesion of the family as a result of emotional attachment or the dominance of the father; (c) family influence on the subject's job choice (scores negatively in the case of a passive, unstimulating social environment); (d) presence or absence of the father; and (e) completeness of the family (is it complete or is it a one-parent family).

In scoring the ties with the primary social environment, one point was given for each of the characteristics above and then an inversion was performed on certain traits, since supposedly strong ties with the primary social environment had negative influence on the chances of upward social mobility of lower or inert social strata. It was understood that in the case of an active, stimulating social environment the variables *a, b,* and *c* would be positively related to social ascent while *d* and *e* would preserve their negative impact. It has to be assessed in each case separately which environment is active and stimulating because deductions may lead to wrong results. Surveys show that in the United States the offspring of fathers working in skilled and semiprofessional occupations have higher aspirations than their parents, while offspring of the superior social strata want to remain at the same socioeconomic level. There are, however, important exceptions as a result of the general political atmosphere or of a childhood spent in laziness and effortless luxury (Werts, 1968). In Britain, in the time of the economic boom, upward mobility was the average or expected experience for unskilled or semiskilled manual workers, while downward mobility was the most likely mobility experience for children born in nonmanual strata (Stacey, 1968).

It would be wrong to look at these data as only a result of economic trends and changes in the technological infrastructure. Social mobility is also the result of conscious activities displayed by families in the transmission of values and aspirations and in making it possible for their offspring to get an appropriate education, sometimes at the price of tremendous sacrifices. It has been already mentioned that in the former Eastern bloc, at the time the aforementioned research was performed, peasantry provided a much more active social environment for their children than urban workers. Our research data showed that their offspring had a greater probability of advancement and even of becoming well-adjusted to their jobs in comparison with the children of urban workers (Krau, Aluas, Latis, and Jurcau, 1969).

In opposition to people aspiring to the upward mobility of an ascent career, individuals belonging to the **horizontal career type** mainly strive to improve their material status and/or also their occupational competence. They want comfortable working conditions and good colleagues, and they do not desire greater responsibility or social power. However, it would be wrong to view the horizontal type as definitely inferior in abilities and skills. It is simply another career type. They view their career in a different manner, and they use it differently as an instrument for achieving self-realization. Yet, it is true that more individuals with poor aptitudes have horizontal careers compared with people having ascent careers. The reason for this is cultural. Our achievement culture encourages persons with good aptitudes to seek the realization of upward mobility aspirations.

The special characteristics of the *horizontal* career type are:

Good practical skills (know-how) at the job

Good adjustment to job requirements, including a good initial adaptation after work entry

A highly positive attitude toward authority figures at the place of work

Low promotional aspirations

Strong ties with the primary social environment (especially in inert social strata)

The last characteristic may introduce some confusion, depending on the social stratum to which the person belongs. The upper strata will ensure so high a career start for their offspring that even a horizontal type of development in lawyers, physicians, or executives in family enterpriese may seem to reflect an ascent career. The question that should be asked in such cases is whether these persons achieved greater social power during their careers by enlarging their enterprises substantially, becoming directors of hospitals or of a law firm, chairpersons of a board, by entering politics, or the like.

Nevertheless, it should by no means be understood that only people belonging to the ascent career type are capable of self-realization. The latter is performed in a self-chosen domain and depends upon the congruence of the individual's achievements with the aims of his reference group. This gives plenty of room for persons belonging to the horizontal career type to realize themselves.

The self-realization of people belonging to the ascent career type mainly concerns hierarchical advancement and the attainment of social power. Unexpectedly, Waterman (1993) associates such aspirations with the eudaimonic form of happiness in self-expression: feeling challenged, feeling competent, investing a great deal of effort, having clear goals. He associates hedonic enjoyment with feeling relaxed, content, happy, losing track of time, and forgetting one's personal problems. From the perspective of a life-career orientation such experiences should be associated with our horizontal type of career. It seems that there are grounds for the assumption that the "eudaimonic" striving of the ascent career is linked to the Type A behavior pattern as implied by the research of Byrne and Reinhart (1989).

We recently investigated the link between type A and B personality styles and the types of ascent and horizontal careers with 113 male subjects (mean age 39.2 years, SD 6.5), including semiskilled, skilled, semiprofessional, and professional-managerial employees. In order to assess their career type a double measurement was used: (a) subjects were asked to evaluate which of the events of their vocational biography were a result of their aspirations for upward mobility, and (b) the career type was determined by evaluators' judgment on the events of subjects' vocational biography. The evaluations (number of promotions) were transformed into standard scores with the mean = 0 and SD = 1, ranging from −3 to +3. People with standard scores higher than the mean were considered to belong to an ascent career type. Most significantly the subjective evaluation of the career type in the light of aspirations correlated highly with the evaluation made by judges ($r = 0.62$ at $p = 0.001$) attesting to the strong link between aspirations, behaviors, and career events.

For the assessment of the personality types A and B, the Jenkins Activity Survey Form C was used (Jenkins, Zyzanski, and Rosenman, 1979). In addition, the subjects' achievement motivation was also assessed using the already-discussed variant of the Mehrabian Risk Preference Scale (Mikula, Uray, and Schwinger, 1974). Finally, there was an assessment of the subjects' salient life domain using Krau's version (Krau, 1989b) of the WIS Salience Inventory.

The link between personality style and the objectively evaluated career type is presented in Table 7.5. The results clearly indicate that the two career types rest on different styles of behavior (personality styles). This conclusion is upheld also by the link between the measurement of personality type and subjectively assessed career events, where again the types of personality style (A, B, inter-

Table 7.5
The Link between Personality Style and the Objective Evaluated Career Type

| Personality type | Career Type Standard Score | | ANOVA | | | | |
	M	SD	Source of variance	Sum of squares	Mean squares	F	P
A*	0.41	0.97	Between groups	18.24	9.12	10.67	0.0001
Intermediary	0.13	0.93	Within groups	95.75	0.85		
B*	-0.55	0.86	Total	113.99			

* Scheffé's method for mean comparisons shows that both the groups A and B significantly differ from any other group.

Table 7.6
Multiple Regression of Personality Style and Achievement Motive on the Type of Career

Predictors	B	ß	T	P	R
Personality style	0.005	0.352	3.81	0.0002	0.40
Achievement motive	0.047	0.098	1.02	0.308	
Interaction	0.054	0.060	0.65	0.514	

mediary) recorded different kinds of career events from the point of view of upward mobility ($\chi^2 = 7.93$, Df $= 2$, significant at $p = 0.05$). There is also a significant correlation between achievement motivation and the standard score of evaluated career events (the career type) ($r = 0.18$ significant at $p = 0.05$). However, a multiple regression of personality style and achievement motivation on the type of the career demonstrated that of the two predictor variables (personality style and achievement motivation) the former one is decisive, contributing $\beta = 0.35$ to the multiple correlation of $R = 0.40$, with the type of the career (16% of the explained variance, see Table 7.6). The personality style A already includes the behavior characterized by high achievement motivation, and in itself the latter does not add to the variance.

The two career types also appeared with significant differences in the choice of the salient life domain. Persons belonging to the ascent career type are much more willing to invest in the domain of work and even more so in studies. At the same time, they do not care less for their family or for leisure activities compared to people belonging to the horizontal career type (see Table 7.7). The outstanding salience of studies should be linked to the recognition that they are a key instrument for getting promoted and thus becoming "successful."

For reasons stemming from the achievement culture of our society, the ascent career constitutes the main ingredient of what in public opinion is considered as success. A career evolving horizontally at the level of the original entry position or close to it will rarely be considered a success. Yet subjectively it may be evaluated as such, if it creates the conditions for gratifying the person's salient aspirations.

There is a certain similarity between our types of ascent and horizontal careers and the career patterns of Driver (1982). His linear and spiral career patterns correspond to our ascent careers, while his stable and variable careers correspond to our horizontal career type. In regard to the spiral career pattern, Driver emphasizes status improvement through circumferential career moves. It will be remembered that in our career typology every advancement of this kind, such as moving to a more prestigious enterprise, is considered an ascent move. Therefore, spiral careers are in fact ascent careers.

Table 7.7
Salient Life Domains in the Two Career Types

| Salient life area | Studies | | Work | | Family | | Community | | Leisure | |
Career type	M	SD	M	SD	M	SD	M	SD	M	SD
Ascent N = 57	3.19	.58	3.23	.60	3.18	.81	1.90	.82	2.42	.78
Horizontal N = 58	2.74	.76	2.89	.74	3.17	.86	1.97	.92	2.38	.90
F (1,111)	12.74*		6.94*		.01		.19		.07	

* p = 0.01

Beyond the correspondence between Driver's career patterns and ours, it ought to be noted that similarity is not identity. Driver mainly focuses on the career process, whereas we link the process to its result from the perspective of achieving the realization of life aspirations. In this sense "stability" or "variability" and "autonomy" characterize a process, but not the content of an achieved end-state. The question is: To what stable or autonomous situation does the person aspire? Apart from this, Driver's patterns are revealed post hoc. They cannot serve for prediction purposes for time intervals of 10, 20, or 30 years ahead. This is precisely one of the important reasons for elaborating a career typology, which should be a reliable auxiliary tool in assisting people in realizing their life aspirations.

Let us turn now to the problem of *career type prediction*. In order to predict the dichotomous career pattern, a normalized ascent score is computed using a C scale with a 5-unit range for every component variable. This procedure refers obtained scores to a common scale that is related to the normal distribution (Guilford and Fruchter, 1973). It was decided to use a rough 5-unit range in view of the fact that these scores had to be used for predictions of events far distant in time.

Each of the five variables of the career-ascent score yields a normalized score on a 5-point scale. To compute the person's general ascent score, the partial scores of the variables are simply added. Theoretically the ascent score could be between 0 and 25. Practically it ranges in most samples between 10 and 23. When plotting these scores against the career events of the follow-up samples, it became evident that upward career mobility (the ascent) decreased with the decrease of the ascent score, and under 16 became a rare event. Thus, generally careers of individuals with scores up to 15 are horizontally oriented, while from

16 upward there is a real possibility of ascent and its possibility increases with the ascent score.

In interpreting the ascent score, special attention has to be given to the fact that it does not express only a mere orientation. It is a prediction score of career events based on the presence of the necessary ingredients to achieve career advancement. The ingredients include those ensuring competence on the job: vocational aptitudes, job involvement, attitudes toward work and authority figures at the place of work, and occupational knowledge. It follows that a high ascent score indicates not only the probability of a strong orientation towards vocational upward mobility, but also the probability of attaining it and, *eo ipso*, the degree of readiness to cope with the intervening vocational problems. *Mutatis mutandis*, the same applies in certain limits to scores under 16. For such subjects hierarchical upward mobility is improbable, not because any of them definitely do not want promotions, but they are unlikely to achieve them; and the probability decreases with the decrease in the ascent score, which signifies lower levels of ingredients ensuring coping with vocational problems (aptitudes, involvement, etc.). There is no identity between lack of ascent chances and horizontal competence on the job at specific scores, yet for overall comparisons one ascent score is preferable to two overlapping measurements of ascent and horizontality.

When the means of the normalized variable scores were compared after the 5 year follow-up, it became clear that no single variable significantly differentiated between the group with promotions and the group without. However, when the scores were aggregated, the difference became significant at the $p = 0.01$ level (see Table 7.8).

After five more years there was a slight erosion in the results. The group with promotions comprised only 30 percent of all sample members who could be located; nevertheless, the comparison of the group ascent profile gave a difference of $t = 2.20$ significant at $p = 0.03$ (Krau, 1977a).

One could possibly ask what happens further, since a career is longer than ten years. One could also wonder whether these results also apply to higher-order occupations such as professions. In order to answer these questions a retrospective inquiry was performed with 40 engineers having seniority between 25 and 40 years. They were asked to record all significant events of their work biography (promotions, more important assignments, moving to more important locations, important salary rises, etc.). It appeared that 72 percent of them continued the trends that appeared during the first seven years in production (Krau, 1977a).

The data obtained in the follow-up studies permit the elaboration of a **model for the prediction of self-realization through vocational careers**. It involves the determination of:

1. The person's type of self-realization aspiration (in a vocational activity, in work concomitants, in a nonvocational life area).

1.1 The content aspects of aspirations in groups II and III (what kind of concomitants, what life area).

2. The individual's career ingredient variables in the light of compensation possibilities, the final measures expressed in standard scores.

3. The type of career to which the individual belongs (ascent or horizontal) by computing the career ascent score.

4. The chances for implementing aspirations, the probabilities for career stability and changes.

The probability of aspirational implementation is related to the success probabilities of each ascent score. However, the latter has to be referred to the special requirements and conditions existing in each vocation and formulated for every career position. If we designate these requirements by Q and the person's abilities, skills, and attitudes by A, S, and T then the formula of career success will include the cumulated conditioned probability of all these variables:

$$P = \{(A + S + T) \mid Q\}$$

Table 7.8
Means of Progressively Cumulated Normalized Scores in Persons with and without Hierarchical Promotions

	1	2	3	4	5	
Sample group	Knowledge in technology	Vocational abilities	Promotional aspiration and attitudes towards supervisor	Initial adjustment to the job	Ascent qualities of social background	Cumulated standard deviation
	1	1+2	1+2+3	1+2+3+4	1+2+3+4+5	
Persons with hierarchical promotions	3.57	6.71	9.71	13.10	17.28*	0.74
Persons without hierarchical promotions	2.60	5.53	8.22	11.10	13.92	3.05
t-test between cumulated scores	0.49	1.38	1.65 $p = 0.10$	2.12 $p = 0.05$	2.89 $p = 0.01$	

* Value inversion to fit the sense of this variable in the ascent career (see text).

Table 7.9
Frequency Distribution of Ascent Scores in People Having Ascent and
Horizontal Careers (N = 166)

Ascent Scores	Frequency Distribution		Probability of Ascent versus Horizontal Careers
	Ascent Careers	Horizontal Careers	
	N = 58	N = 108	
7			
8		4%	
9			
10		12%	
11			
12			
13		67.5%	
14			
15	4%		1 : 3
16	12%		1 : 1
17		12%	4 : 1
18			
19	67.5%	4%	15 : 1
20			
21	12%		
22	4%		
23			

It will be remembered that the measurement of career ingredients is already occupationally specific, satisfying the requirement of conditioning by Q. Therefore, the above formula may be replaced by the computation of the individual's ascent score and the probability of occupational and social vertical mobility attached to it. The latter is different at the various scores of the scale. Table 7.9 presents the distribution of horizontal and ascent career scores in the two samples of the 10-year follow-up. It can be seen that while scores above 20 belong only to ascent careers, there is a "twilight zone" between the scores of 15 and 19. The dispersion of horizontal careers is wider than that of ascent careers. This means that at an ascent score of 18 there is a probability of 4:1 for an ascent career, but also a 20 percent probability that the person will not have a career of vertical mobility. At a score of 16 the chances are 50 percent. However, there is a need to enter a correction for the prediction error inherent in the method. In the empirical follow-up of our samples the prediction error amounted to 7% for a 1-year period, 13% for a 5-year prediction, and 22% for a 10-year prediction. These errors designated incongruence, which is evenly distributed between the two career types; therefore, the prediction error, chosen in accordance with the time interval for which a prediction is desired, should be divided by 2 and the resulting number subtracted from the computed career achievement probability.

The relatively high predictive validities should not astonish one. In several investigations McCrae and Costa (1990) attested to very high stability coefficients of self-report measures of personality, especially in adults, even over time intervals of 30 years. In another study McCrae (1993) concluded that individual change scores appeared to be largely errors of measurement or due to psychiatric episodes. On the "objective side" of predicting behavior on the job, Bartram (1993) has recently drawn attention to the fact that predictive studies have greater validity for the assessment of job satisfactoriness than concurrent selection testing, because in time people learn what behaviors are required of them. Bartram (1993) states that in this context the key role belongs to personality variables that command self-presentation. Thus, the possibility of a high validity in predicting careers rests, first, on the stability of the self-image and the end-state image of self-realization over time and, second, on the gradual improvement of self-presentation in a given framework. However, the latter phenomenon heavily draws on the motivational variable, and it may act in the opposite direction too. It all depends on whether people feel that they are on the right track for their self-realization. The longer the predicted time interval, the greater the chances are for negative judgments to be made and changes to occur in attitudes toward the job and in behavior. Therefore, predictive validity in the judgment of careers decreases over longer time spans.

In order to predict a particular career advancement, the general ascent probability $P\{V\}$, where V designates ascent, has to be completed by adding or subtracting the probability of a particular promotion P_1, conditioned by its specific requirements. The new formula must comprise the specific variables necessary to satisfy the condition Q:

$$P\{V\} \pm P_1 \{(A_1 + S_1 + T_1) \mid Q_1\}$$

If all intermediate steps leading to the desired end-state of self-realization were already known, together with the requirements, then the predictive career formula would merely comprise the total probabilities of all the steps leading to the desired objective. However, the general ascent probability is an approx-

Figure 7.4
A Partial Graph of Technological-Administrative Careers

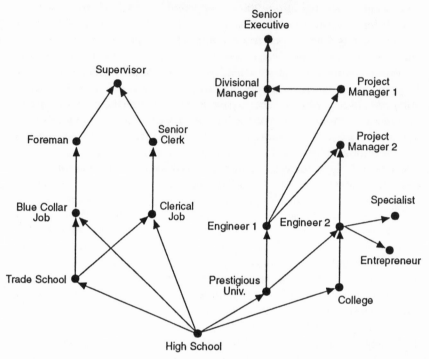

imation of the sum of partial probabilities of advancing through a set of career steps that are not yet known in detail.

It follows that in order to evaluate the chances for a desired end-state of self-realization, it is necessary to assess the probability of every step leading to it, since the latter is the result of a career development process and usually not one single lucky strike: to prepare this calculation one will have first to sketch the envisaged career path. This can be done in the form of a graph that presents all alternatives that lead away from the career start, as well as those leading to the desired end position (see Figure 7.4). Let us consider that somebody aspires to become a CEO. He must ask himself not only whether he has the aptitudes for leading a big organization but also whether he has all the skills and traits for successfully coping with the intermediate steps. In large American industrial organizations CEOs usually were formerly successful divisional managers, and still earlier they had been high-performing creative production engineers, economists, or marketing specialists. A high percentage of them graduated from prestigious universities. It is clear that these three steps of the CEO career ladder ask for different abilities, skills, and personality characteristics. The final probability of attaining the aspired end-state of self-realization is the resultant probability of a graph in which each career position enters the probability of moving to the next step into the combined probability of the graph.

Figure 7.4 presents a career graph with a rough sampling of possibilities open to people with high school studies. The position may lead to ascent or horizontal careers *in specific paths*. Each career position opens some possibilities and closes others. The individual who entered a job without going to college may also have promotions, but only in the narrow field of his path. The same holds for someone who entered the position of Engineer$_2$. He may become a successful entrepreneur or be promoted to Project Manager (for smaller projects), but he has virtually no chances of becoming a senior executive. His chances are for a horizontal career, as are those of the blue-collar worker and of the holder of a clerical job. If we know the requirements for each position in the career path and the personal characteristics of the subject, we may compute the concrete probabilities and predict their career achievement.

In order to assess the paths of self-realization in people aspiring to work concomitants of money, prestige, and power, the career graph will have to outline the paths leading from the individual's career start to positions that entail such concomitants. In this case the condition variables of abilities and skills (including social skills) will be related to the probabilities of obtaining superior positions in the hierarchy of material comfort and peer consideration.

Usually every career graph has prolongations in the direction of extravocational activities. They are of growing importance for persons having aspirations not linked to the vocational domain. The graph of extravocational activities consists of community activity, courtship experiences, the foundation of a family, child rearing, travelling and hiking, amusements, and congenial social relationships.

Figure 7.5 presents such a graph comprising the variables of Family, Children, Hobby, Amusement, Community Work. Its peculiarity is that it can be entered at each position (peak) and interrupted at any other peak, as there is no obligation to cross all the paths. It does not have the rigidity of a career graph, and the paths are not exclusive: From each peak it is possible to move to any other one.

The problem is the linkage between the graph of extravocational life activities and the career graph. People used to need both. Even those who see their self-realization in avocational activities usually need work in order to provide for their subsistence. As for the rest, save for extreme cases of workaholics, everyone has some form of extravocational life. The latter definitely influences the person's vocational decisions, his vocational path. Mathematically the combination of the two graphs is a Cartesian product.

The difficulty is to predict the moment in which a vocational career is seriously influenced by extravocational activities and the direction in which this influence will develop. Personality tests may help to clarify this point.

It is possible to improve career predictions further by forecasting stability versus turnover in occupations and organizations. From the already-described longitudinal follow-up of 110 lathe operators and 479 job leavers from chemical

Figure 7.5
A Graph of Avocational Activities

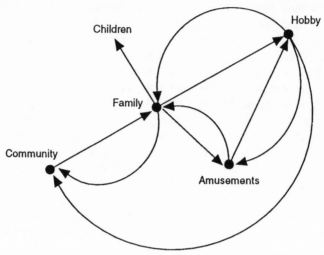

plants, it could be demonstrated that job quitting is a career decision depending upon career type, career stage, and the characteristics of the organization from a career policy point of view (Krau, 1981b). Using this last characteristic as a dummy variable, organizations may be divided into "open" and "inert or closed." In the former, every employee out of seven has a fair chance to get promoted within a 5-year span. In promotionally closed organizations the chances for career advancement are virtually nonexistent as a result of an unceasing policy of retrenchment or of filling vacancies with outside candidates. As it happened, our lathe operators worked in two such enterprises, the one open, the other "inert," although both belonged to the same industrial branch of machine-tool building.

We remind that of the 110 subjects 71 belonged to the horizontal career type and 39 to the ascent type. After eight years of follow-up, 53 subjects had left their places of work. To assert the interaction of career type (expressed through the height of ascent scores) and promotional openness of the organizations (open vs. inert systems), a two-factor ANOVA was performed with job leaving as the dependent variable (see Table 7.10).

The table shows a most significant influence on turnover on the part of the two factors taken separately and by their joint action. Computing the eta coefficient measuring the strength of effect the independent variables have on the dependent one, the two factors together account with certainty for up to 39 percent of the total variance of the phenomenon. However, one should take a closer look also at the interaction of levels of ascent scores with the situational system factor. In Figure 7.6 ascent scores of turnover are plotted against this background.

To interpret these figures we must recall that scores between 10 and 15 char-

Table 7.10

**Two-Way ANOVA of Career Type and Promotional Openness of the
Organizations with Turnover as Dependent Variable**

Source of variance	Sum of squares	DF	Mean square	F	Significance of F
Career type*	2.69	3	0.89	4.47	0.01
Promotional openness of organizations	4.36	1	4.36	21.9	0.001
Joint action of factors	7.30	7	1.04	5.22	0.001
Residual variance	20.30	102	0.199		
Total variance	27.60	109	0.25		

*With a high and low level for each career type.

Reprinted with permission. Courtesy of *Personnel Psychology.*

acterize horizontal careers. If we first look at the score group between 14 and 17, where horizontal leaving can be compared with ascent leaving in both categories of systems, we see that the turnover of capable "horizontal" employees (scores 14–15) is twice as high in companies with few promotional possibilities ("inert systems") when compared with the number of leavers from the same category in open systems. In the case of less-capable horizontal employees (scores 10–13), the situation reverses itself; the very poor men leave open systems but remain in a somewhat greater proportion in inert ones.

At ascent scores of the upward-mobile career pattern, the case becomes reversed. The best workers (scores 18–20), who will not stay in inert systems but will leave them, will leave open systems to a far lesser degree. In relation to the poorer ascent employees (scores 16–17), the phenomenon seen in the analysis of horizontal careers repeats itself; they leave open organizations in a far greater proportion compared to their leaving of inert organizations.

In a system with few promotional possibilities the upward-mobile persons will attain the positions that in open organization are occupied by horizontally developing careers. This causes individuals from the latter category who have somewhat greater abilities (and/or believe that they are very capable) to leave the system. Paradoxically, the turnover rate of the upward mobile is in such systems somewhat lower. In this case, upward-mobile leavers will be mainly among the best workers with the highest ascent scores and high self-assertion, who refuse to compromise over their ascent aspirations and to accept vicarious arrangements.

In organizations with real promotional possibilities, these are offered to the

Figure 7.6
Leaver Category Percentage of Each Career Type from the Two Types of Organizations (see explanations in text)

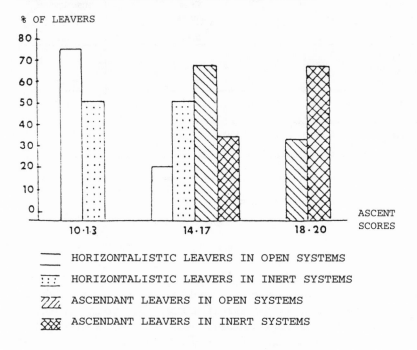

LEAVER CATEGORY PERCENTAGE FOR EACH SYSTEM

— HORIZONTALISTIC LEAVERS IN OPEN SYSTEMS
∷∷ HORIZONTALISTIC LEAVERS IN INERT SYSTEMS
⧄⧄ ASCENDANT LEAVERS IN OPEN SYSTEMS
⊠⊠ ASCENDANT LEAVERS IN INERT SYSTEMS

most capable workers who strive for promotions. Persons who are behind them in abilities have little chance for advancement. If they are ascent oriented, they will desire promotions; but as they cannot get them, they will prefer to leave the company. They feel better in organizations where the scantiness of promotional possibilities may be used to cover their lack of aptitude and does not continuously remind them of their failure.

In taking the decision of staying at a job or leaving it, the two factors that have been considered combine with the person's family and community responsibilities. They put pressure on the person to see his current status and intentions in the perspective of his life aspirations.

At this point it will be objected that in a time of retrenchments in organizations all predictive career computations, especially those regarding stability in organizations, seem entirely irrelevant. However, a more attentive look will show that such a conclusion is unfounded. Throughout this book the vocational career is presented as a tool for achieving self-realization, whatever its objectives may be. In this respect nothing changes, because people will always have aspirations for self-realization, and work (i.e., careers) will continue to provide the means for achieving them. Within the new economic pattern predictions are not easier, but neither are they more difficult. One will have to map the new career, graphing positions of possible changes and transitions and computing the achievement probabilities as indicated. The advantages of such a procedure lie in the mental and emotional preparation for changes while preserving the general aim.

Planning for the fulfillment of life aspirations is a necessity. As a matter of fact, by the end of adolescence, the premises of both career planning and prediction are construed already in the end-state image of self-realization. The task is to make this image more explicit and its implementation a conscious, goal-oriented process. This involves the need to consider the intermediary steps, each of which is instrumental to the fulfillment of self-realization aspirations. All career steps must be prepared through acquaintance with the task, autonomous goal setting, and preparation for implementation. These are the consecutive stages of action on the molecular level, but in addition there is also a need to see the general picture and to ensure that each career step is integrated into the planned general career path. Becoming aware of the probabilities of obtaining the different career positions will ensure a better utilization of potential, time, and energy by avoiding dead-end avenues and the fret and struggle for positions for which the chances are nil.

Finally, the prediction and planning of careers should also be a component of sound organizational policy. In a recent work (Globerson and Krau, 1993) it has been proven that the failure of large Israeli organizations to plan for the career of their staff causes mid-level managers with the highest qualifications to leave and settle in small organizations where they have more autonomy and a greater say in decision making. It is understood that organizational career planning has to be extended to all employees and not just to managers. The reported investigation on employee turnover has shown that organizations with a faulty career policy or no career policy at all remain, in the long run, with the poorest employees.

Planning for employee careers on the basis of predicting their career paths will enable the organization to rationalize the investment in its human assets. It teaches the organization in whom to invest and how, in order to maximize the self-realization of its employees, which in turn maximally benefits the employer.

8

What Went Wrong and Why? The Pathology of Career Adjustment and Self-Realization

In his pervasive analysis of deviant behavior, Merton (1957) sees its causal linkage in the anomie-producing contradiction between society's culture inciting the individual to see certain achievements and the existing social structure precluding such achievements in people who belong to an inferior socioeconomic level. Be the result of this contradiction overconformism, retreatism, or revolt, from our point of view the common denominator of people with socially deviant behavior is that they have a problem, as they cannot adjust their aspirations to the socially sanctioned way of realization. They are maladjusted, and they feel that way.

Generally, a social criterion is used in order to define maladjustment. The UNESCO definition refers to the individual's incapacity to assume the tasks, the statuses, and the roles proposed by society. Emphasizing this aspect, Mury (1965) concludes that maladjustment is not an internal state of the person, but a relationship of inferiority vis-à-vis the requirements of his environment. He writes, ''The individual who in normal housing conditions, lives up to a satisfactory life experience, will appear incapable of coping with the pressure put on him in a shanty town. Finally, the maladjusted individual acquires the behaviors put forward and forced upon him by society, and then the same society holds them against him'' (Mury, 1965).

This point of view is unilateral. Many years ago Allport (1937) had already pointed out that the personality is more than the subjective side of culture. Nevertheless, in each case of maladjustment the individual is in a position of inferiority vis-à-vis the requirements of his social environment, or at least he feels he is. On the other hand, not every relationship of inferiority to social demands means maladjustment. We have argued that the yardstick of self-realization assessment is in the norms of the reference group and not the membership group. Many a fighter against unjust régimes is jailed or even put to death but does not feel maladjusted, as he is sure of the approval of his reference group, the other freedom fighters.

Although the social and economic weakness of the lower social strata facilitates the contradiction between culturally valued aims and the possibility of achieving them, the causal texture of the maladjustment phenomenon may mainly reside within the person as a contradiction between an unarticulated end-state image of self-realization and the necessity for a planned advancement toward the aims it contains and the contradiction between these aims and the existing skill coverage.

In literature, the maladjustment problem is widely discussed in the definition of mental illness, which is usually related to the deviation of behavior from situational requirements in the different areas (vocational, social, partnership). Müller-Suur (cf. Schwarz, Weise, and Thom, 1971) speaks of the "true individual norm" (eigentliche Individualnorm), which comprises the interaction of the individual's needs and striving with collective norms. Mental illness would be the result of unsuccessful endeavors to reach a satisfactory accommodation.

Two things should be added to this definition. First, it does not mention that the failure of strivings and need gratifications causes suffering. This is astonishing in view of the wide impact of Selye's (1956) well-known book on the stress of life. Second, even suffering and the lack of adaptation to social norms does not mean mental illness yet. Szasz (1960) pointed out that mental illness is a myth; the concept functions as a disguise; it provides an impersonal thing (an illness) as an explanation for problems in living. What we do have are problems in living, whether these be biologic, economic, political, or sociopsychological. They originate in people's failure to satisfy the cherished aspirations of their lives.

The process of life-sense fulfillment starts with the crystallization of the end-state image of self-realization, which is the point where also the pathology of self-realization takes its start. The faulty end-state image is not the ultimate cause of the distortions in the whole self-realization process, but it is an important link in the chain.

According to the classification of end-state images of self-realization presented in this book, a first group sees their fulfillment in a well-defined vocational activity. Nonetheless, the image has to be holistic, containing also elements from other life areas, in order to allow the person to live a full and satisfied life. Tinsley and Tinsley (1988) have demonstrated that leisure is not the negation of work but has an independent value of satisfying basic psychological needs such as companionship, self-expression, security, and power. Important as work may be, it cannot satisfy all human needs. Persons whose self-realization image refers only to work find themselves in a double trap: the feeling of not having lived, of having lost the amenities of life, and a possible total crumbling should obstacles and problems materialize in their work careers. Here is the story of such a case out of 54 maladjusted persons interviewed in Israel between the years 1982 and 1984.

Y., aged 53, asked for counseling because of an oppressing feeling that his life was incomplete and that he had lost his way. **Y.** immigrated to Israel from Eastern Europe. He was then 25 and had a diploma for mechanical engineering. Working in this field was his dream, and nothing else was really important to him. He had left his country of origin because he thought he would find better work opportunities in Israel. He was married, but his wife was a homemaker because he felt that only his work was important in the family and that his wife had to provide the conditions for him to devote all his time to his career. In Israel he was employed in a company working on projects in machine building. After working several years at minor tasks and being under observation all the time, he was finally appointed head of a team. As the years went by he became well established in the company and at the time of the interview he had a good salary and a comfortable house, and his two children had successfully finished university studies. Still, he felt that all had gone astray.

His problem started as he became aware that he lagged behind the younger engineers in knowledge. In order to cope with this problem he tried to invest more time in reading technical literature and to work longer hours. However, **Y.** felt that because of his age he was incapable of closing the gap. This caused him frequently to lose his temper and be less tolerant with his coworkers and his family. They responded in the same way, and the relationships with his environment became troubled. His children accused him of never spending enough time with them, and they were disinclined to accept his advice and opinions, especially his son who was an engineer too and gave his father to understand that he surpassed him in professional knowledge. **Y.** asked himself whether these had been his life aspirations, and if so, was that all there was to it? Had it been worthwhile to be solely devoted to his career all these years? He felt trapped and sensed that he had been unfair to his family. Perhaps he had not been fair to himself either, because life had slipped away from him.

It clearly appears that life aspirations have to be wholesome and should include all areas of life for the person to feel fulfilled. However, they must also include work, in a well-defined vocation, or at least accept it and adjust to it even if the individual's main aspirations are in another domain.

It will be remembered that the second type of self-realization end-state images focused on work concomitants such as high income and social status, while the area of vocational activity by which these aims were to be achieved was of little importance. For the life success of these persons it is essential that the link of concomitants to *work* be consciously acknowledged and included in the self-realization image. If this does not happen, life aims are cut off from the ways and means that persons have to use in order to achieve their aspirations. Concomitants are linked to work and energy investments, but the maladjustment-prone reject the latter as not part of their self-realization image. The same happens with some people who aspire to an interesting work activity but unilaterally stress the "interest," which becomes a kind of concomitant aspiration being severed from a specified vocational activity. The content of a vocational activity as a life aspiration is the privilege of the formerly discussed first group, and for them "interesting" is the pursuit of their chosen vocation in itself. They do not need artificially constructed interesting episodes to gain satisfaction. The following two cases illustrate what has been said.

R. asked the employment office of his town for financial assistance because the enterprise where he worked as a driver was retrenching and he had received a notification that his employment was being terminated. He was aged 31, was married, and had five children. His father had an important job in an industrial plant, but even so they lived on a higher level than his salary permitted. His mother therefore worked as a cleaning woman, in another town lest their friends and neighbors would find out. **R.** never dreamed of a specific occupation. He always wanted a lot of money. He told the interviewer that as a child, when he saw people counting money he would sit by their side and imitate them. However, the thought of what he would have to do to have lots of money was never in his mind. He wanted to drop out from school after finishing seven grades, but at the insistence of his father he continued two more years in a trade school, where he learned the locksmith trade. During his military service he learned driving, and after being discharged from the army he was employed as an industrial worker but quit because he was not satisfied with the pay he received. He got a job as a truck driver and left for the same reason. He worked several years as a construction worker for his father-in-law, who promised to buy him a flat, but left this employment immediately after he received the flat and again started a job as a truck driver in a company where the employer allowed him to use the truck after working hours for private business. It was from this company that he was now being discharged. Although he desperately needed a job to provide for his five children, he refused to take one at the same level and lived on unemployment payments. He told the interviewer that he wanted to find "something good." Asked what he intended to do, he replied, "I do not know. I only know what I do not want to do." He added that he came to the employment office only because this was the procedure to receive unemployment pay.

Here is another case from a higher socioeconomic level. **C.**, aged 30, was already unemployed one year. He was single. His parents belonged to the upper middle class with a warm relationship between the members of the family. **C.** was an excellent student in high school and then at university, where he finished graduate studies in social sciences without receiving a diploma for any practical job. Indeed, he did not aspire to working in any definite occupation, but he wanted his work to be interesting and nonroutine, offering the possibility of autonomy and self-development. He did not aspire to organizational advancement or stability in a job. After finishing his studies he held seven jobs: He started as an instructor at a student home and left because of the strain he felt when the work became routine and boring. He then got a job as a tutor of children with learning difficulties. At the end of the school year this job also came to an end, and he was employed in a clerical job in one of the institutes of a university. After two years this job too made him feel bored, so he left and became an aide to the chief of a department in a governmental agency. The work was interesting, demanding responsibility and creativity. He described his job termination as being due to a bureaucratic error in the nomination procedure. From here he went on to be in charge of a seminar in the police force, a common project of the police and the Ministry of Education. He described the work as interesting, but left following a divergence of opinion on substantive matters with his superior. The same Ministry of Education gave him the opportunity to work on another project at a workers' club. This job was again described by him as being interesting, but after two years it again appeared routine and boring. His last job was as a secretary to an organization of volunteers, with responsibility and autonomy, but after two years he quit, charging that the work had become boring and routine. Since then he has had some part-time jobs in educational projects, but in fact he is unemployed and has had to put up with a drastic decrease in his living standard. However, he refuses to compromise his aspirations for "interesting work." Such is the story of a career in which the regulating end-state image of self-realization in interesting work superemphasizes the "interesting" and downgrades the work.

Problems may arise also with the third type of end-state images, those that refer to areas other than work. First of all, here too the area of aspiration must be defined. You cannot realize anything if you do not know what it is that you want. Some people run all the time after novelty and excitement. This is not an area or life activity that permits a lasting motivation and satisfaction because every novelty wears off and the person feels nothing but emptiness instead of self-realization. Second, although for these people work is not a condition for self-realization, they must not reject it; should it become necessary for them to work, they have to adjust to their jobs. Self-realization functions in the framework of adjustment, and maladjustment at one's job inevitably causes psychological problems, which then spread to other life areas. The same happens if the person miscomprehends his true life aims and forces himself, or allows others to force him, into a life career aiming at high achievements in a definite vocational area.

N., a woman, aged 29, from a rural background, unmarried with a neglected physical appearance, worked as a clerk in a shop in one of the squalid quarters of Tel-Aviv. She defined her life aspirations as getting married and being a housewife. After finishing high school she was admitted as a student to the department of economics at a university but left in the fourth semester because the studies did not interest her and she was not able to develop social relationships with her colleagues. She worked in her father's vegetable shop and then asked for vocational guidance in one of the big institutes in the country. They recommended that she work as an x-ray technician, but she did not get the job and started an evening course in accountancy while continuing to work in the vegetable shop. Before finishing the course N. again quit, justifying her decision with a lack of interest in the subject and in the people who participated in the course. Since then, for three years she had been working in her present position as a shop clerk. She was very frustrated and hated the job but did not have the courage to leave. She was separated from her parents, her financial situation was bad, and she refused to attend to her physical appearance, which scared off all possible suitors.

S. was an unmarried woman, aged 30. Her family belonged to the upper middle class and came from the United States. In high school she was rather a poor student, but she finished her studies and got a college degree in sociology. She described her life aspiration as "hedonist," a life of pleasure that was in her own words, more important than status or career. For her it was important to be independent and to have the opportunity to do what she liked. She had no specific occupational interests but wanted whatever she did to be interesting. Job stability, seniority, and organizational affiliation were not important to her. For several months she worked as a chambermaid in a hostel out of curiosity. She then learned photography and had a job as a photographer for the police. However, other areas attracted her curiosity, and she decided that she did not want to be a photographer; for one-and-a-half years she worked at the Defense Ministry and then left because she decided that she wanted to study, but instead she took a temporary job at a museum exhibition. She wanted to continue working there but was refused as she did not have the necessary qualifications. During the summer months she sold paper dragons, then got a job being in charge of the "children's city" park in Tel-Aviv. The project came to an end after nine months, and she decided she did not want to work for the municipality for fear of losing her autonomy. After being unemployed for three months she got a job as a group animator and remained there one-and-a-half years, but then she felt the work was becoming routine. She quit and looked for something new. Apart from this, she could have continued at her job only with a qualification in psychology, but she did not want to study for three more years. She was offered an educational job in the harbor of Ashdod and accepted "until I could figure out what I wanted to do." When she again felt that the job was becoming routine and tedious, she quit. Since then she had been unemployed for one year and had ceased looking for employment because she did not know what she wanted to do. From time to time she answered newspaper ads for temporary jobs in order to support herself. Her financial situation was quite bad, and she had lost much of the confidence that characterized her previously. The prognosis of the case was also anything but optimistic if she would not get thorough psychological assistance.

In answering the question of what went wrong in all these cases, we shall first have to refer to the inappropriately crystallized image of self-realization. This latter stands in the way of correctly resolving the task of realizing the person's aspirations. Yet failure has a negative influence on the person's aspirational system and coping style. This will cause even more severe failure, and so the maladjustment spiral goes on, finally leading to social inadaptation and/

or mental health impairment. The literature has partly described this occurrence as self-fulfilling prophecies (Jones, 1977) and failure neuroses (Mâle, 1966). We are entitled therefore to speak of a **psychopathology of the process of career development**.

We put forward three theses characterizing the psychopathology of the process of career development:

1. Normal and pathologic behavior are meant to cope with problem situations. The difference lies in the social adaptive value of these behaviors. Maladjustment does not follow from the individual's inability to cope with the minimal social requirements but with the ones considered minimal by him.

2. Maladjustment is a devolutionary, spiral-like process starting with superficial, mild forms of suffering—feelings of dissatisfaction and frustration—and it progresses to more severe forms where satisfactory functioning is hampered. Usually job behavior is the first to be affected. This is because the leading human activity is vocational, which puts strain on energy reserves and often has an imposed character both with regard to the nature of work and the social relationships involved. Moreover, it is an overt and publicly exposed activity and less protected. Hence, any disturbance is likely to grow as a problem of urgency for which a solution must be found.

The maladjustment spiral can be halted and normal functioning restored, but only if the external problem that triggered the entire process is solved. If this does not happen, the devolutionary process will continue with an aggravation of dysthymic and psychopathic disturbances.

3. Personality disturbances are mobile and have a certain fluidity between one another as dysthymia and characteropathy (psychopathy) mingle. In the different phases of the devolutionary process, one of them appears as the dominant disturbance. It should be added that when speaking of disturbances, reference is made only to psychogenetic disorders, that is, those that are not caused by primary substratum damage (psychoses, certain severe psychopathies).

The maladaptive spiral is triggered off by the incongruence between what the person claims to be rightfully entitled to and the environmental offer, and as long as the incongruence lasts the spiral will develop and maladjustment will grow worse and worse. It will spill over to other life areas and finally cause psychosomatic diseases. This last aspect indicates that what may be called "career pathology" is a part of a general pathology of the person, including psychological (mental and emotional) and somatic components.

These theses are in line with experimental facts known from the literature. After submitting the symptoms of 600 patients to a factor analysis, Phillips (1968) concluded that they cluster around three groups of factors: turning against oneself (self-depreciative ideas, depression, insomnia, psychosomatic illnesses), turning against others (aggressiveness, self-indulgent socially disapproved behaviors, anger), and avoidance of others (suspicion, withdrawal, daydreaming). The first and the third categories of disturbances coincide with what Eysenck and Rachman (1968) termed dysthymic disturbances; the second category refers to psychopathies, what American authors used to call sociopathic disturbances and the German psychiatric school, moral debility. The disturbances of both these types are subject to evolution. Psychopathy is a rather severe state that evolved from behavior disorders or character disorders. The genuine psycho-pathic personality, as described by Hare (1970), seems to have a hereditary basis. Dysthymic disturbances are expressed in neuroticism, but here too physiological predispositions are usually present as a weakness of the nervous system. Neu-roticism is not a localized nervous disorder. It is defined by Janet as a "down-fall" of the individual's mental energy (tension psychique). In people with high neuroticism, Larsen (1992) found a preferential negative information processing about the self, rumination, and high levels of retrospectively self-reported phys-ical illness. Nevertheless, the dysthymic maladjustment appears at external trau-matic influences only. Eysenck and Rachman (1968) ascribe it to traumatic events that are linked to anxious, maladaptive behaviors. Neutral situations be-come mentally linked to the traumatic ones, and the neurosis spreads.

In connecting the discussion of personality disturbances with the problem of maladjustment at the job, it is understood that its immediate cause is the subject's failure to acquire the necessary vocational skills and to use them ap-propriately. As for these skills, they refer to the already-discussed occupation-specific tasks and also to the general employability skills needed in a job (Herr, 1984; Bingham, 1986). Nevertheless, the acquisition of skills and their use is conditioned by motivational and instrumental career factors.

The already mentioned follow-up of 198 lathe-operators and 40 casters ap-prentices offered the possibility to observe in vivo the establishment and the evolution of the maladjustment process in 42 lathe men and 9 casters (Krau, 1974a). The judgment of adjustment was based on the criterion of exceeding the nominal salary, and it accounted for production results and attendance, com-bined with the evaluation of conduct vis-à-vis superiors and coworkers. In sub-jects who turned out to be maladjusted, a renewed comparison was performed with the tests administered at school entry: tests for vocational aptitudes, vo-cational interests, neuroticism, and the already-described projective personality test, which included the diagnosis of attitudes toward authority figures at the place of work. This comparison showed the following predictors of maladjust-ment: 19 apprentices had failed at the initial aptitude tests, 14 subjects had high scores on neuroticism, 16 had a negative attitude toward authority figures at the place of work. There were 2 subjects whose poor behavior on the job was not predictable with our measurements, a failure rate in prediction of 3.9 percent, which is highly acceptable.

As subjects moved toward maladjustment at school and later in production, their personality profiles showed characteristic deteriorations, that is, tended to reveal lower scores at some of the features measured. In literature this is gen-erally thought of social relationships only (Eysenck and Rachman, 1968). How-ever, the process of gradual deterioration of the individual's links with the outer world does not begin with social relationships. First, pecuniary value attachment seems to be affected, and it is the first to recover. Next follows the individual's reasonable adhesion and positive attitude to his vocation and workplace (an exaggerated vocational involvement is again a sign of disturbance, as it severs other social links). Only now, if unresolved problems persist, do social relationships become affected; and there is (an additional) negativization of attitudes towards authority figures. At this stage, the individual is not insane, but he is occupationally maladjusted, which is a clear caveat that declared insanity may follow if there is no help to solve the underlying problems. Such characteristics are shared in common by neurotics and psychopaths. Both lose links and attachments to values accepted by their social milieu. This shows that there is a single morbid process with common laws. Differences in outcome are due to the different conditions in which that process takes place, including here also constitutional peculiarities.

We traced maladjustment with its symptom formation in preadolescents and adolescents in school activities, in light physical work (turners), and under strong physical stress (casters). The status of these people was not so bad as to need internment in mental hospitals or in special institutions for reeducation, but it was serious enough to cause trouble in school and production.

In school, personality disorders appeared when requirements or a too-high aspiration level exceeded intellectual capacities. If no adequate measures were taken, a process started, mingling up neurotic and characteropathic symptoms, both of which were in response to the social situation stimuli.

Here is one case in support of the statement above: **G.**, 15 years old, attended a general school. A weak nervous system and low intellectual capacity continuously caused her school difficulties. She could hardly grasp the essentials of a lesson, and by the time she would arrive at school she would forget the content of what she had learned at home. At 12 years she developed various physical pains (head- and toothaches, giddiness, etc.) and some time afterwards a highly negativstic attitude towards school, with truancy, lying, and social misconduct. Generally, the girl was known for these conduct deficiencies and regarded as having character disorders. To bring the symptoms to recess, a complex psychological treatment was applied, aiming at the basic problem solution but providing also for a firm frame to fight the psychopathic disturbances (Krau, 1974b).

It appears that ordinarily one can speak of a predominance of neurotic or characteropathic symptoms rather than of a strict categorization. This predominance is situationally bound and changes if the situation with its problems is changing. In our dysthymic subjects at the trade school, neurotic manifestations had appeared earlier in childhood under the influence of an incorrect educational setting, mainly the absence of the father in family life. There already was a negativistic attitude of contempt, but directed only against their fathers and not transferred upon the school situation, which did not interfere with the individual's life habits and desires. At school they expressed various anxieties, defensiveness, and a tendency to avoid efforts. There was an exaggerated care about health and a low interest toward the occupation they were meant to enter. Nevertheless, their school record was pretty good, and one year after leaving school they were adjusted, although at limits, in the lathe trade. In the foundry, however, with its stern physical requirements, they failed; and only 20 percent of the subjects having high scores in neuroticism were able to adjust to their jobs. To the contrary, the characteropathic subjects were well adjusted as casters but astonishingly less so in the far more comfortable conditions of the lathe operators' job, where only 36 percent of the former apprentices with this disorder could adapt.

In their case histories the subjects with predominantly psychopathic features revealed a severe interference with their aspirations, for which somebody was blamed (parents, school). While some of them felt anxieties and aversions, the main symptom was an aggressive behavior. They had also little interest in the trade they learned and longed for a vocation like the military with opportunity to display great physical movement and aggression. School results were poor.

Obviously the reaction of neurotics under physical stress was due to a stimulus that their weak energy could not stand, while the hard working conditions of casters provided an aggression outlet for psychopaths in a way the lathe trade did not.

Although there may be some difference in the constitutional structure of the two categories of subjects, we want to underline here that in events disrupting life habits and images built up earlier, or in situations the subjects could not stand, there was a common response: In both cases quality and quantity of work output were poor and there were more or less severe infringements of plant discipline. Thus, apart from cases of substratum damage, there is no predetermined severage of neurotic and psychopathic disturbances functioning outside definite life situations. Under stress conditions, like those in the physically difficult caster trade, neuroticism turns into psychopathy. Such stress conditions are by no means merely physical. We witnessed the same phenomenon in school activities. Together with the drop in attachment toward school and the establishment of a negativistic attitude, behavior became psychopathologically tainted with lies, slandering, truancy, sex misdemeanor, and outbreaks of violence. Consequently, the experimental evidence does not support distinct lines of evolution for neurotics and psychopaths. Neither must rehabilitation work be separated for the two categories. Symptoms are not epiphenomena, but correspond to an inner reality of mental life based on personality modifications. The curing of anxiety alone does not, therefore, entail the disappearance of psychopathic manifestations that, once established, may function autonomously, as Allport's theory holds for human motivation in general (Allport, 1937).

We may conclude so far that the complexity of the personality structure involves the fluidity of its potential evolution in a dialectical relationship with life situations. Psychogenetic symptom formation is a gradual process taking place under environmental influence, and although it may be conditioned by hereditary factors, the latter are not determining so that the disturbances may evolve in either direction. Since this point was essential for our theory of the holistic and progressive development of maladjustment symptoms, we conducted research with 40 persons who asked for counseling (22 vocational and 18 clinical counselees) and 62 persons who did not, among them 42 students and 20 white-collar employees, all between 22 and 35 years of age, men and women in equal proportion (Krau, 1981c).

It was hypothesized that there would be differences in the status of the personality among these three groups, in their involvement with life problems and with their environment and also in coping with their anxieties and fears, which paralyze the behaviors aiming at goal realization. All subjects were given Krau's projective personality test (Meir and Krau, 1983). Counselees were given Woodworth's Psychoneurotic Inventory (after an adapted form by Laird) for the measurement of neuroticism, and vocational counselees were, in addition, administered ability tests (intelligence, clerical speed and concentration, general vocabulary, English language, and manual skills).

The results of the comparison of personality profiles appear in Table 8.1, and they show significant differences between the groups. People who did not ask for counseling are less extreme in their attitudes toward their vocation. Fewer among them reject it emotionally, but also fewer manifest extreme enthusiasm, which also correlates with high neuroticism ($\varphi = 0.42$ significant at $p = 0.05$). The valuing of money is surprisingly lower in vocational counselees, which may indicate why they asked for counseling: They are supposed to settle down in an occupation but money does not interest them and neither does any vocational activity. The involvement with the social environment is significantly lower in clinical counselees, correlating with the larger percentage of high scores in neuroticism. However, the tendency for increased neuroticism already appears in vocational counselees, although the link is less certain. There is a manifest stepwise increase in disturbances through the group of vocational to the clinical counselees, as proved also by the increase in the incidence of high scores in neuroticism. Thus vocational counselees appear as a middle-of-the-road group between the "normal" situation of absence of deeper personality problems to their overt manifestation in people seeking clinical counseling.

These conclusions are statistical, and therefore it is not an absolute law that every individual asking for advice in matters of his vocational future has personality problems. In our sample 22.6 percent of the counselees actually needed more precise vocational information or the confirmation that they had the necessary ability coverage for their intended vocational choice. Some may see here deficiencies in the clarity of the self-image, a problem recently tackled by Vondracek (1992). It is important, however, that for more than 75 percent of the sample the vocational problem they presented to the counselor was a disguised expression of problems at the level of the personality.

It appears, therefore, that there is one single disadaptive process, the different stages of which became manifest in the job failure of lathe operators and casters and in the problems of vocational and clinical counselees. In lathe operators

Table 8.1

Differences in Personality Traits between People Who Did Not Ask for Counseling, Vocational and Clinical Counselees (in percentages)

Group	Extreme attitudes toward vocation	Valuing of money		Low tendency for thrift	Involvement with social environment		High Neuroticism
		High	Low		High	Low	
A. No need for counseling N = 62	30.6	40.4	19.2	7.9	37.0	29.0	30.8
B. Vocational Counselees N = 22	54.0	14.0	46.2	14.0	31.8	31.8	45.1
C. Clinical Counselees N = 18	60.0	27.3	33.3	45.0	27.0	44.0	63.0
Chi-square test A-B	2.70 P = .10	13.49 P = .001	6.18 P = .02	1.82	1.15	0.01	5.20 P = .07
A-C	5.41 P = .02	1.92	1.47	20.0 P = .001	3.89 P = .05	3.33 P = .07	5.86 P = .05
B-C	0.10	1.01	1.29	5.13 P = .03	0.67	2.70 P = .10	2.43

there was "only" an objective gap between their behavior and situational requirements; the vocational counselees already felt strain and inadequacy at the lowered performance but were still able to function; while in clinical counselees functioning was seriously impaired as the feeling of inadequacy grew in strength and maladjustment spread to most cherished areas of private life.

Maladjustment starts with the objective gap between behavioral performance and environmental requirements, while the individual by all means denies having a problem. In the framework of the experimental program with lathe operators, not only was counseling offered to them, but the trade-school headmaster and the plant managers obliged all unsatisfactory operators to undergo counseling. All of them were given lengthy counseling sessions, but none admitted having any problem, especially not with work activity. In the denial stage, traditional counseling has little effect, but then as the objectively persisting problem makes the situation worse, the person begins to feel strain and will then ask for *vocational* assistance. However, usually vocational problems are part of a general pathology of self-realization.

In most cases of vocational maladjustment the difficulties are not caused by an isolated problem in the area of vocational development but by one at the level of the personality. The proof may be found in that the vocational difficulties are paralleled by difficulties of the same nature in other life areas: a loafing around in jobs is matched by the same behavior in the person's love life or political affiliations. Maladjustment is not limited to an isolated area of life, and it hampers self-realization objectively and subjectively.

Between the years 1982 and 1984 we gathered 54 case histories of maladjustment, of which some have already been presented. The subjects, persons of both genders, were aged between 27 and 53 and belonged to various occupations. They asked for short vocational counseling or were referred for assessment to counselors by their employers as problem employees. In the counseling sessions their occupational history and family background were discussed in detail and then the subjects were administered Krau's projective personality test and the aforementioned form of Woodworth's Psychoneurotic Inventory.

This latter was presented as a health questionnaire. It comprised 11 questions such as, "Are you frequently afraid?" "Do you feel pains in some parts of your body?" "Do you have a detailed plan to achieve your aims?" The subjects were asked to rate the frequency or intensity of the contents asked in each question on a 10-point scale. The tester reversed the score of certain questions such as the one inquiring about planning (if the subject gave the score 8, meaning that he nearly always has a plan for achieving his aims, he would get a score of 2), and then summed up all the ratings into a single score of neuroticism.

The analysis of the coping behaviors in this sample and in that of lathe operators showed that (1) the link between neuroticism scores and maladjustment is not linear and that (2) in 58.5 percent of the cases neurotic symptoms were accompanied by characteropathic manifestations in behavior already apparent in the predictive tests and attesting to the fluidity of symptoms in the devolutionary process of maladjustment.

The following Neuroticism Scale was empirically validated vis-à-vis the behavioral coping styles of our various research samples comprising a total of 378 persons (lathe operators, casters, students, vocational and clinical counselees, maladjusted persons).

Category I (scores 8–15). These scores indicate the absence of neuroticism, a poised, mature self-analysis that is not afraid to admit occasional aches or fears. The behavior is definitely adjusted with mature problem solving.

Category II (scores 22–33). The person has or has had severe problems that caused neurotic episodes with some failures but has succeeded in compensating for his maladaptation. The behavior is one of resistance to maladjustment and of fighting to overcome the barriers to fulfillment of aspirations and to the deployment of a normal lifestyle. However, if these barriers persist, neuroticism increases and the person is aware of it. The prognosis for such a case is not good if the person has also characteropathic disturbances in the form of extreme negative attitudes toward authority figures at the place of work. These will inevitably cause problems, which in time will bring about an increase in neuroticism with all its consequences.

R.A., aged 36, was considered to be a beautiful woman by all who knew her. She was not married, worked in the training department of a big enterprise for electronic products, and took evening courses at the university. Neuroticism score: 30, Attitude score: 0, with the father characterized as well-mannered but not the dominant figure in the family. Her life aspirations centered around high social status and money.

After high school she took courses in modelling and in cosmetics and then worked in promoting cosmetic products. She was successful in her job but quarrelled with her boss about money and left. She lived in England for one year and then returned to Israel and again worked at another cosmetic firm in training sales personnel. Again she quarrelled with her superiors and had to leave. She had been working for three years at her present job but complained of lack of satisfaction and of quarrels with superiors and subordinates. She knew that soon she would leave her job, but was afraid that in the present tough economic situation it would be hard for her to find another suitable job. So far the behavior of **R.A.** was not explicitly maladjusted, but the script for what would happen was already "on the wall." She was still actively involved, fighting and resisting maladjustment, taking initiative, and studying, although she already felt deeply dissatisfied and anxious about the future. As a matter of fact, all her story was told by her test scores: attitude 0, with negative characterization of the father, high scores in self-assertion, sociability, and risk behavior with a high valuation of money.

It may be presumed that her negative attitudes, associated with a personality profile of high self-assertion and money value, would cause further quarrels with superiors, finding employment would be harder and harder, and then neuroticism would deepen and enter categories V and VI, with final apathy and a decreased work capacity. On the other hand, the increase in neuroticism into category V may be her great and last chance. It would make her aware that she had a problem, not only one of getting another job, and she may become receptive to psychological counseling.

Category III (scores 0–7). This category opens the series of maladjusted behaviors. Persons belonging to this category are not adjusted to their jobs but deny it emphatically when inquired. It is impossible not to feel pain, fear, or indigestion sometimes, and who so declares has a confrontational attitude of resistance and denial. Therefore, people with such scores usually also have negative attitudes toward their jobs and authority figures at the place of work. This was the case with two maladjusted individuals in our sample of lathe operators.

C., a lathe operator aged 20, had already had severe discipline problems in the trade school. His parents were divorced, and he characterized his father as a brutal person. In his job discipline problems of attendance and misdemeanor continued. His foreman asked for him to be sent for counseling, where he manifested the same attitude of confrontation. He declared he had no problems, and he did not feel any inadequacy. He contended that all problems rested with his superiors. At this point counseling had to be terminated. Later on he was discharged from his job.

Category IV (scores 16–21). This category actually constitutes a neurotic disadaptation. Objectively the person is not capable of living up to the requirements of his/her job, but emphatically denies it, which is the attitudinal linkage to the former category of maladjustment. Under the surface the feeling of inadequacy is already present, but at this moment there is enough energy left for the compensation of inadequacies, paradoxically conditioned by an increase in neuroticism (into Category II). Until such compensation does not occur, the person is unsatisfactory at the job.

N., aged 27, originated from a family with a lower-middle-class background. He described the relationship with his father as "correct" and had a normally positive attitude toward authority figures at the place of work. His neuroticism score was 21. He had excelled as a student in high school and in college, where he obtained a bachelor's degree in psychology. N. defined his life aspirations as having a model family and obtaining a Ph.D. degree and a senior administrative position. After receiving his B.A. degree he entered a junior position in a psychiatric hospital, where the work was interesting but the salary low. He left this job for a higher-paying one as a social worker in a destitute neighborhood. The work wore him down, and his superiors, who had no understanding of the strain of his work, fired him on the first occasion of retrenching. This was a severe blow for N., who was used to excellence in school, and also a severe blow financially as he had married a student colleague when he finished his studies.

In his personality profile the highest scores were in the valuing of money and impulsivity in behavior regarding money, with a low vocational interest and low sociability. His aspirations were contradictory in themselves. The emphasis was on concomitants, but paired with aspiration to a Ph.D. degree that required quite another order of preferences and quite another "instrumental" profile. These contradictions explained the strain he felt in his employment. He was not satisfactory at his job but denied it and felt under stress. It could be predicted that if the basic contradictions could not be solved, neuroticism would grow stronger as maladjustment deepened, and **N.** would find himself in one of the following categories in which objective failure at the job is paired with the lack of inner resources to fight the situation.

Category V (scores 34–48). Placement in this category marks a decompensation of the coping possibilities evinced in Category II (scores 22–33). The persistence of the external problem causes the maladjustment spiral to deepen, sweeping away the fragile coping balance. Nonetheless, the person does not give up yet. He still fights, but from a position of perceived inferiority, with little hope and a strong sense of inadequacy and maladjustment.

R.I., aged 28, unmarried, had a university bachelor's degree and was employed as a hospital nurse. She had a neuroticism score of 37 and a positive attitude toward authority figures. She hoped for a job in the department of internal medicine, but the only vacancy was in the surgical department. She was very upset. Her superior was extremely demanding and rigid, and loaded work on her beyond her capacity. Her relationships with coworkers were correct, but were bad with her supervisor. She wanted a transfer to another department, but without a recommendation from her supervisor nobody wanted her. She put all her energy into her work, but more and more she felt she could not cope. In the meantime the relationship with her parents also came to a breaking point, and she left the family home. In her personality profile a high regard for money and high self-assertion stood out. Her vocational interest was low, presumably as a result of what happened at her place of work. It has been already mentioned that neurotics become maladjusted when their workload is increased, and this decompensation stage is characterized by the beginning of despair. The person still fights, but inefficiently, and will give in more and more as neuroticism grows.

Category VI (scores 49 and over). Now the fight is over, the surrender and renouncement are complete, and the person enters a state of despair, in which apathy and withdrawal are the response to every problem. They no longer have the energy to take the initiative and change anything in their lives.

J., aged 31, was married and had a little daughter. He had been born to parents in their later years, who had survived the Holocaust but lost their families. They became acquainted in Israel after their emigration from Poland. Their attitude towards their son was loving but overprotective. **J.** had failed in his high school studies and entered a trade school for mechanical operators. He did not finish and tried his luck at a school for technicians, but dropped out after one year. Nevertheless, influenced by his parents, his life aspirations were to become "a great executive" resolving complicated matters while sitting in his office with people showing him respect and admiration. He could not say what kind of manager he would be in his self-realization image, but he was capable of describing his office with much precision: a wall-to-wall carpet, an executive's desk with telephones, a female secretary. Even now he planned to buy a new car and electrical appliances, which would indicate a high standard of living.

In order to come nearer to his dreams he took on a clerical position at the municipality. He liked his job but, in his employer's opinion, he worked slowly and without precision; and after a trial period of six months they dismissed him, advising him not to seek a clerical job. After being unemployed for nearly one year, he decided to try his luck in industry and got a job as a machine attendant. He worked satisfactorily but felt that he was only a little cog, without any responsibility and authority, and quit the job. Again he remained unemployed for a lengthy period and then decided that he wanted to look for "something serious." He went to the employment office but turned down each of their proposals (blue-collar jobs in plants or building sites, jobs as a waiter or clerk). Finally he took on a job as a porter in a transportation company, but the work was physically hard and he could not stand it and had to quit. Since then he had had only occasional jobs and had stopped seriously seeking employment. He felt helpless and depressed and that his cherished dreams had all crumbled and there was no incentive left for him to try again. His neuroticism score was 66, with a positive attitude toward authority figures, low self-assertion, low courage, low sociability, and low vocational interest, but a very high regard for money and spending tendencies.

The question in all these cases is, of course, how much the career events contributed to the increase in neuroticism. There certainly is such a contribution, but one must reckon also with the initial background. Magnus, Diener, Fujita, and Pavot (1993) recently demonstrated that life events cannot be viewed as a source of influence independent of the personality and that neurotics objectively encounter more negative life events. Since neuroticism expresses a low level of psychological tension (Janet) termed as "strength of the nervous system" by Pavlov or as the human "energy capital" by Selye, one has to acknowledge the fact that people are different and that the energy reserves of some are larger, while they are scantier in others. Events that hardly touch some people will topple others. Two things stand out clearly: First, nobody can be endlessly submitted to adverse events without finally collapsing and, second, everybody can reasonably realize himself or herself if assisted to make the best of his or her capacities and can use occurring events in the best way to serve and facilitate the fulfillment of his or her aspirations. More on this will be said in the last chapter.

Prediction of neurotic maladjustment may be advanced by the use of the Pavlovian concepts of Higher Nervous Activity (Pavlov, 1951) applied to a set of objectively recorded behaviors. To this purpose we compared the neuroticism scores of our high school student samples described in Chapter 3, with life events told by them and with the analysis of mistakes in their exam papers in a foreign language (Russian). We also compared neuroticism scores of the lathe operator sample with their recorded on-the-job behavior.

The method of error and misbehavior analysis was largely used by Freud in his endeavor to give a psychoanalytic interpretation to personality manifestations. In the investigation that has been mentioned, the method served to achieve a physiological explanation of behavior.

It is well known that Pavlov classified nervous systems in accordance with the strength and the mobility of the two fundamental nervous processes: stimulation and inhibition. Misbehaviors show the concrete unfolding of nervous processes, since every omission, confusion, contamination, and refusal is the translation of fallacies in the constellation of nervous processes commanding and controlling the behavior.

The physiological analysis of misbehavior in members of our research samples showed that the subjects who in the testing showed various degrees of neuroticism (the scores in categories II–VI) were found to have a weak nervous system with an inert stimulation process and predominance of imagery. In his experiments, Pavlov (1951) pointed out that attrition affects the strength and the mobility of nervous processes and above all the conceptual system as phylogenetically more recent. This results in memory failure, the "narrowness" of conscience (called also "tunnel vision"), when the person is unable to consider the situation as a whole, and in communication deficiencies. Persons who are born with such nervous systems have a high probability of developing neuroticism because the usual conditions of life may hurt them psychologically (their nervous system is weak!). Since their stimulation process is inert, these wounds of the soul persist a long time and are also amplified by their highly developed imagery. This last feature is essential for the appearance of neuroticism: Some of our subjects with an inert weak nervous system manifested good compensation behavior in the face of problems, as they had a highly developed conceptual thinking process with only 14 percent imagery in the administered reasoning test (Krau, 1971). Their school record was satisfactory, although not superior. Obviously the weak nervous system was not an obstacle to the effort required in order to achieve good school progress.

There appeared to be a link between physical illnesses in the subject's history and neuroticism (infectious diseases, forms of influenza). The disease reduces the body's energy and then normal physical environmental conditions may act as factors of oversolicitation. It is hard to tell whether repeated illnesses were precipitated by the scarce initial coping energy, or whether the illnesses weakened the body in a process of attrition. It is probably a combination of both phenomena that eventually leads to the manifestations of a weak nervous system, resulting in neuroticism. Generally neuroticism does not appear in physical examinations, and some neurotic persons are definitely well developed, but there is a tendency for dynamometer examinations to have a predictive value for such ailments (φ/φ max $= -0.30$ significant at $p = 0.07$). In industrial jobs the dynamometer represents a work activity evaluated as too heavy by dysthymics.

Therefore one may find a correlation in the same range between the dynamometer test and the test of the Book Catalogue (φ/φ max $= 0.27$), which in turn has a high negative correlation with neuroticism (φ/φ max $= -.53$ significant at $p = 0.01$). As mentioned previously the Book Catalogue measures emotional involvement with one's vocation.

It will be fully understandable that neurotics form the core of accident-prone people. Certainly, other people also have accidents, but all neurotics recall minor to major accidents if asked to relate life stories of their choice. An accident is an inappropriate response to a risk-involving situation. Because of the neurotic's weak nervous system, the situation is not duly analyzed, security instructions are forgotten, and the inertness of the stimulatory process leads to a deficient motor response. At the same time, the faulty analysis and motor responses persist because of the inertness of the system. In this condition inappropriate behavior has the tendency to be repeated even in situations that bear only a remote resemblance.

Here is the accident story of a worker with a weak inert nervous system, a decompensated neurotic (score 34). The story is drawn from an investigation of the personality factors in causation of accidents. The man, **B.**, worked in the aeronautic industry and described his accidents as follows: ''Once they started the motors of an aircraft and I stood behind it doing some minor work, although I knew it was forbidden in this situation. The motors ignited, and I was instantaneously hurled to the ground and badly hurt. Then, another time, I repaired the electric part of an aircraft motor and thought there was no electric power in that region. However, it so happened that there was power, and I got an electric shock.''

On both occasions **B.**, failed to grasp the whole of the situation. He forgot the safety instructions, made a faulty analysis in overlooking essential indicators, and repeated unsafe behavior. His accidents were definitely not ''accidental'' and rather reflected the weakness of his nervous processes of control and command.

During the years 1984–1986 we conducted research into the personality factors in the causation of accidents. A total of 169 workers participated from the Israeli Waterworks, the international airport, and a big enterprise in the metal industry. Of these workers, 45 had had accidents. All of them were administered Krau's projective personality test and the adapted Woodworth Psychoneurotic Inventory. Table 8.2 presents the distribution of neuroticism, negative attitudes, and low self-assertion (a corollary of the energy drain of neuroticism) in the 45 people who had had work accidents. The comparison with workers who had not had accidents was made with the aid of the χ^2 test for the frequency of the neuroticism categories III–VI in relationship to maladjustment and the frequency of negative attitudes and of low self-assertion in both samples.

The neuroticism categories of V and VI were found to differentiate between workers with and without accidents with $\chi^2 = 4.88$ significant at $p = 0.02$. Negative attitudes vis-à-vis authority figures differentiated with $\chi^2 = 4.80$ sig-

Table 8.2
Stigmas of People with Work Accidents (N = 45)

Stigmas	Neuroticism Categories						Negative attitudes	Low Self-assertion
Subjects	I 8-15 Normal	II 22-33 Compensated	III 0-7 Denial	IV 16-21 Maladjusted but fights	V 34-48 Decompensation	VI 49- Collapse		
Waterworks N = 25	-	8	-	3	7	6	14	11
Metal work N = 10	-	3	1	1	3	2	1	7
Airport N = 10	-	3	-	2	2	3	4	3

nificant at $p = 0.03$, but if adding the criterion of a negative characterization of the father, the differentiation became very meaningful with $\chi^2 = 10.46$ significant at $p = 0.001$. Low self-assertion was also found with a larger incidence in people with accidents ($\chi^2 = 3.76$ significant at $p = 0.05$).

These results mean that high neuroticism (categories V and VI) or a negative attitude toward authority figures, as the father is also negatively characterized, are in themselves highly indicative of an accident-prone behavior at the place of work. The probability of people with neuroticism scores of II, III or IV being involved in an accident is high only if they also have negative attitudes toward authority figures (not necessarily combined with a negative description of the father) and/or a low self-assertion.

It is certainly understood that accident causes are not exclusively internal but the result of the combination of an accident-prone behavior, the "human error" with a situation of potential risk and environmental conditions, making the risk acute (Haddon, Suchman, and Klein, 1964). Therefore, people with "accident stigmas" will not always automatically have accidents, but they tend to be maladjusted and unsatisfactory at their place of work. As a matter of fact, work accidents are particular manifestations of job maladjustment.

Apart from neuroticism, the maladjustment process may also find its expression in the characteropathic-psychopathic direction. We have seen that usually the two forms go together with the mobile dominance of one of the symptoms. In our sample of 54 maladjusted people, the distribution of symptom categories presented in Table 8.3 shows that in 19 cases of positive attitudes in the neurotic maladjustment categories IV, V, and VI the symptoms were predominantly neurotic (35 percent of the total sample). In 9 cases of people with low or compensated neuroticism scores in the categories I and II (16.6 percent of the total sample) the actual maladjustment was caused by characteropathic negative attitudes toward authority figures at the place of work, and in the remaining 26 cases of maladjustment (48 percent of the sample) the symptomatology was combined.

Because of the mingling of neuroticism with characteropathic disturbances, the emerging picture is not only one of energy shrinkage and renunciation flight, but an active attitude of rejecting the stressful job. It is not a mental loss of interest in the job, but its rejection. This characteristic was brought into evidence by the significant negative correlation between neuroticism and the special vocational interest test of the Book Catalogue. The important feature of this test, already described in Chapter 7, is that it measures the emotional involvement with areas of vocational activities. The correlation between the Book Catalogue test and neuroticism scores presented a negative relationship ranging between $\varphi = -.53$ in Romania and $\varphi = -.49$ in Israel, both significant at $p = .01$. This attests to the fact that neuroticism causes rejection of involvement with the duties of the job, which is the common ground between the neurotic-dysthymic and the characteropathic disturbances. The difference between them lies in the consecutive outlet behavior, which is more a flight and self-hurting in the dys-

Table 8.3
Distribution of Symptoms of 54 Maladjusted People

Neuroticism		Characteropathy (negative attitudes toward authority figures)		
		Negativistic attitudes		
Category Scores	Frequency	At_1 + hostility toward father	At_0	Positive attitudes (including At_1 + positively described father)
I. Normal (8-15)	2	1	1	
II. Feels strain but compensated (22-33)	12	4	3	5
III. Denial (0-7)				
IV. Maladjustment with fight (16-21)	7	2	1	4
V. Neurotic decompensation (34-48)	16	5	5	6
VI. Total collapse (49-)	17	3	7	7

thymic, and outward aggression against other people in the characteropathic. The basis of these differences may be found in the features of the nervous system.

The characteropathic individuals of the samples belonged to a nervous system intermediary between weak and choleric (after Hippocrates, "uncontrolled" in Pavlovian terminology). The main feature of a choleric nervous system is the weakness of the inhibitory process, whereby the person is not able to control his excitation. The maladjusted persons in our sample did not have a strong nervous system as had the classic choleric type, but an intermediary one. Every stimulation engendered an immediate response (the "explosiveness" of excitation) because there was no inhibition for a postponement of reaction for the sake of a poised consideration. On stronger stimulation the response activity of such an intermediary system becomes chaotic. Its relative weakness especially concerns the superior integrators of behavior (concepts, principles).

A constitution of this kind does not lead to characteropathy automatically; but through improvised, explosive reactions, it facilitates the formation of negativistic attitudes toward authority figures, which already is an important characteropathic disturbance. Seen from a physiological point of view, the formation of negative attitudes is the reaction of a nervous system with diminished strength, to events producing the overstretching of the inhibitory process.

It follows that the generalized negativistic attitude toward authority figures is not produced by the image of a weak father per se, but by problems associated with this background. The image of a strong father offers the internal support to cope with problems. It is even not always the father who is the source of negativistic attitudes. They may be linked directly to a frustrating condition such as school or reflect the vying after an aggressive gang. In this case the individual usually has a low self-assertion but high sociability, and the gang members constitute his significant others. In opposition to this "aggressive vyer" is the first-described "active" psychopath, with high self-assertion but usually with low sociability.

Again, caution should be used not always to expect pure types. The eventual and actual picture of maladjustment is usually fluent, including symptoms of both categories, and in many a case neuroticism turns into disturbances that may be labelled characteropathic. Fluidity is a basic feature of maladjustive manifestations.

The discussion so far might have given the impression that a reduced energy and/or negative attitudes toward authority figures are the only and sufficient cause and expression of career maladjustment. This is certainly not so. Neuroticism and negative attitudes are measurable indicators of a process that involves the whole of the person's behavior.

We have already pointed out that the manifestation of personality disturbances is preceded by a distortion of his value aspirations. First the material aspiration values of money and property acquisition are affected, followed by the attachment to one's vocation; and if the traumatic problem persists social relationships are affected, and negativistic attitudes appear or strengthen. However, before the latter become a dominant symptom, a highly developed self-assertion and boldness may compensatorily act against neurotic energy attrition. High sociability or high self-assertion compensate also for fearfulness. Low self-assertion increases the speed of neurotic devolution, but career maladjustment is deepened by very high scores of self-assertion, if they are accompanied by negativistic attitudes. In management personnel such a high self-assertion is the actual indicator of negativistic attitudes: They consider themselves the supreme authority at the place of work and direct their hostility toward colleagues and subordinates.

Here is the story of a former lieutenant-colonel released from the army at the age of 38 and incapable of getting established in a civil occupation. A. had a technical education. His studies in mechanical engineering were supported by the army. He aspired to top positions "next to God" (in his words), while the domain was not important to him. He characterized his father negatively as a tyrant and had a negative attitude toward authority figures. In the army he had constant rows with his superiors, which slowed down and finally halted his promotion, so finally he had to leave. For six months he led a project in the aircraft industry, but when it ended they were unwilling to give him another managerial job, and he would not accept anything else. He was offered a managerial position in a company of cleaning services, "office maintenance" as he called it, but after two years he again quarrelled with his subordinates and his employers on matters of power and authority and had to leave. Since then he has had several jobs but after only a few months had to leave them all, for the same reasons. His reactions to his failures were aggressive behavior toward others, daydreaming about his future successes, and cheating on his wife. His psychological profile was high self-assertion, low sociability, moderate valuing of money and moderate vocational interest, low courage, and neurotic decompensation (category V).

Although his psychopathic constitution permitted him to remain in the army for 18 years, his negativistic attitudes and low sociability impeded his advancement, while a self-realization image that did not contain the necessary elements of steady career advancement precluded the achievement of the positions he aspired to. After he left his "office maintenance" job, the maladjustment spiral entered high gear. The destruction was visible in sociability and courage being reduced to nil and neuroticism entering the decompensation phase.

Maladjustment is related to an incorrect career behavior and is not the automatic result of a weak energy basis or of properties of the person's basic nervous system. This means that the achievement of adjustment and self-realization is the result of the activities by which the end-state image of self-realization was crystallized and of the implementation processes involving all the motivational and instrumental ingredients that have been discussed. The physiological condition is only a background, although one that has to be seriously reckoned with, as it requires special adjustments of the person's career plans and activities. Since the person's end-stage image of self-realization constitutes his abbreviated and "infolded" life plan, it is of paramount importance for life success and failure. It sets into motion and controls the process of implementation, and there can be no final achievement if the goal image is faulty.

First, although there is usually no clear representation of the desired end-state with the steps leading to its implementation, as excessive lack of clarity of the self-realization image produces anxiety: One does not know what one really wants, and uncertainty in goals breeds negative emotions (Emmons, 1992). The person feels painful inner torment, which drains off energy. The result is neuroticism, exacerbated by failure provoked by the wrong decisions taken because of an unclear goal representation.

Second, the end-state image of self-realization is a life project; it must have the quality of a plan. This is obvious for people who see their realization in a particular vocational activity, but it also applies to those who see it in career concomitants, and even to the third group who want to realize themselves in a nonwork area of life. The attainment of every goal is conditioned by climbing the rungs of the ladder leading to it. However, all people have come to terms with work. For those who hunt concomitants, the work career is the main vehicle to achieve status and wealth. Those who seek things not linked to work must at least adjust to it lest they become frustrated and destitute and lose their mental health.

There is an essential link between self-realization and mental health (Maslow, 1954), eo ipso, between failure to obtain it and pathology. Since anomie in society is a major cause of deviant social behavior (Merton, 1957), it is also a major cause of individual mental pathology in the form of neuroticism and characteropathy. There are constitutionally conditioned interindividual differences as to the ease with which such forms appear, but society is and remains an important contributor through the barriers it imposes on career advancement.

In the investigated samples there were individuals who gradually became destitute because they refused jobs that in time might have led to the realization of their aspirations. They ruined their lives because the rungs of the ladder leading to their goal attainment simply were not included in their self-realization image as a life project. Others failed in their quest for self-realization because they did not carefully analyze the implications of their somewhat blurred self-realization image and entered vocations with implications not compatible with their initial aspirations.

This having been said, one should also stress the individual's obligation to be committed to a societally useful career. As long as society's well-being depends on work, and of necessity it does, work is man's basic condition, allowing people to achieve the gratification of their choice. Their jobs do not always allow them to obtain all their cherished satisfactions, but without work they are worse off.

It has been stressed already that end-state self-realization images are formed under the influence of the person's significant others. However, not only aspirations are formed this way but also behavioral styles reflecting permanent character traits. There is a certain selectivity in interiorizing behavioral modes seen in others as they fit the constitutional properties of the individual. The so-constituted basic behavior style of the personality is a reflection of both the author and the actor of people's life narrative. In this sense Klages' adage "Dein Character, dein Schicksal" (your character is your destiny) holds much of the truth, and the question, "what went wrong and why?" has to be considered from this angle. The timid will skip opportunities, the gullible will have disappointing experiences with people, and both may turn out to be losers. What this chapter has shown is that the causal mosaic of our life events is not a rigid texture and that there should be room for interventions and improvements.

To begin with, much can be done by parents, the natural significant others of children. Today it seems old-fashioned to preach "family values," but by the law of nature and of society, parents have responsibility vis-à-vis their children, and they should be aware of it. A precarious material condition is no excuse for rejection or indifference. One need not be wealthy to love one's children and one's family. Children are human beings in their own right, neither toys nor "accidents," and they have the right to be loved. Parents should know that divorces destroy not only the family but also the future destiny of their children as they acquire negativistic attitudes toward authority figures that are very prejudicial for later career adjustment. If in their later years many people blame their parents for what went wrong in their lives, they are not far from the truth. Of course, even carrying such a heavy family burden, people are still the masters of their own lives, and blaming one's parents will not improve anything. The winner in the race of life is the person who has the strength to face his or her weaknesses and to say, "Despite all this, what can I correct and how can I use what I have in order to realize my dreams?"

In accordance with all that has been said, it appears to be hard to change an already crystallized self-realization image, but it can be clarified and then completed in its nonessential aspects. Mainly, all its requirements and implications must be made clear. The analysis of implications must also extend to the necessary ability and skill coverage of the intended vocational activity. This is the classical case of vocational counseling, but under the new perspective of the end-state image of self-realization. Another new perspective is introduced by the necessity to consider people's inabilities and not only their aptitudes, a problem raised also by Subich (1992). The statistical data presented on accident causation attested to the link between the latter and certain personality traits hindering the safe performance of job activities in conditions of a particular risk. The airport mechanic whose story has been told had all the skills for repair work, but his behavior was unsafe given the high risk potential in his work setting. In a garage or on a car assembly line he would have been a successful worker, but in the job chosen for reasons of prestige, the final outcome was invalidity and not aspirational realization.

The secret of career success lies in the maximal utilization of one's potential in the direction of a strongly motivated aspiration. A faulty end-state image directs the efforts into directions for which there is no ability coverage or, because of the "missing links" of work, squanders the person's energy. Therefore, the pathology of self-realization actually starts with the pathology of the self-realization end-state image. "What went wrong and why?" begins with this image and continues with the flaws of the implementation process, which include all the factors and causes involved. Yet, fairness and the need to correctly understand what happens makes it necessary to perceive and consider not only the inner, person-bound part of the variance in life occurrences but also their outer part, produced by uncontrollable events in the broader society. As an aftermath of wars, political upheavals, and economic recession, people emigrate and lose their jobs—some even their lives. It is obvious that cohorts living in the economic boom of the 1950s in Western democracies had better chances to realize themselves than those overrun by the Nazis in the 1930s and 1940s or those having to cope with a communist takeover after the war in the countries of Eastern Europe. However, although little could be done to halt these events, some foresaw them, emigrated in time, and mitigated their impact, while others were taken by surprise and crushed. The same applies even to layoffs in times of peace, as attested to by Kroll, Dinklage, et al. (1970) in their analysis of coping styles of workers in the wake of and following the declaration of bankruptcy by their employer.

The more common case, however, is when the plant is not closed altogether but only retrenched. Some employees are laid off, others not, raising the very intriguing question of finding the characteristics that make an individual fit to survive in his organization while others are sacked. Of course, there is the traditional answer, referring to the survival of people with the highest job skills, but life experience teaches that there is more to that than meets the eye. Aged employees are fired regardless of their occupational skills only to "rejuvenate" the organization, and other well-sounding pretenses are found to get rid of immigrants, minority workers, or "uncooperative" women. It is certainly not true that all of them are less skilled occupationally, and yet they lack particular skills that in a crisis situation make the difference between winning and losing.

We shall recall that job requirements extend beyond the officially acknowledged ones to include hidden characteristics that appear only in images: the vocational image in public opinion, but also the organization's image, whence the organizational employee's image in management. The concealed characteristics do not figure in the official worker specification, yet they are sought by management in their employees. In order to be on the winning side, the person must detect these characteristics and develop them if possible or else look for other employment (or another place to live) while there is still time.

All this does not mean that our approach puts the blame for what went wrong in a career on the person only. The blame remains on insensitive regimes, shortsighted, incapable employers, or a discriminatory society as a whole, but apportioning blame does not help the individual realize him/herself.

In our research on immigrants (Krau, 1981a) a major stumbling block in the way of their career reconstruction was a state of cognitive dissonance over status incongruence. They had a home and a job in their country of origin, a position in the community, and a family, but after emigration all went to pieces, and they were left with nothing but the painful question of who they really were: the persons they used to be or the ones in the present state of destitution. More often than not the causes of these difficulties lay with the host society, its unjust discriminatory practices using immigrants only as a cheap labor force while denying them real absorption and advancement. Nevertheless, scores of immigrants succeed in their new homeland. They are the people who apply a positive behavioral strategy of involvement even vis-à-vis an estranging culture and a job with unwanted characteristics. They develop a positive attitude toward authority figures at their jobs and an orientation toward absorbing the values of the new environment. Chances of success are greater if the individual does not lower his self-image; but even if he does, the positive behavioral strategies will help him reconstruct his career (Krau, 1981).

In this complex situation, vocational abilities understandably have importance, but the difference between successful integration or failure and a feeling of misery and hatred is made by adjusting to the host society's *hidden* requirements however unjust, unintelligible, or racist they may be. In many cases, and certainly not only for immigrants, this is "what went wrong and why." Again we are reminded that self-realization functions in the framework of adjustment. The more you adjust and emotionally accept the necessary compromises in the areas not linked to your life aspirations, the greater your chances are to achieve what you really desire.

9

Counseling for Self-Realization

In the domain of health care we are accustomed to hear that it is by far easier to prevent an illness than to cure it. The same holds true for all deviations from normal career behavior. However, the latter area presents additional difficulties. First, there is no consensus as to what constitutes a normal career behavior. Society and the individual may hold different views on this point. Second, in most people's minds there is a clear link between health ailments and the necessity to seek medical assistance, while the link between a broken career and psychological help is less unanimously accepted. This is not to say that if General Motors closes some of its plants and 70,000 people lose their jobs, all of them should see psychologists (perhaps General Motors management should!), but if somebody has repeated career difficulties, one could fairly presume that something is wrong with the programming, the command, and the control of the person's career development process. Maladjustment is not merely a technical problem like recycling or improving the skills for job search; rather, the person has a lifestyle problem of a more holistic nature.

In the 1950s and in the early 1960s there was a general consensus that the gist of career problems was the match of the individual's abilities with the requirements of the job (Meili, 1951; Tyler, 1953). Vocational counseling was considered to deal with the normalities even of abnormal persons, with locating and developing personal and social resources and adaptive tendencies (Super, 1962). Then, toward the end of the 1960s, a new insight gained ground holding that actually vocational problems were personality problems and had to be tackled as such (Crites, 1969; Tyler, 1969). Bordin (1968) went so far as to transform all vocational counseling into psychotherapy. Finally, in the last decade, progress has been made towards a comprehensive model of counseling that reflects developments in four major directions and deals with both the inner and the outer worlds (Crites, 1981).

First, Crites (1974) made a distinction between the content and the process of vocational decision making. A career mismatch may be the result not only of lack of vocational information, abilities, or interests, but of an incompetence in making choices and decisions.

A second development concerned the necessity to go beyond the standard assessment of clients' interests in order to find people's private logic, their "guiding fictions" (Savickas, 1989) indicating the personal sense vocations have for life-goal attainment. In a clinical context, Frankl (1962) emphasized the necessity for defining the sense life has in retrospect for the person. We should like to add that the advantage of vocational counseling is the perspective enabling the person to plan with foresight and to achieve desired goals and not just accept what is irreversible history.

The third breakthrough is related to choosing a career rather than a job. It is true that this issue had already been raised by Anastasi (1964), but then the modern trend of computer-aided counseling reverted the question to overtly declared and acknowledged matches: A computer does not dream and has no emotional interaction with the client. It does not stimulate him to open up and become aware of his hidden motives. It also happens that people prematurely choose a career and omit the development of skills enabling them to make the correct career and life decisions later on. The issue has been raised by Tyler (1978), and her caveat is in place.

The fourth and last important development in counseling theory consists of the broadening of the concept of career and life decisions, as they are not only work and workplace related. In this sense Krumboltz (1993) asks for the integration of personal and career counseling. In the new Person-Environment Correspondence Model (Lofquist and Dawis, 1991), counseling is geared to the client's goal setting, developing plans, pattern matching, and acting.

Today the tendency to consider vocational counseling a part of assisting the person's life development (Goguelin and Krau, 1992) is gaining ground, just as the stages of vocational career are considered parts of Erikson's (1963) life stages (Savickas and Super, 1993). The completion of this model appears in **counseling for self-realization**. Not the momentary match between the person and the job gives reason to one's life, nor even the match between career development and the general development stages of the human individual, but the private sense of the end-state of self-realization, the cherished and concealed life goal revealed in the person's imagery.

The counseling for self-realization model acknowledges that life aspirations are not always related to the vocational career, let alone to career advancement. The counselor should assist counselees in implementing their aspirations, whatever they are, if they do not contravene the law of the land and human ethics.

Not everybody asks for counseling, but the need for assistance in self-realization is universal. This is so because, first, end-state images are blurred, the motives hidden, and people may benefit from clarifying their life goals. The clarification of motives is not an easy task, given the tendency to conceal them.

Second, counselees need help in the customary sense of choosing, deciding, and implementing the best course of action for converting their life project into practice. The two parts of the counseling process must be organically related. In this sense Krumboltz (1993) asks for the integration of personal and career counseling. Failure to recognize this linkage while trying to maintain counseling in the classical match framework leads to sterile verbal exchanges and frustration if counselees' self-realization aspirations are not in the vocational domain or if they have problems with the self-realization image as such, or with its implementation. In the already reported research on counseling (Krau, 1981c), such persons constituted the majority of the sample (77%), and it should be of interest to take a look at the problems for which these people asked for help.

Some 22 percent of the subjects needed reinforcement in their vocational choice, and counseling could develop along the classical pattern. However, here too the problem was not the absence of information on occupations or on the counselee's own aptitudes, but the emotional lack of assurance. This emotional side moved to the forefront with the other counselees, who needed another type of vocational counseling that would use methods of clinical psychology. In this respect, four problem categories could be established, as described in the following paragraphs. In the first two categories the self-realization image was not related to the means of implementation.

1. *Counselees asked for reinforcement of unrealistic aspirations.* **P.** came to the counselor's office asking for an expert opinion on whether she would be able to pass the entrance examination to the Department of Economics. At her request an ability test was administered, but it yielded poor results; the counselor tried to work out another solution together with her. She categorically refused, blaming the ability tests. She said, ''I will try to get in to Economics no matter what the tests say,'' and this is what she did. She failed, as had been predicted. **P.** manifested a strong drive for self-realization in a definite vocational activity without reckoning with the necessary instrumental ability ingredients, and she obstinately resisted all endeavors to enlarge her interest profile.

2. *Counselees felt saturation and disgust for their present job and wanted to change it.* The problem is that generally such saturation is not caused by occurrences in a specific job, but rather has generalized roots in vocational immaturity and/or a neurotic personality. A simple change of job or occupation does not solve the problem, and after a short time the same saturation and disgust appear in regard to the new job. Essentially, these persons do not see any link between their end-state image of self-realization in occupational concomitants and any vocational paths. Any job they enter is rejected after a short time as they feel it is leading nowhere.

M. worked in a clerical job at the university. She felt incapable of continuing because she did not meet enough people. She saw her self-realization in meeting people and having a family, but it seemed to her that she failed in both areas. Recently she had had a fight with her boyfriend. Of work she spoke reluctantly. She said she would like to study, but feared failure; and indeed her scores in ability tests were so low that she had no chance of being accepted as a university student. Her interest scores (S.D.S. Holland) were high in the social and enterprising areas, both related to occupations with people. During the interview she wept several times and spoke of the fear of death. Finally, she revealed her wish to become a medical nurse, but then she declared that she was unable to decide or to register for training. She also thought of becoming an air hostess and to this purpose she took classes in French. The counselor tried to reinforce her autonomous decision capacities and to work out with her a plan of action built on the alternatives she had raised herself. She appeared to agree with this approach, but one month later filed a complaint against the counselor who, as she put it, did not solve her problem and left her with the same doubts about a suitable vocation in spite of the fee she had paid for counseling.

In the following two categories, the link severage between self-realization image and implementation is manifested in the decision-making process. This disturbance has been theoretically analyzed by Crites (1974) and later by Savickas and Jarjoura (1991), who made a distinction between the content and the process of vocational decision making. In our research the flaw in the decision-making process appeared in two forms, as in the following categories. In the first example, a very talented young man fails in his life development because he is unable to reach decisions.

3. *Counselee is unable to reach decisions.* **A.** was an army draftee who came to the counselor's office in order to get help in determining his future path. Asked about his life plans, he told the counselor that he wanted to make a lot of money but did not want to be a salaried employee. His father was a lawyer, who wanted his son to work in the same profession. **A.** considered law as a possible vocational avenue, but in the Ramak test of vocational interests, he surprisingly gave high preference to "waiter" and then explained that he was unable to make up his mind and working as a waiter would give him time to decide. The administered ability tests showed he had good aptitude to work in the domain of law and that he would have no problem in passing the very strict entrance examination for law school. However, the subject declared that he feared law would not satisfy him. Referring to his private life, he told of similar intense doubts that had made him break off his engagement to the girl he had intended to marry. Since, of all his plans, the one concerning the legal profession was the most crystallized and congruent with his psychometric data, the counselor supported this plan. In the follow-up six months later, **A.** wrote a letter to the counselor telling that he had successfully passed the entrance examination to law school, but he added that he was not fully satisfied with his decision to study law and was still thinking of changing the vocation. In fact, this is what he did after two years. He transferred to sociology but did not finish his studies. Finally, he entered an administrative job in which he could not advance because he lacked the necessary qualifications, and he was very dissatisfied.

4. *Decisions are permanently changed.* Another group of counselees who also had problems with their decision-making process took decisions and then

changed them far too easily, as the link between self-realization image and implementation was not clearly articulated, mainly not in a logically compelling manner. These persons "decide" all the time, and each decision is in sharp contrast with the previous one.

L. asked for counseling in order to choose a college major. In his youth he had studied in a religious yeshiva, which he left to enter a lay school because he did not like the religious lifestyle. He left this school too because he reached the conclusion that the matriculation exams were superfluous. He wanted to be a journalist and started studying journalism during his army service, but when he was released from the army he no longer wanted to be a journalist because of the difficulties linked to this profession. He decided to become an instructor to underprivileged youth, but again had second thoughts and began thinking of other avenues. The changes in his vocational plans were paralleled by transformations in his general life conceptions: He became religious, then became secular, was engaged in political activity in one of the right-wing parties, and then went over to a centrist one. Asked about his life plans, he knew only that he wanted money—and quickly. He was worried that so far he had been unable to reach a well-established position.

To conclude from the material presented, counseling for self-realization has two preconditions: (a) the clarification of the end-state image of self-realization and (b) the understanding of the role a work career plays in the achievement of the aspirations that compose the self-realization image. Both conditions have to be resolved before any help can be given to the person in order to make progress on the way to aspirational implementation. Therefore, we should speak of a *maturity for self-realization* in analogy to the customary concept of vocational maturity. It seems that the former has a primary status and determines the efficacity of all vocational moves for what has been termed the "internal career" (van Maanen, 1978), a concept that evaluates objective career attainments in the light of self-realization aspirations.

The maturity for self-realization starts with the crystallization of the self-realization image, that is, people's awareness that they have such an image, its elaboration if they have none, and its articulation. It so happens that people think of elements of their future, such as money or a family, but these elements are not integrated. They must be assisted to establish a hierarchy between the various elements of their self-realization image and to remove existing contradictions. The counselor will make it clear to the counselee that this image is a life plan and that incompatible elements will cause failure.

The establishment of a hierarchy between the elements of the self-realization end-state image helps the person in achieving accepted compromises and adjustment to constraints in the areas of less importance for his life aspirations. Self-realization functions in the framework of adjustment. An imposed compromise always causes frustration; an accepted compromise leaves the person satisfied and ready to achieve what is really important. To circumvent the tendency to conceal the cherished life goals, counselors should use a combined approach of aspiration narrative, life-domain salience inventories, and value inventories, as was done in the investigations presented in this book. Only such a combined approach will show what the person really wants.

The second step in counseling is to convert an image into an explicit plan. It is not necessary to conclude this stage with the adoption of one single life scenario, but with the elaboration of alternative narratives. The aim is for the counselee to realize that there has to be an organized way to achieve one's life goals and that every step has to be evaluated in the light of the ultimate goal. Into this discussion of an organized path toward life achievements, the counselor introduces the role of work in society as an instrument for the acquisition of the gratifications the individual dreamed of. There is no word yet of a specific occupational choice. There must be an acknowledged commitment to a way of life including work before any particular occupational choice can make an efficient contribution to the realization of life purposes.

In the counseling process, the recognition of what self-realization really means for the person is also essential for helping the counselee to resolve the problem of occupational and organizational stability. Presently, counselors are either guided by their own conservative or "liberal" ideas on this topic, or they consider that the question should not be decided in advance but be dependent on intervening events. This, again, is a faulty approach that may cause much harm because for some types of aspirations and careers, stability is a necessary condition, while for others it is not.

To speak of career stability today may seem ludicrous in the face of the massive downsizings in organizations. However, highly skilled people will most frequently be retained in their jobs, because in order to function normally each company must have at least a core of stable competent job holders. As persons belonging to the first group of self-realization aspirations usually possess the highest possible job competence, they have good chances for being offered stability even under the new industrial policy of downsizing. Second, their highly developed vocational knowledge and skills should permit them to turn job loss into career growth (Eby and Buch, 1995) as they move to another organization or become self-employed.

This latter point is important. The stability of career plans must not be equated with the obligation to stay at the same place of work. It does, however, mean the pursuit of a direction in implementing aspirations, even if conditions radically change. Medical research may be conducted in different organizational settings or even in a private practice, as computer programming may be done for a company by an employee or by the same person as a free-lance consultant. Today the key word is career self-management, which does not preclude general career planning and stability in its implementation.

To be more specific, if the person belongs to the first group of self-realization in a well-defined vocational activity and also to the ascent career type, he may be well advised to plan for stability and to waive it only under very adverse conditions. Every change in the place of work reverts the person to the status of a novice, slowing down his advancement or halting it altogether. There usually is no way to catch up with the time lost, and finally frustrating compromises become necessary. Apart from this, permanent changes in environment and the need to adapt to them divert the person's energy from the pursuit of vocational purposes that are the main content of self-realization in this group.

Diametrically, individuals belonging to the third group, aspiring at self-realization in areas not linked to work, should definitely not plan for stability in their jobs, which may only restrict the free pursuit of their family, love, or experience-enriching preoccupations. At the same time they should plan for work and job adjustment while they work, even if they do not bind themselves by thoughts of loyalty to their chosen occupation or to the organization they happen to work for.

Again, one must bear in mind that present economic conditions do not favor career stability. However, they have not abolished, nor can they abolish stability in organizations altogether (and the future may reinstate it, as it warrants higher productivity and therefore higher profits).

Second, we are speaking of the stability of a career design aiming at the achievement of life aspirations according to a plan that must allow for some flexibility in jobs, in organizations, and sometimes even in occupations. For some life aspirations to be implemented and, given the person, the possibilty of deciding her fate, stability may be a preferential strategy. Yet, if changes are imposed, the person should have alternative narratives for realizing the same project, as modifications of the career path are kept as small as possible. In other cases, only the final aspiration remains stable, but the career path and all other conditions may definitely vary.

The counselor's greatest difficulty is to correctly assist people belonging to the second group, who see their self-realization in the attainment of concomitants of work careers. The problem is here to define the particular concomitants they aspire to and their career type. It must be also made clear that their aspirations refer to *work* concomitants and can be fulfilled only by working. While for people in the first group the link between work and self-realization is an organic one, for some in the second group it is not, and they must be helped to see the necessity of this linkage. As for the third group, work and self-realization are indeed not linked, but still these people must be adjusted to their jobs in order to have the freedom for pursuing their different aims. Lecturing on the subject of the importance of work may not prove very effective, but group counseling usually is.

The problem of choosing an occupation appears only now, that is, if, when, and how it is required by the implementation of the self-realization image. Let us remind the reader that less than a third of all people want to realize themselves in a definite vocational activity, and for about 20 percent a vocational career is not related to their life aspirations, either emotionally or logically. Apart from this, some satisfy their existential needs and life goals by marriage, legacies, or winning at lottery, and consequently they may be adjusted and self-realized in the absence of any vocational choice and work activity. However, they constitute a small minority. Some of them may even realize that they have incorrectly read their life aspirations, which actually referred to a situation of comfort obtained as a result of work or to *working* in the household. Therefore, in later years when their children leave the parental home, they desperately seek to enter a work career. For the great majority work is the *via regia* for self-realization as a purpose or in providing the means for it.

In the light of what has been said, the problem of occupational choice appears with some new emphases and characteristics.

First, for the individual the choice of an occupation amounts to a match of images between a self-realization image and the occupation's image in public opinion. It has been shown that the latter also contains vocationally and organizationally irrelevant characteristics, while the existing and relevant ones may be concealed. This fact may prejudice the individual's chances for adjustment and advancement. It is therefore the counselor's task to "divest" occupations of all the mythical features with which they were invested and to see to it that counselees accept the new information and arrange their life plans accordingly. This task is not an easy one for persons who have developed an emotionally loaded tie between certain image characteristics of a vocation and their life aspirations.

A second new emphasis in occupational choice must be to consider the match with a career type. All choices and matches must be geared to a long-term aspirational reality. This means choosing a career that provides answers to the aims depicted in the person's end-state image of self-realization. An ascent career provides gratification for hierarchical advancement, for aspirations motivated by the need for perfection in a certain activity, by a strong need for social power or wealth. A horizontal career gratifies people whose aspirations are mainly oriented toward nonwork life amenities or toward a work life with less effort.

In order to assist the individual to perform such complicated matching correctly, testing may be required. However, in opposition to the usual practice, it should encompass the whole of the subject's personality and aptitudes. It is fallacious to test whether the counselee meets the requirements of a certain occupation only. The occupation has concealed characteristics, and so has the counselee. Testing must be as complete as possible, and the results should be analyzed in the light of the clarification of the counselee's self-realization image. While Strong's general interest profiles may indeed allow for a broader judgment, testing without a previous inquiry into life aspiration narratives reveals the top of the iceberg only. The rest may be congruent with it, or it may not. In the first case, classical methods of counseling would work, in the second they fail. Without being opposed to interest tests as such, we must stress that the problem is not so much to assess people's interests as to find their motivated active interests related to their capabilities, so they may further realistic life aspirations.

Special attention must be given to every contradictory aspect in comparing tests, job requirements, and self-realization aspirations. The latter should be considered not in the form they are declared, but with their real meaning revealed in the counseling sessions. Failure to do so frequently leads to serious problems later in life. Here is such as case for illustration.

E.D. was born in 1946. Her father was an insurance agent. In high school she was a very good student and showed special interest in chemistry, biology, and mathematics. After vocational counseling in school acknowledging her talents for chemistry and in accordance with the advice of her father, she registered at the university to study chemistry "out of her interest to develop an important economic branch." Although her definition of self-realization was only obtained later (in 1987), she affirmed that it had always been "to have a challenging task, offering variation and pleasure, to set up a beautiful family, to love and to be happy."

After finishing her studies at the university, she got a job as a chemist in research and development in one of the important enterprises in the country. All her friends and relatives thought of her work as challenging and pleasant, corresponding to her vocational interests and aptitudes. However, a glance at her value profile would have told otherwise. It is true that the WIS Value Inventory was administered to the subject at the age of 40, and it might be argued that her values had changed since adolescence. However, in Chapters 3 and 4 it has been demonstrated that self-realization end-state images remain stable over time, as do the values intimately related to them. There can be minor shifts in rank positions, but the values linked to the image of self-realization will never leave the upper quartile of preferences.

The upper quartile of **E.D.**'s WIS Value Inventory comprised the values of Ability Utilization, Achievement, Social Interaction, Participation in Decision Making, and Prestige. The rise of this latter value to the upper quartile is very significant because usually it appears between the least preferred values (Krau, 1987, 1989b). No wonder that **E.D.** felt unhappy in her "challenging" job and complained of all kinds of drawbacks, some real like social isolation, some only for the sake of complaining, like unpleasant smells in her laboratory. She continued working there and even succeeded in developing some new products, but more and more she loathed her job. In the meantime she married the manager of a plant in the food industry situated in the southern part of the country. With help from their friends she got a job overseeing the catering of happenings in the Southern University, and now she was happy and rated her work satisfaction at 10 and her self-realization at 6 on a 7-point scale.

In this case interest and aptitude tests oriented the counselee to the wrong track, which occurred because of the hidden, private sense attached to the concept of "challenging, pleasant." In public opinion, a research and development job fits such characteristics, but this is a "public image"; a true match has to correspond to the private self-realization image of the subject. For **E.D.**, "pleasant" and "challenging" were colorful social gatherings in which she might perform a prestigious role. This story ended happily, but one may wonder what would have happened had **E.D.** not have married the plant manager with connections enabling her to get a rather unusual job that gratified her real aspirations. Probably the maladjustment spiral would have been set into motion.

Hitherto we were concerned with the stages and methods for counseling people for self-realization at the start of their careers. However, the greater part of those asking for counseling are having problems with their careers in adult years, some of them rather serious ones.

Customarily there is much said about career crises as the focal point of counseling. Three such crises used to be considered: the first after entering work, the second at mid-career, and the third when the individual prepares for retirement. These crises used to be linked to the age of "passages" (Sheehy, 1976) or to changes in the person's self-concept (Murphy and Burk, 1976), but they are simply the aftermath of bad career planning, starting with an unclear end-state image of self-realization. How otherwise could it happen that after longing for a particular vocation, the individual undergoes a crisis just when he gets the job? Or that after remaining for 10–15 years in an occupation, some feel that they did not obtain what they had hoped for and that they must make a radical change while there is still time? Did they not know what the vocation had to offer, and if it indeed disappointed them, why had they waited so long?

One may follow up these events, comparing organizational turnover figures with the demographic characteristics of the work force. We performed such an investigation (Krau, 1981b) in 1967 in two medium-sized plants, one chemo-pharmaceutical, the other in the metal industry, both in an industrial region of Romania, where all enterprises were state-owned. As both plants were relatively new, the workforce was composed mostly of young people. The upper age limit of subjects comprised in this study was 40 years.

The importance of this now "antique" research is that it permits us to judge stability at work in itself, determined by employees' wishes alone, as it is not obscured by sometimes necessary and sometimes unnecessary downsizings.

In the chemical plant the research comprised 426 leavers from various jobs on the production line over a 2-year period (considering only leavers for whom all data were available). Information was collected on age, education, family background, marital status, previous production experience, and work output while staying on the job.

In the metal plant the research comprised 53 lathe operator leavers, all from the same mechanical workshop at the plant, and during the same period of two years. Specific to this group was the fact that all its members belonged to one workshop.

It was assumed that the job change behavior did not occur automatically at certain ages, but was moderated by factors bearing on vocational and life maturity and on the realization of the worker's career type. The tight link between vocational and general life maturity has been stressed in several studies (Sheppard, 1971; Heath, 1976; Munley, 1977). Therefore, it was assumed that events such as family responsibilities and life experience in production would accelerate the process of general and vocational maturity and foster an early stability on the job in the Establishment stage. Acquiring vocational qualification (the knowledge and skills needed on the job) should have the same effect. Conversely, the lack of all these qualities should enhance turnover.

There were dissimilarities between the curves of leavers in the chemical plant and in the metallurgical plant as well as important common features. What was different seemed to be conditioned by the special settings in the two companies: in the metal plant the greatest quitting rush was in the age group of early twenties, but later the personnel were more stable in this company. In the chemical plant, employment began earlier because there was no stringent need for trade school qualification. However, a substantial number of people apparently did not wish to make a career of their jobs and quit to qualify for other occupations. Apart from dissimilarities, bimodality with one peak at 18–21 years and the other at 35 years was a common characteristic of the curves. Between these peaks turnover decreased and there was in both plants a period of relative stability ($\chi^2 = 5.87$ significant at $p = 0.03$). The first rush of turnover takes place apparently at an age when an individual generally does not consider himself "settled" in life, and these resignations are characterized mostly by a short stage with the job they quit. In the chemical plant 49 percent of the leavers stayed less than one year with the job, and 92 percent of them fell in age categories under 25 years. As to the characteristics of the job leavers at this age, the relationship in departure of skilled and unskilled workers at the early turnover rush was approximately 1:3. At the age beyond 35, it became 1:2. These data did not reflect company policies in training. In the described setting, management gave equal consideration to any job applicant (there was a shortage of applicants) and always welcomed the acquisition of broad job qualifications through trade school or evening school courses. This was, however, an individual decision for the workers, who were not always prepared to engage in such "investments." At any rate, the probability of remaining with the company was greater for those who agreed to qualify thoroughly for the job. It must be added that not only did skilled workers leave their jobs in a smaller proportion, but they stayed significantly longer. The conclusion has to be that those whose life-career aspirations were matched by what the occupation had to offer decided to invest in it and stayed significantly longer in the organization. However, when comparing the earnings of the leavers with those of the sample of stable employees, the proportion of lathe operators with higher earnings was significantly greater among the leavers ($\chi^2 = 8.38$ significant at $p = 0.01$). This finding emphasized the importance of the turnover rush at 35 years, but its significance went beyond the link with the age variable, since fewer workers left the metallurgical plant in the age groups over 30 (when they supposedly earned more) compared with the younger age groups (see Figure 9.1).

In Figure 9.1, age groups of leavers were plotted against the size of earnings, holding constant trade school qualification. The main finding that deserves

Figure 9.1
Relationship of Income and Age to Job Turnover of Skilled Workers in the
Chemical Plant

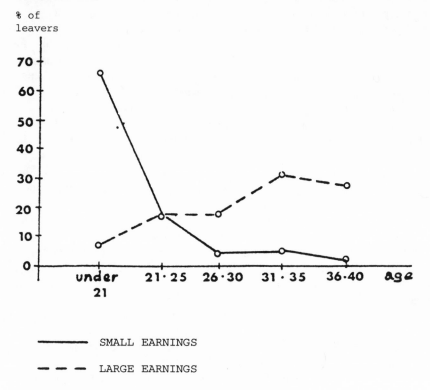

Reprinted by permission. Courtesy of *Personnel Psychology.*

attention in this figure is that after the age of 30 the skilled workers left, having
attained the best material situation a worker in that plant could obtain. The
earnings categorized here as ''high'' reflected the highest possible income for
workers in that plant. Employees who remained stable at the job had no greater
earnings.

Let us now analyze the mid-life crisis of those people. The turnover peak
between 30 and 35 years comprised the workers who had achieved all that their
occupation had to offer. Therefore, the feeling of a mismatch is evident. As it
was, they would only now see that the return from their vocation was not what
they wanted. Given the difficulties of job quitting at that time under a communist
régime, they had to have been in a real crisis. However, midlife crises are pretty
much ubiquitous and therefore not dependent upon a political regime. A common ground has to be assumed, and it is rooted in career planning deficiencies.
It is precisely this planning deficiency that explains why the crisis appears in
midlife when there is a compelling necessity to take stock of one's realizations

as time is running out. It is the *Torschlusspanik* mentioned in German literature—[In medieval Germany, cities use to be surrounded by walls and the gates were closed for the night. Travellers panicked at the thought that they would not arrive at the gate in time and be trapped.]—accompanied by the confidence that something may still be done. Some take sharp turns and quit their job or else emigrate and look for an entirely new start. In an investigation on emigration decisions, 31 percent of the motives were related to lack of satisfaction with career realization and perspectives (Krau, 1991). In the face of possible skepticism regarding the possibility of planning in a world of change, we must reach the conclusion that, for the sake of achieving life aspirations, career decisions have to be weighed carefully to planfully implement a life project. An emotional rush for change is seldom sustained. While change is legitimate, it has to be carefully prepared and implemented. This is not the case with many emigrants who make their decisions to quit on insufficient information regarding their target society and later on find themselves in a state of culture shock and cognitive dissonance. These factors and the unforeseen external difficulties due to discrimination, differences in occupational requirements, and the scarceness of jobs, make adaptation look anything but a smooth task (Krau, 1991). Success is more easily achieved by individuals who planned and were prepared for the general direction of their lives at least, and the same has to be said of people living today in a permanent job-at-risk situation (Hartley et al., 1991).

In this context, counseling plays a very important role. Counseling for self-realization assists people in planning for the implementation of their aspirations and thus constitutes an important instrument for the prevention of crises and for career self-management. This clearly means that people should not wait for crises to ask for help.

Nonetheless, it frequently happens that counseling is requested in the aftermath of negative life events, like dismissal from a job. It goes without saying that in this situation the process of counseling must have some distinctive features. This follows from the fact that a crisis has taken place at the junction between a traumatic event and a particular personality profile, and this constellation of conditions determines the choice of counseling methods and techniques. The process will have to go through the common stages of building maturity for self-realization and its implementation. While these are the stages also in counseling adolescents who are assisted in making their way into the future, maladjusted people must rebuild it, which makes a great difference. During the failures of the past, habits were acquired and so were behavior patterns laden with negative feelings. Counseling has to be adapted to the nature of maladjustment symptoms, to the cultural level, and the personality profile of the counselee. If the problems affect the person very seriously, a period of supportive counseling is appropriate. It is essentially a client-centered counseling. The counselor does not try to orient and lead the client, but the therapeutical process is controlled by the counselor, who expresses opinions in support of the client; he shows understanding and acceptance of the client's point of view and confidence in his abilities, insisting that he is sure the client's problems will be resolved. However, after a certain period of relaxation, the counselor has to use methods designed to resolve the problems themselves and not only to allay the client's anxieties. Now the nature of the client's disturbances have to be taken into account. With problems that have produced neurotic symptoms, the nondirective Rogerian method has the best chances of success. In characteropathic (psychopathic) disturbances such an approach is ineffective, and counseling has to rely on directive methods.

The Rogerian counseling conception assumes that human individuals have the capacity to become aware of the causes of their maladjustment, that is, of the lack of congruence between their self-concept and the totality of their experience. They then develop a tendency to reorganize their self-concept in order to stop the incongruencies (Pagès, 1965). This is a process of growth, the cornerstone of the Rogerian therapy. Nondirectivity is not only a technique; it is the counselor's fundamental attitude, which leaves the client in control of the therapeutical process. In the nondirective interview, the counselor may ask the client to tell more of himself, of his life experiences, even of his dreams—or they may discuss projective materials. The counselor does not express opinions, nor does he introduce his own values. He intervenes only in order to induce the client to deepen his analysis. The attitude of understanding and accepting the client as a person is the best instrument for reducing defensiveness and stimulating progress toward a clarification and a possible reformulation of his aims (Pagès, 1965).

The great advantage of this method is that it does not try to impose any change from without but leaves the decision of change and its implementation to the person while emotionally assisting the person and facilitating the process. This is one of the few ways in which changes in the end-state image of self-realization can be achieved. Outside intervention is doomed to failure, with the exception of intervention backed by an absolute authority. The cause lies in our defense mechanisms, starting with perceptual defensiveness and the refusal to perceive unwanted things.

It has been established that perception is an essentially selective process. The perception threshold is reduced for stimulations congruent with our values and attitudes, while it is heightened for incongruent ones. The latter are not perceived or are distorted in the direction of our wishes and preoccupations (Krau, 1977b). This phenomenon has been much discussed in consumer psychology (Engel, Kollat, and Blackwell, 1968), where it has been proven that people resist stimuli threatening their value systems and attitudes and that this resistance is greater the closer the affected values and attitudes are to the core of personality.

Counseling is not about advertisements for promoting the sale of furniture or cosmetics. Everything that is said refers to most central and therefore passionately defended areas of the personality. This is why many important objects or messages are misperceived or not perceived at all, and therefore it is futile to give advice to people having problems. Not only is advice not implemented, but from the start it is erroneously perceived. Obviously, perception and knowledge is more than information; it implies affectivity, choice, and axiology.

All this means that a genuine change in the personality seldom occurs. McKinney (1965), who has followed 20 student counselees over 20 years, concluded that counseling had been for all of them a valued experience, especially when a close relationship had emerged with the counselor. However, none of them had achieved a restructuring of his personality. The author was impressed in finding a certain continuity in the personalities known from counseling interviews. What had changed was the attitude toward life's difficulties, and many of the former counselees had found new avenues for satisfaction, mainly through better coping behaviors.

While a basic change in the end-state of self-realization is infrequent, nevertheless counseling can achieve its clarification, the hierarchical arrangement of its elements, and the addition of "missing links" like work, which allows for the achievement of high-priority aspirations. This is what can and what must be achieved as a basis for the consecutive stages in the process of counseling dealing with the solution of the special problems the counselee has raised.

The Rogerian method of counseling has its limitations and should not be looked upon as a universal remedy. Haentschke points out that the individual's growth forces may be too reduced as a result of very unfavorable living conditions or of a nervous breakdown that has occurred (Legewie and Ehlers, 1972). Apart from this, the method very much relies on verbal skills and therefore also on the subject's cultural level. People with a low cultural level are disadvantaged. In a certain sense this is true of all verbal methods of counseling.

Client-centered counseling methods do not work with people presenting characteropathic disturbances. Hare (1970) has systematized the reasons for this as follows:

1. While clients with other disturbances suffer because of their state and want to change, the psychopath does not feel he has a problem and is not motivated to change.

2. The behavior of counselees used to be influenced by aspirations concerning the future and by expectations; the psychopath lives in the present, and future status, expectations, or consequences of his acts do not influence his behavior.

3. Effective counseling implies a complex relationship of an intellectual and emotional nature between counselor and counselee, but the psychopath is incapable of the warmth, the empathy, and the sincerity necessary for such a relationship to emerge.

4. It may be possible that the largely shared doubts about counseling psychopaths negatively influence counselors' attitudes and failure becomes a self-fulfilling prophecy.

It seems to us that this last point is essential to the general negative appraisal of chances in counseling people with characteropathic disturbances. It has been proven only that *some* counseling methods, especially in the nondirective field, do not succeed with this type of counselee. However, there is some proof that the very outdated directive methods do.

Directivity is the oldest method of counseling, based on the assumption that in order to produce a change in somebody's attitudes and behaviors, the individual has to acquire new patterns of adaptive behavior, and this process is much facilitated under the lead of an experienced and qualified person. The concept of directivity implies the existence of somebody who discovers the cause of disturbances, the alternatives to solutions, and who sees to it that the right alternative is chosen and implemented.

However, the problem presents another facet, and one may ask who has the authority to determine when, how, and where the life of a person has to be changed? If followed to their extremes, these positions are irreconcilable and amount to a scholarly discussion on the *liber arbiter*, the freedom of will or in a more modern version personal rights versus the rights of the public. Instead of pursuing this discussion, we shall put forward the argument of reality and refer to the research findings of the previous chapter showing that for a majority of the subjects with characteropathic disturbances, the latter mingled with neurotic undertones as, according to the law of fluidity, symptoms of one category mingle and transform into another. Since neuroticism is expressed in subjective suffering, those people asked for counseling in order to be relieved of their suffering and resolve their problems. They left to the counselor the choice of the appropriate method, and a greater number of them asked for his active intervention.

For a minority of counselees (in prisons they may be a majority), characteropathy is heavily dominant, and those people certainly do not invite counselors of their own free choice. However, it is in the public's best interests that such individuals acquire aspirations and behavior patterns that conform with the rules of civilized social life, and it should be in their own best interest too.

In all cases where characteropathy is involved, counseling has to be backed by reward-punishment pressure and the counselor must play a more active role. This involves introducing values, putting forward behavior requirements, and demanding implementation. Compliance is rewarded, refusal is punished. Of course, the counselor should take on this role in order to serve the client because he feels empathy and warmth and not for the sake of his own ego-aggrandizement or because he rejects the client as a person.

In this context the problem of an enforced counseling relationship has to be brought up. It gives good results if the source who sends the subject to counseling has genuine authority over the subject. Such facts are already known from the Hawthorne counseling program (Roethlisberger and Dickson, 1964), but they have been reported also in a school setting (Krau, 1974b). In Britain, even the counseling of convicts has yielded noteworthy results when a forced relationship was used (Younghusband, 1966).

The authoritative counselor may be replaced by the group the way it was done in Makarenko's (1949) colonies or in the modern sociotherapeutic communities (Edelson, 1970). Both are "total institutions," their members being in very intense social interaction that provides strong pressure for conformity with certain rules. In both cases the rules were initially set by educators and then taken over and enforced by the group.

It should be kept in mind that neither these forms nor the much vaunted milieu-therapy are a universal panacea. Groups may be very sensitive but also cruel, irresponsible, and destructive, especially when they are not led by an actively involved counselor. It is also not always possible to organize milieu-therapy and therefore group counseling is generally preferred as regular group meetings and not as a total institution. Its chances of success very much depend on the previous selection of the group. Experience teaches that it is possible to select a group of 5–10 members with a good working relationship between members out of a pool of 40–45 individually interviewed people. If there is no such previous selection, hostile relationships may develop and the whole counseling process may turn out to be psychonoxious (Hepner, 1966; Laxenaire and Picard, 1969–1970).

Essentially, group counseling is individual-centered. The group is a means to reach the individual, to further his social integration, his self-awareness, and (in our case) the necessity to plan for his life career. In the group discussions, participants are invited to talk about their problems, to comment on and react to the stories and events told by the others. A permissive climate is created that enables counselees to discover that their difficulties are not unique and that each may learn something from the other participants. In order to deepen the therapeutic effect, Moreno proposed the "ad-hoc theater" or psychodrama as it is called (Ancelin-Schützenberger, 1969–1970).

This method uses five instruments: the stage (the counseling room rearranged), the actors, the script roles, the counselor-director, and the public consisting of the other group members. The counselor-director invites the actors to play roles from their private lives or from the lives of other people known to them. He names the roles, but the development of the script is left to the improvisation of the actors. Such scripts may also refer to the future and how the individual prepares for it, for the achievement of his/her life aspirations, for the choice of vocation, or for marriage. The group must be prepared for the "theater show," and all actors go through a "warming up." The group discussion following the "performance" is an important part of the method. Attention should be paid not only to factual representations, but also to the feelings expressed through omissions, verbal redundancies, or voice inflections. In this sense, authors point out that a psychoanalytic formation of the counselor is a definite advantage (Weil, 1969–1970).

The structuring, completion, or restructuring of the end-state image of self-realization creates only the premises for counseling, which has to give the person psychological assistance in the implementation of the now-recognized life aspirations. If this stage seems easier, it is only because counselor and counselee have agreed on what is to be achieved, and the counselee is therefore more cooperative and highly motivated. This is the time when the external problem must be attacked, and the counselee should acquire the skills to solve it. The advantage of this counseling stage is its greater face validity; its difficulty is that its efficiency has to be measured against external standards. The manipulation of psychological concepts is over: It is the real problem that must be solved. How far should the counselor go in this direction? The question remains open. Barron (1968) records the case of a counselor who nearly always succeeded with his clients despite his rough manner. He sometimes went so far as to telephone a client's supervisor, rudely requesting him to stop bullying the client, or inviting a client's wife and scolding her for her behavior.

Of course, counseling is not social work. Nonetheless, counselors have to realize that they have a social responsibility and that also from a professional point of view the results of counseling have to be judged by the successful coping with external circumstances, which sometimes the client alone is not capable of mastering. The dilemma remains, and counselors should heed their hearts in deciding what to do.

However, in many instances the problem is of a more limited nature and may be brought under control with relative ease: the choice of new occupation or the transfer to a new job, moving to a new place, or sorting out career-family priorities. In solving such problems, skill acquisition may be involved. Counselees should be given assistance in deciding on taking training courses and in acquiring appropriate learning methods. In the cases involving the acquisition of social skills like getting along with the boss or with coworkers or succeeding in employment interviews, the above-discussed group counseling and ad hoc theater may be of help. Some will need training in self-assertion, using one of the techniques devised after Salter. They teach the spontaneous expression of emotions, ideas, and gestures. The client learns to oppose suggestions or opinions with which he does not agree, to accept praise without blushing or mitigating, and to express his own opinions without attributing them to writers, friends, or the newspapers.

If the client's problem is the acquisition or the elimination of a well-defined behavior, the counselor should consider the use of behavioristic techniques like operational conditioning, desensitization, implosion, or aversion therapy. Such is the case when the person's career resumption, advancement, or simply adjustment at the place of work is impeded by some of his manners or gestures or by the way he speaks or dresses. It may be conjectured that removing these obstacles by means of a localized behavior correction will improve people's chances for realizing their aspirations.

The use of behavior therapy does not mean that the counselor must adhere to the theoretical framework of this method, which holds that (a) symptoms are not the expression of an underlying neurosis, but the neurosis itself, which appeared as the result of faulty learning processes, and (b) the neurosis will disappear if certain behaviors are relearned (eliminated or acquired) using the methods of conditional reflexes. Leonhard (1965) pointed out that together with the elimination or the acquisition of certain behaviors we also transmit to the client a new attitude, enabling him to develop the correct behavioral style in the future.

Here is the *punctum saliens*. The main problem of behavior therapy is that behaviors learned in the counseling setting by imagining them or thinking of them in a state of relaxation (e.g., in the desensitization technique of Joseph Wolpe) are not transposable to the real world. Therefore, the correction of Bandura, requiring the manipulation of real objects, is most important. The method is famous in relieving patients of the fear of snakes. Alas, even were the boss a snake, he would hardly be available for touch manipulation in the laboratory.

The Russian school of psychotherapy emphasizes the positive influence of explanations and directions given to counselees for changing their behavior. In this conception the developmental history of the counselees is important as a basis for the explanations to be given. They include information on physiological processes and on clients' possibilities of improving their behavior and attitude toward life. In the treatment of neurotic disorders the counselor explains that the disturbances are not unique but typical. The counselor clarifies every symptom, gives a positive appreciation to clients' self-criticism, and shows them how they can cope with their problems (Konstorum, 1962). The efficacy of this method leans on the intellectual level of the clients, but apart from this, the kind of "medical moral preaching" used in old times by Paul Dubois and the giving of advice rarely solve external problems. The reader will, however, observe that we have mentioned this method in the context of problems with the implementation of plans at a time when personality difficulties have already been removed in the previous type of counseling. At this stage the person may definitely be receptive to advice. Physiological explanations can be helpful even in the previous stage of counseling for coping with neurotic psychosomatic disturbances, because they relieve anxiety. Therefore, "explanatory counseling" should retain an important place in the methodological repertoire of the counselor.

All this should mean that counseling cannot and must not be confined to a particular methodological outlook, even if the counselor has strong preferences in the field. Psychologists must accept what, in the medical profession, has become commonplace, that there are no diseases, only sick people. Therefore, the counseling approach has to be adapted to the peculiarities of each case. Even in counseling the same person there is usually need for several methods and techniques to be applied as the counselee progresses through various stages of the process (Howard, Nance, and Myers, 1987).

In the face of theoretical developments, but also of shrinking financial support from governments, the evolution of the counseling domain is marked by the integration of approaches and strategies and by the shortening of procedures in psychotherapy, focusing on specific developmental crises and passages (Peake and Archer, 1988). In this sense, Erskine and Moursund (1988) integrate psychoanalytical concepts with client-centered, behavioral, gestalt, family therapy and transactional analysis into their "integrative psychotherapy," while Ivey (1983), still holding on to the traditional aim of vocational counseling to "help normal people cope with normal problems," includes states of loneliness and depression within the counselor's area of concern, as they are treated by the reflection of sentiments, the exploration of goals, and the change of beliefs followed by assistance given in skill acquisition.

By the same token, in every counseling approach, including the directive ones, counselors' attitudes should be characterized by correct empathy, unconditional human warmth, and authenticity, as put forward by Truax and Carkhuff (1968). This means that the counselor has to understand and to accept the client's world and the feelings he expresses overtly or by hints, without conditioning this acceptance on the counselee's compliance with counselor's directives. Above all, the counselor has to be sincere and involved with the client throughout the entire process. If he merely plays a professional role, if his smile is phony and he judges the client and speaks from a position of superiority, the basis of the counseling process is wrecked and its continuation is a mere waste of time. Therefore "training" counselors has a certain ambiguity. Empathy is a positive feeling of acceptance with a well-defined physiological base (Levenson and Ruef, 1992), which students of college age either have or do not have. It is a vocational aptitude, irreducible to an intellectual capacity à la Sherlock Holmes, of guessing what the other is thinking or feeling. More often than not our training amounts to training people to wear masks. To improve the situation, greater emphasis should be put on vocational selection of the right people for the counseling profession and also on training for authenticity.

Time and again we used to hear that counselors must not be emotionally involved in the problems of their clients lest they become quickly burned out. Burnout may be felt only by counselors whose half-hearted commitment is met by the anger, loathing, and rejection expressed by counselees. Neither Albert Schweitzer nor Mother Theresa ever complained of burnout. To help people in need was their self-realization. The particularity of the counseling profession is that it cannot be chosen for the sake of concomitants and still fulfill its destination truly. Counseling is not like running a drugstore and selling two pounds of comfort the way one would sell flour or candy.

In this context there again arises the question of how to evaluate the success of counseling. Volsky, Magoun, et al. (1965) support the position of evaluation by objective indicators leading to the logical extreme consequence of a successful counseling improving the subjects' adjustment to their environment even if they will not feel happier. On the other hand, for Barron (1968) the revitalizing transaction of counseling takes place in the emotional sphere begetting a feeling of "how good it is to live," which cannot be registered on any tape recorder, photograph, or electric muscle potential.

These opinions are unilateral. In the domain of the personality, the objective and subjective aspects cannot be separated as the objective is always refracted and reflected by the subjective, the internal conditions (Rubinstein, 1962). To neglect the subjective is not only contrary to science, but also to the aim of psychology: Of what use would a better adjustment be if the person feels miserable and frustrated? By the same token, neglecting the objective aspect also leads to the absurd. What use is there in an elevated disposition if it is not derived from the outcome of objective behaviors complying with the standards of success in the individual's group of reference? It would be obviously a pathological sign of link severance with reality.

Counseling for self-realization has to be evaluated by the progress clients make toward the attainment of aspirations. Self-realization is expressed in objective attainments leading to satisfaction and to the feeling of happiness. It is not the counselor who must be satisfied with the results of counseling, but the counselee. Otherwise Jerome D. Frank would be right in his foreword to the book of Truax and Carkhuff (1968), when he says that for years the domain of counseling and psychotherapy has presented the confusing spectacle of unabated enthusiasm for treatment techniques, the efficacy of which cannot be objectively demonstrated. Others more bluntly state that psychological assistance can also be psychonoxious (Ginott, 1961) and that evidence suggests that psychotherapy may turn out to be deleterious with the same frequency with which it is curative, having a mean effect comparable to no help received (Truax and Carkhuff, 1968; Eysenck, 1972). In his book, Eysenck described how he was nearly beaten up by angry colleagues when he put this truth before them.

Such is the mirror of counseling given by uninvolved counselors whose only purpose is to gratify their own needs of self-realization in concomitants of wealth status and of playing the "happy, healthy animals" at the expense of counselees overwhelmed by their troubles.

What has been said does not refer to clinical counseling only. A majority of vocational counselees also have personality problems. Therefore vocational counseling, especially in its form of counseling for self-realization, has to be of a more holistic nature, extended in depth and in width. In this latter direction the counselee should be assisted to live a complete life, especially today when there is a threat of diminishing satisfactions stemming from the job. Work is assigned the role implied by the individual's aspirations of self-realization, but there is life also outside and after work: courtship, the family, amusement, sport. These preoccupations ensure the necessary psychological commutation by which the stagnant excitation in the brain, produced by our worries on the job, is extinguished and new energy is accumulated. Therefore, a night's sleep, the passive form of rest, is also very important, despite its negative valuation by modern culture. People do not realize how much the quality of wakefulness depends upon the sleep that preceded it. Very appropriately the ancient Greeks depicted sleep as a god with wings and closed eyes.

The nonwork areas of life appear with an important therapeutical role, especially in career problems for which it is very difficult to find a solution. In this respect the Russian writer Boris Pasternak coined the term of "internal immigration" as a way used by his hero, Dr. Zhivago (and by himself obviously), to cope with the pressure and the misery caused by an inhuman but omnipotent régime. It certainly must not mean link severance with reality, but construction of a domain into which all that hurts the person is not permitted to enter. Far from being a flight, it is a form of adjustment and confrontation if this private haven—be it the family, religion, or a hobby—allows the person to spare his/ her energy and mental health in order to resume the fight under more favorable conditions.

By and large the success of counseling is unthinkable without the education of the public. It should emphasize the right of people to self-realization on their own terms and according to their own values, without being judged according to the achievement values of the majority. A horizontal career and/or realization in nonwork areas are no less legitimate avenues for self-realization than ascent career realizations, and they have to be acknowledged as such by society, openly and plainly.

It is also a matter for public conscience to accept the fact that life worries and problems are not stigmata. Everybody can have life difficulties, and they do not lower the people's value or weaken them automatically. Nonetheless, problems must be solved immediately, precisely in order not to undermine the personality and cause deeper disturbances. Usually individuals need qualified help for solving their traumatic situations even if ultimately it is they themselves who find and apply the solution. It is important, therefore, that the relationship among the client, the public, and the counselor should be freed of any denigrating association.

In an article significantly entitled "Caveats in the purchase of psychotherapy," Silverman (1969) wrote that in confrontation with maladaptive responses that became chronic, with situations and consequences of decisions from which there is no return, psychologists may see themselves as preachers of false hopes, illusionists. It is our conviction that the abundance of counseling methods and techniques known today permits the assistance of clients in their most complicated problems and that there is a solution for every situation. Even if there is no road back, there is always one forward. To help people see this road clearly and to assist them in taking it, such is the counselor's task.

> Says Demokritos, "Happiness is not in flocks or in gold, it dwells in our soul." Says Euripides, "You cannot be happy without working hard," and then Seneca says, "The one is miserable who does not consider himself most happy, however he may rule the world": *Miser est qui se non beatissimum iudicat, licet imperet mundo.*

References

Adler, I., and Kraus, V. (1985). Components of occupational prestige evaluations. *Work and Occupations, 12*, 23–39.

Aganbegian, A. G., Osipov, G. V., and Shubkin, V. N. (1966). *Quantitative methods in sociology* (orig. in Russian). Moscow: Izd. Nauka.

Alderfer, C. P. (1969). An empirical test of a new theory of human needs. *Organizational Behavior and Human Performance, 4*, 142–175.

Allen, R. E., and Keaveny, T. J. (1980). The relative effectiveness of alternative job sources. *Journal of Vocational Behavior, 16*, 18–32.

Allport, G. W. (1937). *Personality: A psychological interpretation.* New York: Holt.

American Assembly, Columbia University (1974). *The worker and the job: Coping with change.* Englewood Cliffs, NJ: Prentice Hall.

Amerio, P. (1968). Componenti psicologiche dei fenomeni di "irrealtà" evidenziati in esperienze di livello di aspirazione. *Bolletino di psicologia applicata, 88–90*, 64–71.

Anastasi, A. (1964). *Fields of applied psychology.* New York: McGraw-Hill.

Ancelin-Schützenberger, A. (1969–1970). Présentation du psychodrame. *Bulletin de psychologie, 13–16.*

Anohin, P. K. (1963). EEG analysis of cortico-subcortical relations in positive and negative conditioned reactions. In P. K. Anohin (Ed.), *Higher nervous activity* (orig. in Russian). New York, Moscow: Medical Literature Publishing House.

Arhangelski, L. M., and Petrov, I. P. (1967). Life plans and ideals of school youth (orig. in Russian). *Sovietskaia Pedagogika, 6*, 60–75.

Atkinson, J. W. (1977). Motivation for achievement. In Th. Blass (Ed.), *Personality variables in social behavior.* Hillsdale, NJ: Lawrence Erlbaum.

Atkinson, J. W., and Raynor, J. O. (Eds.) (1974). *Motivation and achievement.* Washington, DC: Winston.

Baily, M. N., and Chakrabarti, A. K. (1988). *Innovation and the productivity crisis.* Washington, DC: Brookings.

Balchin, N. (1970). Satisfactions in work. *Occupational Psychology, 44*, 166–171.

Bandura, A. (1989). Self-regulation of motivation and action through internal standards and goal systems. In L. Pervin (Ed.), *Goal concepts in personality and social psychology*. Hillsdale, NJ: Erlbaum.

Baron, J. (1993). Why teach thinking? An essay. *Applied Psychology: An International Review, 42,* 191–237.

Barron, F. (1968). *Creativity and personal freedom.* Toronto, Melbourne: Van Nostrand.

Bartlett, F. C. (1932). *Remembering: A study in experimental and social psychology.* Cambridge, England: Cambridge University Press.

Bartram, D. (1993). Introduction: The validity and utility of personality assessment in occupational psychology. *European Review of Applied Psychology, 43,* 183–187.

Bass, B. M. (1962). *The orientation inventory.* Palo Alto, CA: Consulting Psychologists Press.

Bauer, A. R. (1982). *The new man in Soviet psychology.* Cambridge: Harvard University Press.

Bauer, J. P., Wetta, J. M., Bucher-Andlauer, M., Philonenko, J., and De Bousingen, R. D. (1965). Le rôle du père dans la désadaptation universitaire. *Révue de Neuropsychiatrie Infantile, 10–11.*

Baumgarten, F. (1928). *Die Berufseignungsprüfungen: Theorie und Praxis.* München, Berlin: Oldenburg.

Bedni, G. Z. (1975). *Engineering psychology* (orig. in Russian). Kiev: Visha Shkola.

Beehr, T. A., Taber, T. D., and Walsh, J. T. (1980). Perceived mobility channels: Criteria for intraorganizational job mobility. *Organizational Behavior and Human Performance, 26,* 250–264.

Bell, D. (1973). *The coming of post-industrial society.* New York: Basic Books.

Bengston, V. (1971). Inter-age perceptions and the generation gap. *The Gerontologist, 11,* 85–89.

Betz, E. L. (1984). Two tests of Maslow's theory of need fulfillment. *Journal of Vocational Behavior, 24,* 204–220.

Binet, A. (1911). *Les idées modernes sur les enfants.* Paris: Flammarion.

Bingham, W. C. (1986). Employability and transition from school to work. *Educational and Vocational Guidance, 45–46,* 131–138.

Birenbaum, A. (1974). The making of a professional identity: The pediatric nurse practitioner. *Sociological Symposium, 11,* 98–110.

Booth, R. F., McNally, M. S., and Berry, N. H. (1978). Predicting performance effectiveness in paramedical occupations. *Personnel Psychology, 31,* 581–593.

Bordin, E. S. (1968). *Psychological counseling,* 2nd ed. New York: Appleton-Century-Crofts.

Brim, O. G., and Wheeler, S. (1966). *Socialization after childhood: Two essays.* New York, London: Wiley.

Bronfenbrenner, U. (1960). Freudian theories of identification and their derivatives. *Child Development, 31,* 15–40.

Brook, J. A. (1991). The link between self-esteem and work/nonwork perceptions and attitudes. *Applied Psychology: An International Review, 40,* 269–280.

Bühler, Ch. (1933). *Der menschliche Lebenslauf als psychologisches Problem.* Leipzig: Hirzel.

Burstein, G. (1963). Fear of failure, achievement motivation and aspiration to prestigeful occupations. *Journal of Abnormal and Social Psychology, 67,* 189–193.

Byrne, D. G., and Reinhart, M. J. (1989). Work characteristics, occupational achievement and the type A behavior pattern. *Journal of Occupational Psychology, 62,* 123–134.

Campbell, A., Converse, Ph. E., and Rodgers, W. L. (1976). *The quality of American life.* New York: Russell Sage Foundation.

Campbell, J. P., Dunnette, M. D., Lawler, E. E., III, and Weick, K. E. (1974). Theories of motivation. In R. Dubin (Ed.), *Human relations in administration,* 4th ed. Englewood Cliffs, NJ: Prentice Hall.

Campbell, M. E. (1971). Study of the attitudes of nursing personnel towards the geriatric patient. *Nursing Research, 20,* 147–156.

Cherns, A. B. (1973). Better working lives: A social scientist's view. *Occupational Psychology, 1–2,* 24–28.

Choubkine, V. (1966). Enquête sur le choix de la profession. *Recherches internationales à la lumière du marxisme, 53,* 70–82.

Cochran, L. (1994). What is a career problem? *Career Development Quarterly, 42,* 204–216.

Cochran, L. R. (1990). Narrative as a paradigm for career research. In R. A. Young and W. A. Borgen (Eds.), *Methodological approaches to the study of career.* New York, London: Praeger.

Cole, L. (1970). *Psychology of adolescence.* New York, London: Holt, Rinehart.

Collins, E., and Scott, P. (1978). Everyone who makes it has a mentor. *Harvard Business Review, 56,* 89–101.

Cooley, W. W. (1967). Interactions among interests, abilities and career plans. *Journal of Applied Psychology, 5,* Monograph.

Corruble, D. (1971). Les motivations professionnelles des élèves-maîtres de l'enseignement primaire. *Révue Internationale de Psychologie Appliquée, 2,* 110–122.

Crites, J. O. (1969). *Vocational psychology.* New York, London: McGraw-Hill.

Crites, J. O. (1974). A reappraisal of vocational appraisal. *Vocational Guidance Quarterly, 22,* 272–279.

Crites, J. O. (1981). *Career counseling: Models, methods and materials.* New York, London: McGraw-Hill.

Crow, L. D., and Crow, A. (1965). *Adolescent development and adjustment,* 2nd ed. New York: McGraw-Hill.

Crowne, D. P. (1979). *The experimental study of personality.* Hillsdale, NJ: Erlbaum.

Crowne, D. P., and Marlowe, D. A. (1960). A new scale of social desirability independent of psychopathology. *Journal of Consulting Psychology, 24.*

Curry, E. W., and Walling, D. (1984). Occupational prestige: Exploration of a theoretical basis. *Journal of Vocational Behavior, 25,* 124–138.

Davis, J. A. (1965). *Undergraduate career decisions: Correlates of occupational choice.* Chicago: Aldine.

Deci, E. L., and Ryan, R. M. (1985). The general causality orientation scale: Self-determination in personality. *Journal of Research in Personality, 19,* 109–134.

Dickinson, J. (1990). Adolescent representations of socioeconomic status. *British Journal of Developmental Psychology, 8,* 351–371.

Docherty, P., Fuchs-Kittowski, K., Kolm, P., and Mathiassen, L. (Eds.) (1987). *System design for human development and productivity.* Amsterdam, New York: North Holland.

Driesch, H. (1921). *Philosophie des Organischen.* Leipzig: Engelmann.

Driver, M. J. (1982). Career concepts, a new approach to career research. In R. Katz

(Ed.), *Career issues in human resources management.* Englewood Cliffs, NJ: Prentice Hall.

Dubin, R. (1956). Industrial workers' world: A study of central life interests of industrial workers. *Social Problems, 3,* 131–142.

Dumazedier, J. (1967). *Toward a society of leisure.* London: Collier Macmillan.

Duncan, O. D. (1961). A sociometric index for all occupations. In A. J. Reiss, O. D. Duncan, P. K. Hatt, and C. C. North (Eds.), *Occupations and social status.* New York: Free Press.

Duncan, O. D. (1971). Path analysis: Sociological examples. In H. M. Blalock, Jr. (Ed.), *Causal methods in the social sciences.* Chicago: Aldine.

Dupont, J.-B., Bersier, P.-A., and Müller, B. (1987). Types de personnalité et types d'études. *Universitas Lausanae, 50,* 36–49.

Eby, L. T., and Buch, K. (1995). Job loss as career growth: Responses to involuntary career transitions. *Career Development Quarterly, 44,* 26–43.

Eckert, R., and Marshall, T. (1938). *When you leave school.* New York: McGraw-Hill.

Edelson, M. (1970). *Sociotherapy and psychotherapy.* Chicago, London: Chicago University Press.

Edwards, A. L. (1957). *The social desirability variable in personality assessment and research.* New York: Dryden.

Emmons, R. (1992). Abstract vs. concrete goals: Personal striving level, physical illness and psychological well-being. *Journal of Personality and Social Psychology, 62,* 292–300.

Engel, J. F., Kollat, D. T., and Blackwell, R. D. (1968). *Consumer behavior.* New York: Holt, Rinehart and Winston.

Erikson, E. H. (1963). *Childhood and society,* 2nd ed. New York: Norton.

Erskine, R., and Moursund, J. (1988). *Integrative psychotherapy in action.* London: Sage.

Eysenck, H. J. (1972). *Psychology is about people.* London: Allen Lane.

Eysenck, H. J., and Rachman, S. (1968). *Neurosen, Ursachen und Heilmethoden.* Berlin: Deutscher Verlag der Wissenschaften.

Feather, N. T. (1982). Reasons for entering medical school in relation to value priorities of students. *Journal of Occupational Psychology, 55,* 119–128.

Ferguson, G. A. (1971). *Statistical analysis in psychology and education,* 3d ed. New York: McGraw-Hill.

Fitzgerald, L. F. (1986). On the essential relations between education and work. *Journal of Vocational Behavior, 28,* 254–284.

Flude, R. A. (1977). The development of an occupational self-concept and commitment to an occupation in a group of skilled manual workers. *Sociological Review, 25,* 41–49.

Frankl, V. E. (1962). *Man's search for meaning: An introduction to logotherapy.* Boston: Beacon Press.

French, E. G. (1958). The interaction of achievement motivation and ability in problem-solving success. *Journal of Abnormal and Social Psychology, 57,* 306–309.

Freyre de Andrade, E. (1965). Un falso dilema en la orientación vocacional. *Psicología y educación, 5.*

Friedmann, G. (1961). *The anatomy of work: Labor, leisure and the implications of automation.* New York: Free Press.

Fromm, E. (1947). *Man for himself.* New York: Rinehart.

Fryer, D. (1986). Employment deprivation and personal agency during unemployment. *Social Behavior, 1,* 3–23.

Fürstenberg, F. (1969). *Das Aufstiegsproblem in der modernen Gesellschaft,* 2nd ed. Stuttgart: Ferdinand Enke.

Galperin, P. Ia. (1957). An experimental study in the formation of mental actions. In *Psychology in the Soviet Union.* London: Routledge and Kegan Paul.

Gati, I. (1991). *Career compromises.* Paper presented at the International AEVG Conference, Lisbon.

Gillis, M. (1973). Attitudes of nursing personnel toward the aged. *Nursing Research, 22,* 517–520.

Ginott, H. G. (1961). *Group psychotherapy with children.* New York: McGraw-Hill.

Ginzberg, E., Ginsburg, S., Axelrad, S., and Herma, J. (1963). *Occupational choice.* New York, London: Columbia University Press.

Globerson, A., and Krau, E. (1993). *Organizations and management: Towards the future.* Aldershot, Sydney: Avebury.

Goffman, E. (1959). *The presentation of self in everyday life.* Garden City, NY: Doubleday-Anchor.

Goguelin, P., and Krau, E. (1992). *Projet professionnel, projet de vie.* Paris: Editions Sociales de France.

Goodman, P. S., Salipante, P., and Paransky, H. (1973). Hiring, training and retraining the hard-core unemployed. *Journal of Applied Psychology, 58,* 23–33.

Gottfredson, L. S. (1981). Circumscription and compromise: A developmental theory of occupational aspirations. *Journal of Counseling Psychology, 28,* 545–549.

Gottfredson, L. S., and Becker, H. J. (1981). A challenge to vocational psychology: How important are aspirations in determining male career development? *Journal of Vocational Behavior, 18,* 121–137.

Gribbones, W. D., and Lohnes, P. R. (1965). Shifts in adolescents' vocational values. *Personnel and Guidance Journal, 44,* 248–252.

Guilford, J. P., and Fruchter, B. (1973). *Fundamental statistics in psychology and education,* 5th ed. New York: McGraw-Hill.

Guttman, L. (1968). A general nonmetric technique for finding the smallest coordinate space for a configuration of points. *Psychometrika, 33,* 469–506.

Hackman, J. R., and Oldham, G. R. (1976). Motivation through the design of work: Test of a theory. *Organizational Behavior and Human Performance, 16,* 250–279.

Haddon, W., Suchman, E. E., and Klein, D. (1964). *Accident research.* New York, London: Harper and Row.

Haldane, B. (1974). *Career satisfaction and success: A guide to job freedom.* New York: Amacom.

Hall, D. T. (1976). *Careers in organizations.* Glenview, IL: Scott, Foresman.

Hall, D. T., and Nougaim, K. E. (1968). An examination of Maslow's need hierarchy in an organizational setting. *Organizational Behavior and Human Performance, 3,* 12–35.

Hare, R. D. (1970). *Psychopathy: Theory and research.* New York, London: Wiley.

Hartley, J., Jacobson, D., Klandermans, B. and van Vuuren, B. (1991). *Job insecurity— Coping with job at risk.* London: Sage.

Haug, M. R., and Sussman, M. B. (1967). The second career: Variant of a sociological concept. *Journal of Gerontology, 4,* 438–445.

Havighurst, R. J. (1964). Youth in exploration and man emergent. In H. Borow (Ed.), *Man in a world at work*. Boston: Houghton Mifflin.

Hayes, J. (1973). Work experience in the perception of occupations. *Occupational Psychology, 47,* 121–129.

Heath, D. H. (1976). Adolescent and adult predictors of vocational adaptation. *Journal of Vocational Behavior, 9,* 1–13.

Hepner, H. W. (1966). *Psychology applied to life and work*, 4th ed. Englewood Cliffs, NJ: Prentice Hall.

Herr, E. L. (1984). Links among training, employability and employment. In N. C. Gysbers (Ed.), *Designing careers: Counseling to enhance education, work and leisure*. San Francisco: Jossey Bass.

Herzberg, F., Mausner, B., and Snyderman, B. (1959). *The motivation to work*, 2nd ed. New York: Wiley.

Hesketh, B., Elmslie, S., and Kaldor, W. (1990). Career compromise: An alternative account to Gottfredson's theory. *Journal of Counseling Psychology, 37,* 49–56.

Hill, J.M.M. (1969). *Transition from school to work*. London: Tavistock.

Hofstede, G. (1980). *Culture's consequence*. Beverly Hills, London: Sage.

Holland, J. L. (1966). A theory of vocational choice. In J. Peters and C. Hansen (Eds.), *Vocational guidance and career development*. London: Macmillan.

Holland, J. L. (1973). *Making vocational choices: A theory of careers*. Englewood Cliffs, NJ: Prentice Hall.

Holland, J. L. (1976). Vocational preferences. In M. D. Dunnette (Ed.), *Handbook of industrial and organizational psychology*. Chicago: Rand McNally.

Homans, G. C. (1950). *The human group*. New York: Harcourt, Brace.

Howard, G. S. (1993). *Career counseling as meaning making*. Symposium at the 101st Annual Convention of the American Psychological Association, Toronto.

Howard, G. S., Nance, D. W., and Myers, P. (1987). *Adaptive counseling and therapy: A systematic approach to selecting effective treatments*. London: Jossey Bass.

Hughes, E. (1949). Queries concerning industry and society growing out of study of ethnic relations in industry. *American Sociological Review, 14,* 219 sqq.

Hughes, E. (1958). *Men and their work*. Glenco, IL: Free Press.

Inglehart, R. (1977). *The silent revolution*. Princeton, NJ: Princeton University Press.

Inhelder, B., and Piaget, J. (1958). *The growth of logical thinking from childhood to adolescence*. New York: Basic Books.

Ivey, A. E. (1983). *Intentional interviewing and counseling*. Monterey, CA: Brooks/Cole.

Jackson, P. R. (1986). Towards a social psychology of unemployment: A commentary on Fryer, Jahoda, Kelvin, and Jarrett. *Social Behavior, 1,* 35–39.

Jacob, P. E. (1965). Does higher education influence student values? In J. Raths and J. D. Grambs (Eds.), *Society and education*. Englewood Cliffs, NJ: Prentice Hall.

Jacobs, J. A., and Powell, B. (1985). Occupational prestige: A sex neutral concept? *Sex Roles, 12,* 1061–1071.

Jaide, W. (1966). *Die Berufswahl*, 2nd ed. München: Juventa.

James, W. (1890). *Principles of psychology*. New York: Holt.

Janne, H. (1967). Morale du travail, morale des loisirs, un nouveau type humain en perspective. In *La civilisation des loisirs*. Paris: Marabout Université.

Jans, N. A. (1982). The nature and measurement of work involvement. *Occupational Psychology, 55,* 57–67.

Jenkins, C. D., Zyzanski, S. J., and Rosenman, R. H. (1979). *Jenkins Activity Survey, Form C*. Psychological Corporation.

Jepsen, D. A. (1992). Practice and research in career counseling and development. *Career Development Quarterly, 41*, 98–129.

Jones, R. A. (1977). *Self-fulfilling prophecies*. Hillsdale, NJ: Lawrence Erlbaum.

Jung, C. G. (1954). *The development of personality*. London: Routledge and Kegan Paul.

Jung, J. (1978). *Understanding human motivation*. New York: Macmillan.

Kadushin, C. (1969). The professional self-concept of music students. *American Journal of Sociology, 5*, 389–404.

Kafry, D., and Pines, A. (1980). The experience of tedium in life and work. *Human Relations, 33*, 477–503.

Kanekar, S., Kolsawalla, M. B., and Nazareth, T. (1989). Occupational prestige as a function of occupant's gender. *Journal of Applied Social Psychology, 19*, 681–688.

Kanungo, R. N. (1982). Measurement of job and work involvement. *Journal of Applied Psychology, 67*, 341–349.

Kapes, J. T., and Strickler, R. E. (1975). A longitudinal study of change in work values between ninth and twelfth grades as related to high school curriculum. *Journal of Vocational Behavior, 6*, 81–93.

Kapr, J. (1969). Occupational prestige (orig. in Czech). *Sociologicky časopis, 6*, 740–747.

Kasser, T., and Ryan, R. M. (1993). A dark side of the American dream: Correlates of financial success as a central life aspiration. *Journal of Personality and Social Psychology, 65*, 410–422.

Katzell, R. A. (1964). Personal values, job satisfaction and job behavior. In H. Borow (Ed.), *Man in a world at work*. Boston: Houghton Mifflin.

Kelly, G. A. (1955). *The psychology of personal constructs*. New York: Norton.

Keynes, J. M. (1936). *General theory of employment, interest and money*. New York: Harcourt Brace.

King, W. L., and Hautaluoma, J. E. (1987). Comparison of job satisfaction, life satisfaction and performance of overeducated and other workers. *Journal of Social Psychology, 127*, 421–433.

Kluckhohn, C. (1962). *Culture and behavior*. New York: Free Press.

Knasel, E. G., Super, D. E., and Kidd, J. M. (1981). *Work salience and work values: Their dimensions, assessment and significance*. National Institute for Careers, Education and Counseling (USA).

Kohn, M. L. (1969). *Class and conformity: A study in values*. New York: Dorsey.

Konstorum, S. I. (1962). *Practical psychotherapy*, 2nd ed. (orig. in Russian). Moscow: Ministry of Health.

Kopelman, R. C. (1977). Psychological stages of careers in engineering: An expectancy theory taxonomy. *Journal of Vocational Behavior, 10*, 270–286.

Kram, K. E. (1985). Mentoring alternatives: The role of peer relationships in career development. *Academy of Management Journal, 28*, 110–132.

Kram, K. E. (1986). Mentoring in the work place. In D. T. Hall (Ed.), *Career development in organizations*. San Francisco: Jossey-Bass.

Krau, E. (1962). The problem of illusions (orig. in Romanian). *Analele Romano-sovietice, Psihologie-Pedagogie, 2*, 89–102.

Krau, E. (1967). The experimental diagnosis of personality traits through a projective completion test. *Révue Roumaine des Sciences Sociales, 2,* 177–188.

Krau, E. (1970a). Experimental research in vocational adjustment. *Studia Psychologica, 3,* 293–306.

Krau, E. (1970b). Thinking in representations—an alternative way of reasoning. *Studia Psychologica, 3,* 199–204.

Krau, E. (1974a). The fluidity of psychogenetic disturbances and the social and vocational adjustment. *Studia Psychologica, 4,* 241–244.

Krau, E. (1974b). On problems connected with the start of maladjustment in adolescents and the fight against it (orig. in Romanian). *Revista de psihologie, 3,* 337–348.

Krau, E. (1977a). Le point de vue de la carrière dans la prédiction de l'adaptation professionnelle. *Travail Humain, 1,* 107–121.

Krau, E. (1977b). Subjective dimension assignment through set to objective situations. In D. Magnusson and N. S. Endler (Eds.), *Personality at the crossroads: Current issues in interactional psychology.* New York, London: Wiley.

Krau, E. (1981a). Immigrants preparing for the second career: The behavioral strategies adopted. *Journal of Vocational Behavior, 18,* 289–303.

Krau, E. (1981b). Turnover analysis and prediction from a career developmental point of view. *Personnel Psychology, 34,* 771–790.

Krau, E. (1981c). Vocational counseling at the crossroads (orig. in Hebrew). *Israeli Journal of Psychology and Counseling in Education, 14,* 92–194.

Krau, E. (1982a). Motivational feedback loops in the structure of action. *Journal of Personality and Social Psychology, 43,* 1030–1040.

Krau, E. (1982b). The vocational side of a new start in life: A career model of immigrants. *Journal of Vocational Behavior, 20,* 313–330.

Krau, E. (1983a). The attitudes towards work in career transitions. *Journal of Vocational Behavior, 23,* 270–285.

Krau, E. (1983b). How important is vocational success to the overall satisfaction of immigrants? *Journal of Applied Social Psychology, 13,* 473–495.

Krau, E. (1984). Commitment to work in immigrants: Its functions and peculiarities. *Journal of Vocational Behavior, 24,* 329–339.

Krau, E. (1985). The feeling of low quality of life and industrial progress: Are they linked? *International Journal of Sociology and Social Policy, 5,* 29–43.

Krau, E. (1987). The crystallization of work values in adolescence: A socio-cultural approach. *Journal of Vocational Behavior, 30,* 103–123.

Krau, E. (Ed.) (1989a). *Self-realization, success and adjustment.* New York, London: Praeger.

Krau, E. (1989b). The transition in life domain salience and the modification of work values between high school and adult employment. *Journal of Vocational Behavior, 34,* 100–116.

Krau, E. (1991). *The contradictory immigrant problem: A sociopsychological analysis.* New York, Bern: Peter Lang.

Krau, E., Aluas, I., Latis, I., and Jurcau, N. (1969). Sociopsychological variables of vocational choice and achievements in vocational training (orig. in Romanian). *Revista de psihologie, 1,* 45–61.

Krau, E., Latis, I., Jurcau, N., and Czitrom, I. (1972). A four-year experiment concerning the introduction of a psychological entrance examination in trade schools (orig. in Romanian). *Revista de psihologie, 2,* 139–148.

Krau, E., and Ziv, L. (1990). The hidden selection of the occupational appeal: The paradigm of nurses. *International Journal of Sociology and Social Policy, 7,* 1–29.

Kraus, V. (1978). Occupational prestige. *Social Forces, 56,* 900–918.

Krech, D., Crutchfield, R. S., and Ballachey, E. L. (1962). *Individual in society.* San Francisco, Toronto: McGraw-Hill.

Kroll, A. M., Dinklage, J. B., Lee, J., Morley, E. D., and Wilson, E. H. (1970). *Career development: Growth and crisis.* New York: Wiley.

Krumboltz, J. D. (1988). *Career beliefs inventory.* Palo Alto, CA: Consulting Psychologists Press.

Krumboltz, J. D. (1993). Integrating career and personal counseling. *Career Development Quarterly, 42,* 143–149.

Kuhl, J. (1992). A theory of self-regulation: Action vs. state orientation, self-discrimination and some applications. *Applied Psychology: An International Review, 41,* 97–129.

Kulik, C. T., Oldham, G. R., and Hackman, J. R. (1987). Work design as an approach to person-environment fit. *Journal of Vocational Behavior, 31,* 278–296.

Künkel, H. (1939). *Die Lebensalter.* Jena: Fischer.

Kuvelesky, W. P., and Bealer, R. C. (1966). A clarification of the concept "occupational choice." *Rural Sociology, 3,* 265–275.

Lamb, M. E. (Ed.) (1976). *The role of the father in child development.* New York, London: Wiley.

Larsen, R. J. (1992). Neuroticism and selective encoding and recall of symptoms: Evidence for a combined concurrent-retrospective study. *Journal of Personality and Social Psychology, 62,* 480–488.

Lawler, E. E. (1966). Ability as a moderator of the relationship between job attitudes and job performance. *Personnel Psychology, 19,* 153–164.

Lawler, E. E. (1971). *Pay and organizational effectiveness: A psychological view.* New York: McGraw-Hill.

Laxenaire, M., and Picard, F. (1969–1970). Transfer en psychothérapie de groupe et psychodrame. *Bulletin de psyhologie, 13–16.*

Legewie, H., and Ehlers, W. (1972). *Knaurs moderne Psychologie.* München-Zürich: Droemer Knaur.

Leonhard, K. (1965). Stellt die Beseitigung des Symptoms in der Psychotherapie eine Heilung dar? *Psychiatrie, Neurologie und medizinische Psyhologie, 9.*

Leplat, J. (1990). Skills and tacit skills: A psychological perspective. *Applied Psychology: An International Review, 39,* 143–155.

Levenson, R. W., and Ruef, A. M. (1992). Empathy: A physiological substrate. *Journal of Personality and Social Psychology, 63,* 234–246.

Levinson, D. J., Darrow, C. N., Klein, E. B., Levinson, M. H., and McKee, B. (1978). *The seasons of a man's life.* New York: Knopf.

Lévy-Leboyer, C. (1986). A psychologist's analysis of the work value crisis. *International Review of Applied Psychology, 35,* 53–61.

Lévy-Leboyer, C. (1988). Looking at work motivation from a wider angle. *British Journal of Guidance and Counseling, 16,* 241–249.

Lewin, K., Dembo, T., Festinger, L., and Sears, P. S. (1944). Level of aspiration. In J. V. Hunt (Ed.), *Personality and the behavior disorders,* Vol. 1. New York: Ronald Press.

Lewis, Ch., and O'Brien, M. (Eds.) (1987). *Reassessing fatherhood*. London, Beverly Hills: Sage.

Linton, R. (1945). *The cultural background of personality*. New York: Appleton-Century-Crofts.

Lipset, S. M., and Bendix, R. (1953). *Class, status and power: A reader in social stratification*. Glencoe: Free Press.

Locke, E. A. (1976). The nature and causes of job satisfaction. In M. D. Dunnette (Ed.), *Handbook of industrial and organizational psychology*. Chicago: Rand McNally.

Lofquist, L. H., and Dawis, R. V. (1978). Values as second-order needs in the theory of work adjustment. *Journal of Vocational Behavior, 12,* 12–19.

Lofquist, L. H., and Dawis, R. V. (1991). *Essentials of person-environment correspondence counseling*. Minneapolis: University of Minnesota Press.

Lofquist, L. H., and England, G. W. (1961). *Problems in vocational counseling*. Dubuque, IA: W. C. Brown.

Lyon, R. (1965). Beyond the conventional career: Some speculations. *Journal of Counseling Psychology, 12,* 153–158.

Magnus, K., Diener, E., Fujita, F., and Pavot, W. (1993). Extraversion and neuroticism as predictors of objective life events: A longitudinal analysis. *Journal of Personality and Social Psychology, 65,* 1046–1053.

Makarenko, A. S. (1949). *Selected pedagogical works* (orig. in Russian). Moscow: Outchpedghiz.

Mâle, P. (1966). *Psicoterapia del adolescente*. Barcelona: Luis Miracle.

Mangham, I. L. (1978). *Interactions and interventions in organizations*. New York: Wiley.

Marques, F. J. (1986). *The relative importance of work in Portuguese students*. Paper presented at the Twenty-first International Congress of Applied Psychology, Jerusalem.

Maslow, A. H. (1954). *Motivation and personality*. New York: Harper.

Maslow, A. H. (1962). *Toward a psychology of being*. Princeton, NJ: Van Nostrand.

Maslow, A. H. (1991a). The nature of happiness (Edited by E. Hoffman). *Humanistic Education and Development, 29,* 99–102.

Maslow, A. H. (1991b). Critique of self-actualization theory (Edited by E. Hoffman). *Humanistic Education and Development, 29,* 103–108.

Maupeou-Leplatre, N. de (1963). *Le cheminement professionnel des jeunes ouvriers*. Université de Paris: Institut des Sciences Sociales.

McClelland, D. C. (1961). *The achieving society*. Princeton, NJ: Van Nostrand.

McCormick, E. J. (1964). *Human factors engineering*. New York, London: McGraw-Hill.

McCrae, R. R. (1993). Moderated analyses of longitudinal personal stability. *Journal of Personality and Social Psychology, 65,* 577–585.

McCrae, R. R., and Costa, P. T., Jr. (1990). *Personality in adulthood*. New York: Guilford Press.

McKinney, F. (1965). *Understanding personality*. Boston: Houghton Mifflin.

Mead, G. H. (1967). *Mind, self and society*. Chicago, London: University of Chicago Press.

Meili, R. (1951). *Psychologie der Berufsberatung*. Basel: Krager.

Meir, E. I., and Krau, E. (1983). Some Israeli contributions to the measurement of interests and personality. *Bulletin de la Commission Internationale des Tests, 18,* 9–22.

Meissner, M. (1971). The long arm of the job. *Industrial Relations, 10,* 239–260.

Merton, R. K. (1957). *Social theory and social structure.* New York: Free Press.

Meyer, W. N. (1973). *Leistungsmotiv und Ursachenerklärung von Erfolg und Misserfolg.* Stuttgart: Klett.

Mikula, G., Uray, H., and Schwinger, Th. (1974). Die Entwicklung einer deutschen Fassung der Mehrabian Risk Preference Scale. *Berichte aus dem Institut für Psychologie der Universität Graz,* Graz.

Milkovich, G. T., Anderson, J. C., and Greenhalgh, L. (1976). Organizational careers: Environmental, organizational and individual determinants. In L. Dyer (Ed.), *Careers in organizations: Individual planning and organizational development.* Ithaca: NYSSILR.

Miller, D. C., and Form, W. H. (1951). *Industrial sociology.* New York: Harper and Row.

Miller, G. A., Galanter, E. and Pribram, K. H. (1967). *Plans and the structure of behavior.* New York: Holt, Rinehart and Winston.

Minor, C., and Neel, R. C. (1958). The relationship between achievement motive and occupational preference. *Journal of Counseling Psychology, 5,* 34–43.

Mirande, A. (1968). On occupational aspirations and job attainments. *Rural Sociology, 3,* 347–355.

Mischel, W. (1968). *Personality and assessment.* New York: Wiley.

Moore, G. A. (1976). An anthropological view of urban education. In J. J. Roberts and S. K. Akinsaya (Eds.), *Educational patterns and cultural configurations.* New York: McKay.

Mortimer, J. T., and Lorence, J. (1979). Work experience and occupational value socialization: New York: A longitudinal study. *American Journal of Sociology, 84,* 1361–1385.

MOW International Research Team (1987). *The meaning of working.* London: Academic Press.

Munley, P. H. (1977). Erikson's theory of psychosocial development and career development. *Journal of Vocational Behavior, 10,* 261–269.

Münsterberg, H. (1913). *Psychology and industrial efficiency.* Boston: Houghton Mifflin.

Murphy, P. P., and Burk, D. H. (1976). Career development of men at mid-life. *Journal of Vocational Behavior, 9,* 337–343.

Mury, G. (1965). Notes sur l'inadaptation. *Nouvelle critique, 175.*

Musgrave, P. W. (1967). Towards a sociological theory of occupational choice. *Sociological Review, 15,* 33–46.

Musgrave, P. W. (1972). *The sociology of education.* London: Methuen.

Myers, C., and Davids, K. (1993). Tacit skill and performance at work. *Applied Psychology: An International Review, 42,* 117–139.

Nevill, D., and Super, D. E. (1986). *The salience inventory manual.* Palo Alto, CA: Consulting Psychologists' Press.

Noeth, R. J., Engen, H. B., and Noeth, P. E. (1984). Making career decisions: A self-report and factors that help high-school students. *Vocational Guidance Quarterly, 32,* 240–248.

Osgood, Ch. E. (1964). Semantic differential technique in the comparative study of cultures. *American Anthropologist, 66,* 171–200.

Osgood, Ch. E., May, W. J., and Miron, M. S. (1975). *Cross-cultural universals of affective meaning*. Chicago: University of Illinois Press.

Osgood, Ch. E., Suci, G. J., and Tannenbaum, P. J. (1971). *The measurement of meaning*. Chicago: University of Illinois Press.

Pagès, M. (1965). *L'orientation non-directive en psychothérapie et en psychologie sociale*. Paris: Dunod.

Palmer, S., and Cochran, L. (1988). Parents as agents of career development. *Journal of Counseling Psychology, 35,* 71–76.

Pareto, V. (1919). *Traité de sociologie générale*. Lausanne, Paris: Payot.

Parker, S. (1971). *The future of work and leisure*. New York: Praeger.

Parmentier-Beloux, M. (1963). *Médicine d'orientation scolaire et professionnelle*. Paris: Masson et Cie.

Parsons, T. (1954). An analytical approach to the theory of social stratification. In T. Parsons, *Essays in sociological theory*. Glencoe, IL: Free Press.

Parsons, T., and Bales, R. F. (1955). *Family, socialization and interaction process*. New York: Free Press.

Paterson, D. G. (1957). The conservation of human talent. *American Psychologist, 12,* 134–144.

Pavlov, I. P. (1951). *A twenty-years long experience of objectively studying higher nervous activity* (orig. in Russian). Moscow: Medgiz.

Peake, Th. H., and Archer, R. P. (1988). *Brief psychotherapies: Changing frames of mind*. London: Sage.

Pearson, G. H. (1958). *Adolescence and the conflict of generations*. New York: Norton.

Perrow, C. (1970). *Organizational analysis: A sociological review*. Belmont, CA: Brooks/Cole.

Phillips, A. (1968). *Human adaptation and its failures*. New York, London: Academic Press.

Phillips-Jones, L. L. (1982). *Mentors and protégés*. New York: Arbor House.

Piaget, J. (1967). *Biologie et connaissance*. Paris: Gallimard.

Poole, M. E., and Cooney, G. H. (1985). Careers: Adolescent awareness and exploration of possibilities for self. *Journal of Vocational Behavior, 26,* 251–263.

Prause, G. (1969). *Niemand hat Kolumbus ausgelacht*. Düsseldorf-Wien Econ-Verlag.

Pryor, R. (1982). Values, preferences, needs, work ethics and orientations to work: Toward a conceptual and empirical integration. *Journal of Vocational Behavior, 20,* 40–52.

Rainville, J. M. (1974). La satisfaction à l'égard de la tâche et la satisfaction à l'égard de la carrière. *Relations Industrielles, 29,* 83–98.

Raven, J. (1981). The most important problem in education is to come to terms with values. *Oxford Review of Education, 7,* 253–272.

Raynor, J. O. (1974). Motivation and career striving. In J. W. Atkinson and J. O. Raynor (Eds.), *Motivation and achievement*. Washington, DC: Winston.

Roberts, K. (1968). The entry into employment: An approach towards a general theory. *Sociological Review, 16,* 165–184.

Robinson, J. P. (1969). Occupational norms and differences in job satisfaction: A summary of survey research evidence. In J. P. Robinson and K. B. Head (Eds.), *Measurement of occupational attitudes and occupational characteristics*. Ann Arbor, Michigan: Institute for Survey Research.

Rodriguez-Tomé, H. J. (1965). Le rôle des adultes significatifs privilégiés. *Enfance, 5.*

Roe, A. (1962). *The psychology of occupations*. New York, London: Wiley.

Roe, A. (1966). Early determinants of vocational choice. In J. Peters and C. Hansen (Eds.). *Vocational guidance and career development*. London: Macmillan.

Roethlisberger, F. J. and Dickson, W. J. (1964). *Management and the worker*. New York: Wiley.

Rokeach, M. (1973). *The nature of human values*. New York: Free Press.

Roman, C. (1971). *Nobel prize winners answer to the question: Is there a secret of celebrity?* (Orig. in Romanian). Bucharest: Political Publishing House.

Ronen, S. (1979). Cross-national study of employee's work goals. *International Review of Applied Psychology, 28,* 1–13.

Rosenberg, M. (1957). *Occupations and values*. Glencoe, IL: Free Press.

Rosencranz, H. A. and McNevin, F. E. (1969). A factor analysis of attitudes toward the aged. *The Gerontologist, 9,* 55–59.

Rossman, G. E. and Kirk, B. A. (1970). Comparison of counseling seekers and nonseekers. *Journal of Counseling Psychology, 17,* 184–188.

Rothstein, W. G. (1980). The significance of occupations in work careers: A theoretical review. *Journal of Vocational Behavior, 17,* 328–343.

Rotter, G. B. (1966). Generalized expectancies for internal versus external control of reinforcement. *Psychological Monographs, 80,* 1.

Rotter, G. B., Chance, J. E. and Phares, E. J. (1972). *Applications of social learning theory of personality*. New York: Holt, Rinehart and Winston.

Rubin, I. M. and Morgan, H. G. (1967). A projective study of attitudes towards continuing education. *Journal of Applied Psychology, 6,* 453–460.

Rubinstein, S. L. (1962). *Grundlagen der allgemeinen Psychologie*. Berlin: Volk und Wissen.

Rumberger, R. W. (1982). *The structure of work and the underutilization of college-educated work force*. Stanford, CA: Institute for Research on Educational Finance and Governance.

Rychlak, J. F. (1982). *Personality and life style of young male managers*. New York, London: Academic Press.

Saleh, S. D., and Hyde, J. (1969). Intrinsic vs. extrinsic orientation and job satisfaction. *Occupational Psychology, 1,* 47–52.

Salomone, P., and Slaney, R. B. (1981). The influence of chance and contingency factors on the vocational choice process of nonprofessional workers. *Journal of Vocational Behavior, 19,* 25–35.

Sarason, B. S. (1977). *Work, aging and social change*. New York: Free Press.

Savickas, M. L. (1989). Career style assessment and counseling. In T. Sweeney (Ed.), *Adlerian counseling: A practical approach for a new decade*, 3d ed. Muncie.

Savickas, M. L. (1993). *Career counseling as meaning making*. Symposium at the 101st Annual Convention of the American Psychological Association, Toronto.

Savickas, M. L., and Jarjoura, D. (1991). The career decision scale as a type indicator. *Journal of Counseling Psychology, 38,* 85–90.

Savickas, M. L., and Super, D. E. (1993). Can life stages and substages be identified in students? *Man and Work, 4,* 71–78.

Schaefer, J. (1983). Schul-und Berufsberatung in der Bundesrepublik Deutschland. *Bulletin IAEVG, 40,* 23–27.

Scharmann, T. (Ed.) (1966). *Schule und Beruf als Sozialisationsfaktoren*. Stuttgart: Enke.

Schein, E. H. (1968). *The individual, the organization and the career: A conceptual scheme.* (Working paper No. 326–68). Cambridge, MA: M.I.T., Sloan School of Management.

Schlesinger, I. M., and Guttman, L. (1969). Smallest space analysis of intelligence and achievement tests. *Psychological Bulletin, 71,* 95–100.

Schulenberg, J., Vondracek, F. W., and Kim, J.-R. (1993). Career certainty and short-term changes in work values during adolescence. *Career Development Quarterly, 41,* 268–285.

Schwarz, B., Weise, K., and Thom, A. (1971). *Sozialpsychiatrie in der Gesellshaft.* Leipzig: Thieme.

Seidlitz, L., and Diener, E. (1993). Memory for positive vs. negative life events: Theories for the differences between happy and unhappy persons. *Journal of Personality and Social Psychology, 64,* 654–664.

Selye, H. (1956). *The stress of life.* New York: McGraw-Hill.

Sewell, W. H., Hauser, R. M., and Featherman, D. L. (Eds.) (1976). *Schooling and achievement in American society.* New York, London: Academic Press.

Sheehy, G. (1976). *Passages.* New York: Bantam Books.

Sheppard, D. J. (1971). The measurement of vocational maturity in adults. *Journal of Vocational Behavior, 1,* 399–406.

Silverman, H. (1969). Caveats in the purchase of psychotherapy. *Contemporary Psychology, 14,* 671–672.

Simpson, R. L. (1962). Parental influence, anticipatory socialization and social mobility. *American Sociological Review, 27,* 517–522.

Smith, P. C., Kendall, L. M., and Hulin, C. L. (1969). *The measurement of satisfaction in work and retirement.* Chicago: Rand McNally.

Stacey, B. G. (1968). Inter-generation occupational mobility in Britain. *Occupational Psychology, 1,* 40–46.

Stefflre, B. (1966). Vocational development: Ten propositions in search for a theory. *Personnel and Guidance Journal, 44,* 611–616.

Stoetzel, J. (1983). *Les valeurs du temps présent.* Paris: P.U.F.

Strong, E. K. (1960). An eighteen-year-long longitudinal report on interests. In W. L. Layton (Ed.), *The Strong vocational interest blank: Research and uses.* Minneapolis: University of Minnesota Press.

Subich, L. M. (1992). Holland's theory: "Pushing the envelope." *Journal of Vocational Behavior, 40,* 201–206.

Super, D. E. (1954). Career patterns as a basis for vocational counseling. *Journal of Counseling Psychology, 1,* 12–20.

Super, D. E. (1962). Transition from vocational guidance to counseling psychology. In J. F. McGowen and L. D. Schmidt (Eds.), *Counseling: Reading in theory and practice.* New York, London: Holt, Rinehart and Winston.

Super, D. E. (1963). Toward making self-concept theory operational. In D. E. Super, R. Starishevski, N. Matlin, and J. P. Jordaan (Eds.), *Career development: A self-concept theory.* Princeton, NJ: College Examination Board.

Super, D. E. (1970). *Work values inventory.* Chicago: Riverside.

Super, D. E. (1980). A life span, life-space approach to career development. *Journal of Vocational Behavior, 16,* 282–298.

Super, D. E., Crites, J. O., Hummel, R. C., Moser, H. P., Overstreet, P. L., and Warnath, C. F. (1957). *Vocational development: A framework for research.* New York: Teachers College.

Super, D. E., Starishevsky, R., Matlin, N., and Jordaan, J. P. (1963). *Career development: A self-concept theory.* Princeton, NJ: College Examination Board.

Swann, W. B., Jr. (1983). Self-verification: Bringing social reality into harmony with the self. In J. Suls and A. G. Greenwald (Eds.), *Social psychological perspectives on the self,* Vol. 2. Hillsdale, NJ: Erlbaum.

Swann, W. B., Jr. (1987). Identity negotiation: Where two roads meet. *Journal of Personality and Social Psychology, 53,* 1038–1051.

Szasz, Th. S. (1960). The myth of mental illness. *American Psychologist,* February, 113–118.

Tausky, C., and Dubin, R. (1965). Career anchorage: Managerial mobility motivations. *American Sociological Review, 5.*

Taylor, N. B., and Pryor, R.L.G. (1985). Exploring the process of compromise in career decision making. *Journal of Vocational Behavior, 27,* 171–190.

Teplov, B. M., and Gurevitch, K. M. (1966). *The problem of vocational fitness in the operational personnel of energy systems* (orig. in Russian). Moscow: Prosveshchenie.

Thurstone, L. L. (1960). *The measurement of values.* Chicago: University of Chicago Press.

Thurstone, L. R., and Chave, E. (1929). *The measurement of attitudes.* Chicago: University of Illinois Press.

Tice, D. M. (1992). Self-concept change and self-presentation: The looking glass self is also a magnifying glass. *Journal of Personality and Social Psychology, 63,* 435–451.

Tiggemann, M., and Winefield, A. H. (1984). The effects of unemployment on the mood, self-esteem, locus of control and depressive affect of school leavers. *Journal of Occupational Psychology, 57,* 33–42.

Tinsley, H.E.A., and Tinsley, D. J. (1988). An expanded context for the study of career decision making, development and maturity. In W. B. Walsh and S. H. Osipow (Eds.), *Career decision making.* Hillsdale, NJ: Lawrence Erlbaum.

Toffler, A. (1970). *Future shock.* New York: Random House.

Trentini, G. (1986). *The work importance study in Italy.* Paper presented at the XXI International Congress of Applied Psychology, Jerusalem.

Truax, Ch. B., and Carkhuff, R. R. (1968). *Toward effective counseling and psychotherapy.* Chicago: Aldine.

Turner, R. H. (1964). *The social context of ambition.* San Francisco: Chandler.

Tyler, L. (1953). *The work of the counselor.* New York: Appleton-Century-Crofts.

Tyler, L. (1969). *The work of the counselor,* 3d ed. New York: Appleton-Century-Crofts.

Tyler, L. (1978). *Individuality.* San Francisco, London: Jossey-Bass.

Vallerand, R. J., Pelletier, L. G., Deshaies, P., Cuerrier, J.-P., and Mongeau, C. (1992). Ajzen and Fischbein's theory of reasoned action as applied to moral behavior: A confirmatory analysis. *Journal of Personality and Social Psychology, 62,* 98–109.

van Maanen, J. (1978). *Organizational careers: Some new perspectives.* Chichester, New York: Wiley.

Vardi, Y. (1980). Organizational career mobility: An integrative model. *Academy of Management Review, 5,* 341–355.

Venables, E. (1968). *Leaving school and starting work.* Oxford: Pergamon.

Volsky, Th., Magoon, Th. M., Norman, W. T., and Hoyt, D. T. (1965). *The outcomes of counseling and psychotherapy.* Minneapolis: University of Minnesota Press.

Vondracek, F. W. (1992). The construct of identity and its use in career theory and research. *Career Development Quarterly, 41,* 130–144.

von Neumann, J. (1958). *The computer and the brain.* New Haven: Yale University Press.

Vroom, V. H. (1964). *Work and motivation.* New York, London: Wiley.

Wallon, H. (1955). *De l'acte à la pensée.* Paris: Flammarion.

Wanous, J. P. (1973). Effects of realistic job preview on job acceptance, job attitudes and job survival. *Journal of Applied Psychology, 58,* 327–332.

Ward, E. (1966). Men and computers. In R. M. Gagné and A. W. Melton (Eds.), *Psychological principles in system development.* New York: Holt, Rinehart and Winston.

Warr, P. (1982). A national study of non-financial employment commitment. *Journal of Occupational Psychology, 55,* 297–312.

Warr, P., and Jackson, P. (1984). Men without jobs: Some correlates of age and length of unemployment. *Journal of Occupational Psychology, 57,* 77–85.

Warren, G. D., Winer, J. L., and Dailey, K. C. (1981). Extending Holland's theory to the later years. *Journal of Vocational Behavior, 18,* 104–114.

Waterman, A. S. (1993). Two conceptions of happiness: Contrasts of personal expressiveness (eudaimonia) and hedonic enjoyment. *Journal of Personality and Social Psychology, 64,* 678–691.

Weaver, Ch. N. (1977). Occupational prestige as a factor in the net relationship between occupation and job satisfaction. *Personnel Psychology, 30,* 607–612.

Weber, M. (1930). *The Protestant ethic and the rise of capitalism.* New York: Scribner.

Weil, P. G. (1969–1970). Psychodrame et psychanalyse. *Bulletin de psychologie, 13–16.*

Weiner, B., and Kukla, A. (1970). An attributional analysis of achievement motivation. *Journal of Personality and Social Psychology, 15,* 1–20.

Wellbank, H. L., Hall, D. T., Morgan, A., and Hamner, W. C. (1978). Planning job progression for effective career development and human resources management. *Personnel,* March–April, 54–64.

Werts, Ch. E. (1968). Paternal influence on career choice. *Journal of Counseling Psychology, 15,* 48–52.

Wheeler, L., and Miyake, K. (1992). Social comparisons in everyday life. *Journal of Personality and Social Psychology, 62,* 760–773.

Wiener, N. (1961). *Cybernetics or control and communication in the animal and the machine.* New York, London: MIT Press and Wiley.

Wijting, J. P., Arnold, C. R., and Conrad, A. K. (1978). Generational differences in work values between parents and children and between boys and girls across grade levels 6, 9 and 12. *Journal of Vocational Behavior, 12,* 245–260.

Wilensky, H. (1960). Work careers and social integration. *International Social Science Journal, 12,* 543–560.

Wolfbein, S. L. (1967). *Education and training for full employment.* New York, London: Columbia University Press.

Wollack, St., Goodale, J. G., Wijting, J. P., and Smith, P. C. (1971). Development of the survey of work values. *Journal of Applied Psychology, 4,* 331–336.

Woodworth, R. S. (1958). *Dynamics of behavior.* New York: Holt.

Wylie, R. C. (1961). *The self concept.* Lincoln: University of Nebraska Press.

Yankelovich, D. (1974). The meaning of work. In American Assembly, Columbia University (Ed.), *The worker and the job: Coping with change*. Englewood Cliffs, NJ: Prentice Hall.

Younghusband, E. (1966). *New developments in casework*. London: Allen and Unwin.

Zaleznik, A., Christensen, C. A., and Roethlisberger, F. J. (1958). *The motivation, productivity and satisfaction of workers*. Boston: Harvard University, Graduate School of Business Administration.

Zubin, J. (1967). Classification of the behavior disorders. *Annual Review of Psychology, 19,* 373–407.

Zytowski, D. G. (1970). The concept of work values. *Vocational Guidance Quarterly, 18,* 176–186.

Index

About the Author

EDGAR KRAU is professor of labor studies, Tel-Aviv University. He has published widely in the areas of self-realization, career development, and social adjustment.

ISBN 0-275-95700-4

9 780275 957001

HARDCOVER BAR CODE